Principles in Practice

The Principles in Practice imprint offers teachers concrete illustrations of effective classroom practices based in NCTE research briefs and policy statements. Each book discusses the research on a specific topic, links the research to an NCTE brief or policy statement, and then demonstrates how those principles come alive in practice: by showcasing actual classroom practices that demonstrate the policies in action; by talking about research in practical, teacher-friendly language; and by offering teachers possibilities for rethinking their own practices in light of the ideas presented in the books. Books within the imprint are grouped in strands, each strand focused on a significant topic of interest.

Adolescent Literacy Strand

Adolescent Literacy at Risk? The Impact of Standards (2009) Rebecca Bowers Sipe
Adolescents and Digital Literacies: Learning Alongside Our Students (2010) Sara Kajder
Adolescent Literacy and the Teaching of Reading: Lessons for Teachers of Literature (2010) Deborah Appleman
Rethinking the "Adolescent" in Adolescent Literacy (2017) Sophia Tatiana Sarigianides, Robert Petrone, and Mark A. Lewis
Restorative Justice in the English Language Arts Classroom (2019) Maisha T. Winn, Hannah Graham, and Rita Renjitham Alfred

Writing in Today's Classrooms Strand

Writing in the Dialogical Classroom: Students and Teachers Responding to the Texts of Their Lives (2011) Bob Fecho
Becoming Writers in the Elementary Classroom: Visions and Decisions (2011) Katie Van Sluys
Writing Instruction in the Culturally Relevant Classroom (2011) Maisha T. Winn and Latrise P. Johnson
Writing Can Change Everything: Middle Level Kids Writing Themselves into the World (2020) Shelbie Witte, editor
Growing Writers: Principles for High School Writers and Their Teachers (2021) Anne Elrod Whitney
Cultivating Young Multilingual Writers: Nurturing Voices and Stories in and beyond the Classroom Walls (2023) Tracey T. Flores and María E. Fránquiz
Mentoring Youth Writers: Six Strategies to Bring Out the Author in Every Student (2025) Wendy R. Williams

Literacy Assessment Strand

Our Better Judgment: Teacher Leadership for Writing Assessment (2012) Chris W. Gallagher and Eric D. Turley
Beyond Standardized Truth: Improving Teaching and Learning through Inquiry-Based Reading Assessment (2012) Scott Filkins
Reading Assessment: Artful Teachers, Successful Students (2013) Diane Stephens, editor
Going Public with Assessment: A Community Practice Approach (2018) Kathryn Mitchell Pierce and Rosario Ordoñez-Jasis

Literacies of the Disciplines Strand

Entering the Conversations: Practicing Literacy in the Disciplines (2014) Patricia Lambert Stock, Trace Schillinger, and Andrew Stock

Real-World Literacies: Disciplinary Teaching in the High School Classroom (2014) Heather Lattimer

Doing and Making Authentic Literacies (2014) Linda Denstaedt, Laura Jane Roop, and Stephen Best

Reading in Today's Classrooms Strand

Connected Reading: Teaching Adolescent Readers in a Digital World (2015) Kristen Hawley Turner and Troy Hicks

Digital Reading: What's Essential in Grades 3–8 (2015) William L. Bass II and Franki Sibberson

Teaching Reading with YA Literature: Complex Texts, Complex Lives (2016) Jennifer Buehler

Teaching English Language Learners Strand

Beyond "Teaching to the Test": Rethinking Accountability and Assessment for English Language Learners (2017) Betsy Gilliland and Shannon Pella

Community Literacies en Confianza: *Learning from Bilingual After-School Programs* (2017) Steven Alvarez

Understanding Language: Supporting ELL Students in Responsive ELA Classrooms (2017) Melinda J. McBee Orzulak

Writing across Culture and Language: Inclusive Strategies for Working with ELL Writers in the ELA Classroom (2017) Christina Ortmeier-Hooper

Students' Rights to Read and Write Strand

Adventurous Thinking: Fostering Students' Rights to Read and Write in Secondary ELA Classrooms (2019) Mollie V. Blackburn, editor

In the Pursuit of Justice: Students' Rights to Read and Write in Elementary School (2020) Mariana Souto-Manning, editor

Already Readers and Writers: Honoring Students' Rights to Read and Write in the Middle Grade Classroom (2020) Jennifer Ochoa, editor

Children's and YA Literature Strand

Challenging Traditional Classroom Spaces with YA Literature: Students in Community as Course Co-Designers (2022) Ricki Ginsberg

Restorying Young Adult Literature: Expanding Students' Perspectives with Digital Texts (2023) James Joshua Coleman, Autumn A. Griffin, and Ebony Elizabeth Thomas

Deepening Student Engagement with Diverse Picturebooks: Powerful Classroom Practices for Elementary Teachers (2023) Angie Zapata

Technology in the Classroom Strand

Reimagining Literacies in the Digital Age: Multimodal Strategies to Teach with Technology (2022) Pauline S. Schmidt and Matthew J. Kruger-Ross

Literacies Before Technologies: Making Digital Tools Matter for Middle Grades Learners (2023) Troy Hicks and Jill Runstrom

Mentoring Youth Writers

Six Strategies to Bring Out the Author in Every Student

Wendy R. Williams
Arizona State University

1 E. Main St., Suite #260, Champaign, Illinois 61820
www.ncte.org

Staff Editors: Cynthia Gomez and Emmy Gilbert
Manuscript Editor: Bonny Graham
Imprint Editor: Cathy Fleischer
Interior Design: Victoria Pohlmann
Cover Design: Pat Mayer
Cover Images: iStockphoto.com | SDI Productions

ISBN (print): 978-0-8141-0253-4; ISBN (EPUB): 978-0-8141-0254-1; ISBN (PDF): 978-0-8141-0255-8

It is the policy of NCTE in its journals and other publications to provide a forum for the open discussion of ideas concerning the content and the teaching of English and the language arts. Publicity accorded to any particular point of view does not imply endorsement by the Executive Committee, the Board of Directors, or the membership at large, except in announcements of policy, where such endorsement is clearly specified.

NCTE provides equal employment opportunity (EEO) to all staff members and applicants for employment without regard to race, color, religion, sex, national origin, age, physical, mental or perceived handicap/disability, sexual orientation including gender identity or expression, ancestry, genetic information, marital status, military status, unfavorable discharge from military service, pregnancy, citizenship status, personal appearance, matriculation or political affiliation, or any other protected status under applicable federal, state, and local laws.

Every effort has been made to provide current URLs and email addresses, but because of the rapidly changing nature of the web, some sites and addresses may no longer be accessible.

Library of Congress Control Number: 2025936259

For Fio Moulton

Dear Reader,

As a former high school teacher, I remember the frustration I felt when the gap between Research (and that is how I always thought of it: Research with a capital R) and my own practice seemed too wide to ever cross. So many research studies were easy to ignore, in part because they were so distant from my practice and in part because I had no one to help me see how that research would make sense in my everyday practice.

That gap informs the thinking behind this book imprint. Designed for busy teachers, Principles in Practice publishes books that look carefully at NCTE's research reports and policy statements and puts those policies to the test in actual classrooms. The goal: to familiarize teachers with important teaching issues, the research behind those issues, and potential resources, and—most of all—make the research and policies come alive for teacher-readers.

This book is part of the strand that focuses on Writing in Today's Classrooms. Each book in this strand highlights a different aspect of this important topic and is organized in a similar way: immersing you in the research principles surrounding the topic (as laid out in the NCTE *Position Statement on Writing Instruction in School*) and then showing you how the principles play out with actual teachers and students. Each book closes with a teacher-friendly bibliography to offer you even more resources.

Good teaching is connected to strong research. We hope these books help you continue the good teaching that you're doing, think hard about ways to adapt and adjust your practice, and grow even stronger and more confident in the vital work you do with kids every day.

Best of luck,

Cathy Fleischer

Cathy Fleischer
Imprint Editor

Contents

Acknowledgments

This book would not have been possible without a number of people. Thank you to Cathy Fleischer, my series editor, who saw the potential in this project from the beginning and who provided fantastic advice and guidance along the way. She has been an incredible mentor to me. Thank you to Kurt Austin, Emmy Gilbert, Cynthia Gomez, Bonny Graham, Barbara Frazier, and the rest of the team at NCTE for their hard work on this project. Many thanks to Pauline Schmidt for recommending the Principles in Practice series and for all of her support over the years. Thank you also to the four reviewers who provided thoughtful feedback that helped make this book better.

Thank you to the adolescents who participated in the Young Authors' Studio (YAS) program at Arizona State University (ASU) and their families. I am also grateful to the university students who served as YAS mentors, especially those who worked so hard in that first year to build a new program for youth. In addition, thank you to the classroom teachers who agreed to be interviewed for this book: Carrie Deahl, Scott Wade, Kimiko Warner-Turner, Matt Hamilton, Andrea Box, April McNary, and Jennifer Ochoa.

I am grateful to the National Council of Teachers of English Assembly for Research, especially Jennifer VanDerHeide and Tonya Perry, for the opportunity to share my research on YAS at an invited keynote presentation. Also, thank you to the ELATE Commission on Arts and Literacies group for providing a professional space within NCTE where I could pursue my interests in creativity, the arts, and multimodality.

Several ASU College of Integrative Sciences and Arts summer grants supported the research shared in this book. In addition, a K–12 literacy grant provided by Arizona Humanities, as well as contributions from donors, made special projects in YAS possible in later years of the program.

I am grateful to two innovative programs at ASU that fueled the idea for YAS and served as important models: the Eleanor A. Robb Children's Art Workshop and Patricia Murphy's Superstition Review internship program. Also, thank you to the National Writing Project for inspiring many of the principles that guided our work in YAS.

Thank you to Maureen Roen and Janice Frangella for their assistance and to Stephanie Reid for her visits and encouragement. Thank you to Tracey Flores for listening to my wacky idea for YAS back in her doctoral student days and responding with enthusiasm.

Thank you to Joanna Grabski, Duane Roen, and Brooks Simpson for their mentorship and to Manu Avilés-Santiago and Vanessa Fonseca-Chávez for their support. Thank you to the ultimate mentor, Jim Blasingame, a professor who is beloved by his students and for good reason.

Thank you to my friends who were patient with me during the writing of this book and who cheered me on, especially Michele Redmond, Kerry Wilcoxon, and my Maricopa County Master Gardener cohort. Thank you to Patty Friedrich, Luiz Mesquita, Juliann Vitullo, Taylor Corse, Cora Fox, Bob and Gigi Bjork, Kim and Gregory Casale, and Mary Traphagan for their friendship and kindness over the years. Thank you to Heather, Mike, Kenny, and Ethan Thoe. Also, I am incredibly grateful for the many ways my parents, Bruce and Judy Williams, supported and nurtured me.

One of my hopes for the YAS program was that it would become a space where writers and artists like my own son, Fio Moulton, would thrive. Fio, I am constantly in awe of your intelligence, kindness, creativity, and humor. The sky is the limit. Don't ever stop writing, drawing, and dreaming!

As always, my deepest gratitude goes to my husband, Ian Moulton, who is unfailingly patient, thoughtful, clever, and funny. With you by my side, all things are possible.

Finally, thank you, cats. And you, too, coffee. You are the unsung heroes of this story.

NCTE *Position Statement on Writing Instruction in School* (2022)

Overview

How writing is conceptualized has consequences, especially in educational settings. Yet, despite decades of research and scholarship on writing, writing instruction, and writing assessment, misperceptions about writing and its purpose in schools persist. In 2008, NCTE's James R. Squire Office of Policy Research, then directed by Anne Ruggles Gere, developed a policy research brief entitled *Writing Now*. This brief defined writing, particularly school-based writing, as it is understood in the twenty-first century, and offered recommendations for classroom teachers, school administrators, and policymakers to promote effective writing assessment and instruction. Since the publication of the *Writing Now* policy research brief, two NCTE position statements on writing instruction—*Professional Knowledge for the Teaching of Writing*[1] (2016) and *Understanding and Teaching Writing: Guiding Principles*[2] (2018)—have expanded on key aspects of the original brief as they relate to teachers and the teaching of writing. This position statement is directed primarily toward an external audience of school administrators and policymakers. It describes problems with how writing is often perceived and taught in schools, identifies challenges educational leaders and educators face in trying to address these problems, and offers recommendations for educational leaders committed to addressing these misperceptions about writing and improving student learning, using the lenses of culturally relevant pedagogy and antiracist writing assessment.

Statement

Writing is an important form of self-expression and communication as well as a tool for thinking, reflecting, and learning. Its use as a process, a practice, and a product is essential in the classroom and beyond. However, in school settings, writing is often perceived and enacted as a gatekeeping device, which contributes to achievement gaps and other inequities. This happens when writing instruction and assessments focus on the *writing*—the products that are ultimately assessed and evaluated—rather than on the *writers* themselves. Writing instruction and assessments also serve as gatekeeping devices when they are built around deficit notions surrounding students' languages and literacies. Narrow definitions of and attitudes about writing and language too often perpetuate white, Eurocentric ideologies about what it means to write "well" or "effectively" (Chavez, 2021), upholding racist and linguistic barriers and inequities for students whose writing does not easily assimilate to dominant norms.

The National Council of Teachers of English (NCTE, 1974) supports "students' right to their own language—to the dialect that expresses their family and community identity, the idiolect that expresses their unique personal identity." Moreover, NCTE advocates for writing instruction that builds on students' strengths, that values their many ways of using language, that promotes a broad view of what constitutes "text," and that promotes young people's voices and purposes for writing within authentic contexts. The recommendations that follow aim to help administrators and policymakers support quality writing instruction and cultivate authentic and culturally sustaining conceptions of writing in schools and beyond.

Challenges to Authentic and Culturally Sustaining Writing Instruction

The aspects of classroom writing instruction described below can lead students to reject identifying as a writer, possess a limited ability to transfer writing processes and compositional decisions to new situations and contexts beyond those they learn in school, and conceive of writing as an exclusively school-based practice rather than a practice that can be personally meaningful and can transform and liberate individuals and communities.

Test-Driven Curriculum, Instruction, and Assessment:

- The ubiquity of standardized assessments, including high-stakes standardized assessments, perpetuates a limited view of composition and continues to heavily influence curricular, instructional, and assessment decisions (Scott, 2008).
- Writing instruction often mirrors test preparation, with students filling in templates and following formulas rather than making important and intentional decisions about writing for authentic audiences and purposes. This kind of writing instruction focuses almost exclusively on "the production of first and final drafts with less scope for an elaborated writing process" (Applebee & Langer, 2009, p. 24).
- Standardized writing assessments inaccurately delineate between modes of writing listed in state standards—e.g., positioning "narrative" and "informational" writing as mutually exclusive (Newkirk, 2014).
- Many K–12 educators feel a lack of efficacy in regard to teaching student writers, which too often leads to the purchase and implementation of prepackaged writing programs, often perpetuating the issues inherent in most standardized assessments of writing and composition (Achinstein & Ogawa, 2006; Stillman, 2011).

Consequences for Student Writers:

- Writing instruction focused on standardized tests fails to prepare a culturally diverse population of students for the college and career writing they'll be asked to do and, more broadly, to cultivate diverse communities of capable, engaged writers who write for their own purposes.
- When students cannot envision authentic purposes for writing or are not invited to make choices about their own writing, they can become disengaged in school-based writing (Behizadeh, 2014).

Narrow Definitions of and Limited Practices for Writing:

- Writing instruction in many English language arts classrooms rarely includes opportunities for children and youth to write often (Gallagher & Kittle, 2018), engage in a variety of writing processes exploring a wide range of forms and modes (Coppola, 2017), write for authentic audiences, or make complex decisions about composition.

- K–12 schools often promote limited and narrow notions of what "good" writing is. "Good" or "legitimate" writing is equated almost exclusively with so-called "academic" forms of writing (e.g., analytical essays, research papers), which perpetuates harmful ideas about what kinds of writing are useful and valued in the world (Coppola, 2019) and delegitimizes the writing that children and youth engage in outside of school spaces (Haddix, 2018; Skerrett & Bomer, 2013; Weinstein, 2006).
- Many professional development opportunities related to teaching writing focus more on the teaching of products and forms—i.e., the *writing*—than they do on building students' decision-making processes as *writers* (Wahleithner, 2018).

Consequences for Student Writers:

- An overly narrow focus on products—and particular types of products—leaves young people underprepared to understand the rhetorical nature of writing, to make decisions about their own writing, and to transfer their writing knowledge to new contexts, especially contexts beyond the classroom.
- When students are offered infrequent opportunities to engage in multimodal composition, they experience a disconnect between school-based writing and the kinds of composition that most children and youth engage in outside of school spaces (Coppola, 2019).

Dominant Ideologies around Writing and Language:

- So-called Standard American English continues to dominate academic institutions, despite the lack of a formally recognized national language (Baker-Bell, 2020; Davila, 2012; Inoue, 2015; CCCC, 2021).
- The dominant language and literacy of school is rooted in an uncritical and almost universal acceptance of white, Eurocentric norms[1] embedded in notions around what makes writing "good" or what constitutes writing "quality" (Chavez, 2021)—what composition scholar Asao B. Inoue (2019) calls "habits of white language." These habits include the privileging of Western logics and a focus on individual production, reason, order and control, and directness of language.

Consequences for Student Writers:

- When educators exclusively define "good" or "effective" writing and language use as that which matches white, Eurocentric norms, students are more likely to be perceived as possessing inherent deficits when their writing and language use does not match those norms (Paris, 2012).
- Student writers' voices, literacies, and compositional practices may not be valued in school settings, inhibiting their confidence and growth as writers, or, worse, students, families, and communities may be penalized, punished, excluded, and oppressed based on their language use.

Recommendations for Administrators and Policymakers

- Despite the aforementioned challenges, there are ways to support writing instruction that can mitigate the potential consequences outlined earlier in this statement and, more important, *actively cultivate* young writers' efficacy and engagement. This kind of instruction builds on students' racial, cultural, social, and linguistic resources, provides opportunities for students to engage in complex writing processes within communities of other writers, and offers frequent opportunities for students to make decisions about composing for authentic purposes and audiences. This more inclusive, authentic view of writing instruction is outlined in NCTE's *Understanding and Teaching Writing: Guiding Principles*[2] and in the position statement *Professional Knowledge for the Teaching of Writing*.[1]

- In attempting to disrupt the ways in which narrow definitions of writing and dominant instructional practices around the teaching of student writers perpetuate harm for both students and educators, this position statement offers educational leaders and policymakers a variety of concrete ways to use policies, practices, and funding to counter these ideologies:

Foster a Culture of Authentic and Culturally Sustaining Writing Instruction

- Promote curriculum and instruction that broaden definitions of *writing* to include visual, aural, and multimodal compositions and to include a wider variety of purposes for writing (e.g., writing to discover, writing for change, writing to learn, writing to reflect).
- Advocate for writing instruction that is process- (rather than product-) oriented and that invites students to become writers who (1) write for authentic purposes and (2) make authentic choices about processes and products.
- Make writing a collective responsibility and a collaborative activity across faculty and academic departments by fostering writing-across-the-curriculum and writing support programs, such as writing centers, writing groups, and peer coaching, for student writers and writing teachers.
- Recognize and value the cultural and linguistic assets that writers bring to their texts by highlighting published writing and student writing that reflect diverse perspectives, voices, experiences, and linguistic practices.
- Adopt approaches to writing assessment that provide qualitative data about students' processes and growth as writers, include students in assessment decisions, and create more equitable assessment experiences for developing writers. See NCTE's position statement on writing assessment.[3]

Support Faculty/Instructional Staff

- Hire professionalized literacy and writing teachers who will recognize and build on students' strengths and their cultural and linguistic resources.
- Support faculty engagement with professional organizations, especially those centered on literacy and writing, such as the National Council of Teachers of English and the National Writing Project.
- Provide professional learning opportunities for all instructional staff centered on culturally responsive pedagogy, universal design for learning, and antiracist writing instruction and assessment.

- Respect and value teachers' professional expertise and knowledge of student writers and classroom practice. Invite teachers to contribute their knowledge and expertise to decisions about writing curriculum, instruction, and assessment.
- Invest in professional learning opportunities that allow teachers to learn together, share practices, and build knowledge collaboratively with one another. While professional development workshops may be useful, teachers benefit from spending time in ongoing inquiry communities.

Note

For example, a hyperfocus on developing independence as writers, notions around developing a "neutral" or "objective" voice/stance, particularly when composing informational texts, etc.

References

Achinstein, B., & Ogawa, R. (2006). (In) fidelity: What the resistance of new teachers reveals about professional principles and prescriptive educational policies. *Harvard Educational Review, 76*, 30–63.

Applebee, A., & Langer, J. (2009, May). What is happening in the teaching of writing. *English Journal, 98*(5), 18–28.

Baker-Bell, A. (2020). *Linguistic justice: Black language, literacy, identity, and pedagogy.* Routledge and NCTE.

Behizadeh, N. (2014). Adolescent perspectives on authentic writing instruction. *Journal of Language and Literacy Education, 10*(1), 27–44.

Chavez, F. R. (2021). *The anti-racist writing workshop: How to decolonize the creative classroom.* Haymarket Books.

Conference on College Composition and Communication.[4] (2021). *CCCC Statement on White Language Supremacy.*

Coppola, S. (2017). *Renew! Become a better—and more authentic—writing teacher.* Stenhouse Publishers.

Coppola, S. (2019). *Writing, redefined: Broadening our ideas of what it means to compose.* Stenhouse Publishers.

Davila, B. (2012). Indexicality and "standard" Edited American English: Examining the link between conceptions of standardness and perceived authorial identity. *Written Communication, 29*, 180–207.

Gallagher, K., & Kittle, P. (2018). *180 days: Two teachers and the quest to engage and empower adolescents.* Heinemann.

Haddix, M. (2018). "What's radical about youth writing?" Seeing and honoring youth writers and their literacies. *Voices from the Middle, 23*(3), 8–12.

Inoue, A. B. (2015). *Antiracist writing assessment ecologies: Teaching and assessing writing for a socially just future.* WAC Clearinghouse and Parlor Press.

Inoue, A. B. (2019). *Labor-based grading contracts: Building equity and inclusion in the compassionate writing classroom.* WAC Clearinghouse and University Press of Colorado.

National Council of Teachers of English. (1974, November 30). *Resolution on the students' right to their own language.*[5]

Newkirk, T. (2014). *Minds made for stories: How we really read and write informational and persuasive texts.* Heinemann.

Paris, D. (2012). Culturally sustaining pedagogy: A needed change in stance, terminology, and practice. *Educational Researcher, 41*(3), 93–97.

Scott, T. (2008). "Happy to comply": Writing assessment, fast-capitalism, and the cultural logic of control. *Review of Education, Pedagogy, and Cultural Studies, 30*(2), 140–161.

Skerrett, A., & Bomer, R. (2013). Recruiting languages and lifeworlds for border-crossing compositions. *Research in the Teaching of English, 47*, 313–337.

Stillman, J. (2011). Teacher learning in an era of high-stakes accountability: Productive tension and critical professional practice. *Teachers College Record, 113*(1), 133–180.

Wahleithner, J. M. (2018). Five portraits of teachers' experiences teaching writing: Negotiating knowledge, student need, and policy. *Teachers College Record, 120*(1), 1–60.

Weinstein, S. (2006). A love for the thing: The pleasures of rap as a literate practice. *Journal of Adolescent & Adult Literacy, 50*, 270–281.

Statement Authors

Carolyn Calhoon-Dillahunt, Chair, Yakima Valley College, WA

Shawna Coppola, The Educator Collaborative

Amber Warrington, Boise State University, ID

Robert P. Yagelski, University at Albany, SUNY

Article printed from National Council of Teachers of English: **https://ncte.org**

URL to article: **https://ncte.org/statement/statement-on-writing-instruction-in-school/**

URLs in this post:

[1] *Professional Knowledge for the Teaching of Writing*: **https://ncte.org/statement/teaching writing/**

[2] *Understanding and Teaching Writing: Guiding principles*: **https://ncte.org/statement/teachingcomposition/**

[3] position statement on writing assessment: **https://ncte.org/statement/writingassessment/**

[4] Conference on College Composition and Communication: **https://cccc.ncte.org/cccc/white-language-supremacy**

[5] Resolution on the students' right to their own language: **https://ncte.org/statement/righttoownlanguage/**

Introduction

Mentoring Youth Writers

Imagine your ideal writing classroom. For just a moment, put aside all thoughts of class size, mandated curricula, standardized tests, and pressures to conform to a team of teachers.

If there were no limits on your teaching, what would your ideal writing classroom look like? What would you do to help all students thrive? What would they spend their time doing? How would students interact? What materials would they have access to? What would they learn?

Who would *you* be in that space?

Becoming a Writing Mentor

The book that is in your hands is the one I didn't know I needed when I was a middle school and high school English teacher. It is the product of a journey outside of those classrooms and into the unknown, where people write because they want to. Places where there are no bells. No homework assignments. No red pens. No tests. No attendance. No standardized curriculum. No grades. And yet, learning happens in these spaces. Really amazing writing takes shape. And people learn a lot from each other.

In graduate school, I started looking at the writing practices of adolescents in out-of-school spaces. I noticed that adolescent rappers were willing to go to impressive lengths to write, perform, and hone their skills in their lives outside of school (Williams, 2013). I became fascinated, too, with how learning and identity work together. I went on to study youth poets (Williams, 2018) and found that the teaching artists who guided them had a unique approach to writing instruction. These artists were very much writing mentors, fellow practitioners supporting the younger writers who looked up to them.

Many writing researchers pay attention to the writing that people do in community, extracurricular, and out-of-school spaces so we can break free from some of the constraints that come with formal, school-based learning (Hull & Schultz,

2001). When doing research in schools, it can be easy to take all of the norms of school for granted, such as separating kids by grade level, teaching subjects in isolation from each other, the power dynamics of teacher versus student, a set curriculum, mandated attendance, and so forth. Studying learning outside of the regular school day and in nontraditional spaces can open up opportunities to question and challenge the conditions we are typically working under in education (Hull & Schultz, 2001).

Drawing on insights gained through my research, including ideas related to mentoring, I started the Young Authors' Studio (YAS) program in the fall of 2017. This free seven-week writing program for students in grades 5–12 took place on Saturday mornings at Arizona State University (ASU), where I work as an associate professor of English. Joining me on this journey were four undergraduate students and one graduate student who were enrolled in my Mentoring Youth Writers internship (see Figure I.1). They earned course credit for serving as writing "mentors" in YAS, developing curriculum, promoting the program, and teaching in it.

Initially, I selected the title "mentors" for these university students because they were not preservice teachers, and I wanted to quickly be able to distinguish between the two levels of students in YAS (the university students versus the adolescent writers). However, embedded in the term *mentor* is also a slightly different meaning than *teacher*. To be a mentor is to be a guide, a fellow learner, and a practitioner of the craft. By taking on this title, the university students were invited to enter teaching from

FIGURE I.1. YAS program mentors.

a different perspective. Being a "mentor" gave them a road map for how they should approach curricula and engage with youth. A mentoring lens offers a way of seeing teaching that would have helped me when I entered the field many years ago.

As it turned out, the mentors developed a seven-week writing program that made a difference to participants. The youth writers showed improvement in their attitudes toward writing and toward themselves as writers—all in a really short time frame, approximately ten hours of instruction. Those who entered the program disliking writing were much more positive toward it when they left. How could that be?

In the study of the YAS program that I conducted (see Appendix A to learn more about the study's design), data analysis revealed that mentors supported the youth writers in a variety of ways. In particular, they attended to the following:

- Variation in activities
- Choice
- Community
- Funds of knowledge and student interests
- Supporting student writing attitudes and projects
- Brokering (making connections to outside groups and opportunities) and performance

These practices that mentors used to support students in the YAS program need not be limited to extracurricular or out-of-school writing programs. All students can benefit from variation in activities, the freedom to make choices, a supportive community, respect for their knowledge and interests, having their writing taken seriously, and exposure to opportunities beyond the classroom. This is the sort of deeply immersive learning in a practice that can make instruction motivating and meaningful for today's secondary students.

A few years into the YAS program, the National Council of Teachers of English (NCTE) released their *Position Statement on Writing Instruction in School* (2022). I remember when I first read this policy document. It was validating to see so many ideas that were relevant to our YAS program reflected there. Both the program and the position statement were formed from developments in writing research (ideas shared through NCTE, the National Writing Project, and so forth), so even though the two arose independently, it is no wonder they have much in common.

NCTE's *Position Statement on Writing Instruction in School* urges teachers to rethink how they teach writing, and it addresses several issues. In particular, it warns against "test-driven curriculum, instruction, and assessment," "narrow definitions of and limited practices for writing," and "racist and linguistic barriers." The statement also includes suggestions for addressing these challenges. Specifically, it advocates for multimodal composition, it centers student writers, and it points out the need for authentic purposes and audiences for writing. Moreover, the position statement supports student agency and choice, the formation of writing communities, and honoring "students' strengths and their cultural and linguistic resources." This statement is a powerful tool because it highlights several key principles for effective writing instruction, principles that were important to us in the YAS program as well.

This book presents teachers with a framework for mentoring youth writers using six strategies. These strategies are rooted in research findings from the YAS program, and they are supported by writing theory and research, including the NCTE *Position Statement on Writing Instruction in School* (2022), which is reprinted in the front matter. This book devotes one chapter to each strategy:

1. Use a wide range of writing forms and modes with students.
2. Encourage student choice and decision-making.
3. Build a supportive writing community.
4. Honor student knowledge, experience, and interests.
5. Nurture students as writers.
6. Connect writers to opportunities beyond the classroom.

This book shows how mentors (novice teachers) used these strategies in the YAS program and how they can be implemented in the writing classroom. Each chapter also introduces readers to an experienced classroom teacher who has used the strategy with secondary students. These teachers demonstrate how to move from principle to practice, which this NCTE book series is so well known for.

I stated earlier that this is the book I did not know I needed when I was teaching at the secondary level. The reason is that these strategies would have brought writing to life in my classroom. They would have helped me better support the writers right in front of me and made my job more rewarding, giving me permission to be a fellow writer who was learning alongside my students. When we approach teaching and learning through a mentoring lens, school becomes much more meaningful for everyone involved.

Seeing education through a mentoring lens allows us to view teaching and learning from a new perspective. This is a particularly useful lens for writing instruction. Are you ready? Let's get started!

Seeing Writing Instruction through a Mentoring Lens

Viewing writing instruction through a mentoring lens focuses attention on the role of the teacher as a guide and fellow learner (i.e., a more experienced practitioner). Mentors inspire and guide their mentees. Writing mentors are knowledgeable about writing, trust mentees to make decisions, cultivate supportive spaces for writing, respect the knowledge and experiences of mentees, provide validation, and present opportunities for mentees to have meaningful learning experiences. Teachers instruct, whereas writing mentors guide students into deeper participation in a practice.

Wenger (2008) writes, "Being an active practitioner with an authentic form of participation might be one of the most deeply essential requirements for teaching" (p. 277). Applying this idea to writing instruction means that writing teachers write (Cremin, 2006; Gardner, 2014; Pytash et al., 2017; Street & Stang, 2009). Teachers who write can usher students into the practice of writing because they bring a "lived authenticity" (Wenger, 2008, p. 276) to this work. They guide youth writers from a place of knowledge and experience while still being open to continuing to grow as writers themselves. They have firsthand knowledge of their subject and realize that people write for many reasons—including to vent, to heal, and to learn. Teachers who write know that writing offers many benefits, that writing is a messy and difficult process, and that writers have unique preferences, approaches, and styles.

Mentoring is not a new idea in education. In *What a Writer Needs*, Fletcher (1993) explains that teachers are "in a unique position to be mentors" to student writers (p. 10). He notes that the relationship between mentor and mentee varies, but there are some similarities across these relationships. Namely, "a mentor has high standards," "builds on strengths," "values originality and diversity," "encourages students to take risks," "is passionate," and "looks at the big picture" (pp. 13–18).

Robinson (2009) points out four ways that mentors guide learners:

1. **Recognition:** "Mentors recognize the spark of interest or delight and can help an individual drill down to the specific components of the discipline that match that individual's capacity and passion" (p. 180).
2. **Encouragement:** "Mentors lead us to believe that we can achieve something that seemed improbable or impossible to us before we met them. They don't allow us to succumb to self-doubt for too long, or the notion that our dreams are too large for us. They stand by to remind us of the skills we already possess and what we can achieve if we continue to work hard" (pp. 181–182).
3. **Facilitating:** "Mentors . . . [offer] advice and techniques, paving the way for us, and even allowing us to falter a bit while standing by to help us recover and learn from our mistakes" (p. 182).
4. **Stretching:** "Effective mentors push us past what we see as our limits" (p. 183).

Applied to writing instruction, English teachers who are writing mentors know that students already have writing knowledge, preferred practices, and personal interests. They give encouragement and advice to youth writers. And since they are writers themselves, they know that writing is difficult, that students will make mistakes and face struggles, and they will be there for them when that happens. "Mentors open doors for us and get involved directly in our journeys. They show us the next steps and encourage us to take them" (Robinson, 2009, p. 186). This book provides English teachers with strategies for mentoring writers so they can guide students into deeper participation in the authentic practice of writing.

Mentoring Youth Writers in the Young Authors' Studio Program

The mentors who were enrolled in the Mentoring Youth Writers internship and who helped build and run the YAS program voluntarily signed up for this elective. Mentors Amir, Emma, Henry, Miranda, and Nari (pseudonyms are used for all mentor names) came to campus for twelve Saturdays during the semester. In the first five weeks, we planned the program together. While the program was in session over the next seven weeks, they taught in it as well. Each two-hour YAS workshop (9:30–11:30 a.m.) took place during the mentors' four-hour class on campus (9:00 a.m.–1:00 p.m.). See Figure I.2 for the typical schedule for prepping and teaching.

The YAS program included five themed writing workshops (narrative, poetry and music, art and writing, drama and film, and genre study). Week six focused on revision and rehearsal, and week seven consisted of two back-to-back culminating events: a writing gallery and performance. In this first iteration of the program, eighteen youth writers participated.

FIGURE I.2. YAS program schedule.

	Schedule
9:00–9:25	Mentors meet to go over the day's activities and set up the room
9:25–9:30	Student drop-off/check-in
9:30–10:00	YAS Workshop: Overview and journal
10:00–10:05	YAS Workshop: 30-second breakout pitches
10:05–10:30	YAS Workshop: Breakout session round 1
10:30–10:55	YAS Workshop: Breakout session round 2
10:55–11:15	YAS Workshop: Writing stations (brainstorm, write, polish, or share)
11:15–11:30	YAS Workshop: Team check-in and reflection
11:30–11:35	Student pick-up/check-out
12:15–1:00	Mentors meet to debrief and review plans for workshops

The mentors brought their own dreams for the program along with their unique experiences, talents, and skills (see Figure I.3). While the mentors entered the ASU internship with little to no teaching experience (three were English or creative writing majors, one was studying engineering, and one was in theater for youth), they learned a lot about writing instruction during our intensive planning in the first five weeks of the semester and through hands-on teaching throughout the seven weeks of the YAS program.

This book serves multiple purposes and audiences. It explores mentoring strategies that can be used with writers in schools and community programs. In addition, teacher educators may be interested to learn about a field experience that could give preservice teachers confidence as they plan curriculum and work with students. Scholars may be interested in learning more about the mentoring lens, which could be applied to research in education more broadly. A smaller group of readers might be interested in launching their own YAS-style program. Plenty of materials and suggestions have been included to support that work as well, including workshop plans, guiding principles, and more.

FIGURE I.3. YAS breakout session.

Structure of This Book

In each chapter of this book, one of the six mentoring strategies is explained in terms of the research and theory behind it. I then take readers inside the YAS program to see the concept in action with adolescents. Next, a secondary teacher discusses why the strategy is important and how to implement it in secondary classrooms. Finally, I share a selection of sample activities to help readers consider how to use these ideas in their own teaching contexts.

Chapter 1 explores the practice of using a **variety of writing forms and modes** with students, demonstrating how the mentors incorporated different kinds of writing into their workshops on narrative, poetry and music, art and writing, drama and film, and genre study. In addition, it considers the importance of experimentation and play in these workshops, the use of mentor texts and props, and students' reactions to working with different writing forms and modes. This chapter then moves to an interview with Carrie Deahl, an English teacher at Maryvale High School in Phoenix, Arizona, who uses many writing forms and modes in their teaching. It closes with some suggestions for ways teachers can use different writing forms and modes in the secondary classroom, including spoken word poetry, songwriting, and comics/graphic narratives.

Chapter 2 considers some ways to encourage **student choice and decision-making** in writing instruction. In the YAS program, mentors offered a choice of activities, let students decide what work was needed on a piece, and gave students the option to share (or to opt out). This chapter discusses how to nurture student creativity through structure and choice, and it argues that teachers need to be free to make choices, too. An interview with Scott Wade, a secondary teacher at Newcomer Academy in Louisville, Kentucky, explores how to support student choice and decision-making in the classroom. The chapter closes by sharing activities in line with this practice, including creative projects, reflections, and conferences.

Chapter 3 considers ways to **build a supportive writing community** in the classroom. It looks at how YAS mentors supported one another, established trust with students, provided validation, grouped students to promote interaction, and maintained a positive atmosphere. The chapter features an interview with Kimiko Warner-Turner, a secondary teacher and master teaching artist from Los Angeles County High School of the Arts in Los Angeles, California, who is an expert at building community in the classroom. Finally, the chapter shares activities for building community, including tableaux, scene writing, and obstacle courses.

Chapter 4 explores how **student knowledge, experience, and interests** can be welcomed into the writing classroom. This chapter shows some of the ways YAS mentors engaged in this practice, beginning with articulating clear guiding principles and learning about students. The program honored students' languages and cultures and promoted writing from experience. It also focused on students' interests in art, music, and film. This chapter argues that teachers have distinct knowledge, experiences, and interests, and these unique features enrich our teaching. An interview with Matt Hamilton, who is an education programmer for the Michigan Learning Channel and a former classroom teacher, offers insight into ways to support student knowledge, experience, and interests. The chapter closes with suggestions for implementing this practice in instruction, including using assignments such as food memory narratives, how-to demonstrations, and stop-motion animation.

Chapter 5 examines ways to **nurture students as writers** and highlights how mentors did this in the YAS program. It takes a closer look at welcoming out-of-school projects into school spaces, exploring writing identity, building writing confidence, setting writing goals, and noticing changes in attitudes toward writing. The chapter includes an interview with Andrea Box, an English teacher at Westwood High School in Mesa, Arizona, who is an expert at nurturing students as writers. It closes with tips for implementing this practice in the classroom through writing surveys, portfolios, and career exploration.

Chapter 6 focuses on **connecting writers to opportunities beyond the classroom**. It shows how mentors in the YAS program put students in touch with writing events, programs, contests, and publishing opportunities. It demonstrates how mentors created opportunities for adolescent writers on our campus, hosting a public writing gallery and final performance for them. This chapter includes an interview with April McNary, English teacher at Sunnyslope High School in Phoenix, Arizona, who helps students find new audiences for their work and who puts students in touch with opportunities for writing around campus and beyond. The chapter closes by discussing ways to honor and engage writers on campus through celebrations of writing, student film screenings, and filling the campus with words.

The book's conclusion reviews the six mentoring strategies that teachers can use to encourage, challenge, and inspire youth writers. Specifically, teachers can put students in touch with a wide range of writing forms and modes; encourage student choice and decision-making; build a supportive writing community; honor student knowledge, experience, and interests; nurture students as writers; and connect writers to opportunities beyond the classroom. Readers are encouraged to use a mentoring lens in education, as it can bring issues to light and offer a way forward.

Additional information about the program and the study can be found in Appendix A. There, I discuss the YAS program's origins, different iterations of the program over the years, and challenges the program faced. In addition, Appendix A provides an overview of the study's design, including sections that address the research site, participants, data sources, and data analysis. This study overview offers additional context for the findings shared throughout this book, especially in the "Mentoring in Action: Inside the Young Authors' Studio Program" sections of Chapters 1 through 6.

A bonus interview on authentic writing is provided in Appendix B. Jennifer Ochoa, a middle school English teacher in New York City, offers advice on centering authentic writing in the classroom, which can be helpful to those facing the constraints of a mandated curriculum.

Chapter One

Using a Wide Range of Writing Forms and Modes with Students

A few years ago, a student—let's call her "Anna"— was nervous about having to compose visual narratives in her English course. She emailed her teacher, worried that her "poor art skills" would count against her. Her teacher reassured her that it would be okay; the projects were flexible enough that she would be able to work at her level of comfort with art.

As it turned out, Anna went on to compose some of the most beautiful visual narratives her instructor had ever seen. Her picturebook about Winston the Wondercat who was fighting crime and saving the day was hilarious. Inspired by Dav Pilkey's *Kat Kong* (2003) and *Dogzilla* (1993), she took photos of her pets (a cat, dogs, a snake, a hedgehog), printed them, cut them out, and placed them against a simple colored-pencil background she had drawn. Her second creative project, a stop-motion animation that featured figurines such as Groot, took the form of a quest narrative in her backyard. She got down and shot the stop-motion animation at the characters' eye-level, the grass in her face. This student inserted title cards to help narrate the story and chose music that conveyed a fun and light tone.

Anna was in my class, and it is fascinating to me that someone who was so nervous initially went on to produce some of the most beautiful and interesting visual narratives I have come across. This experience helped me to realize a couple of things about teaching visual storytelling in English classes:

1. Students may be nervous about trying something new, but if they are challenged within reason, have some room to experiment without fear of punishment, and have access to lots of models to learn from, they can achieve great things.

2. If I were the kind of teacher who said, "I'm not an artist, so I have no business exploring visual storytelling with students," Anna's striking visual narratives might never have come into existence. One of our jobs as writing mentors in the classroom is to give students access to multiple writing forms and modes. We open doors that lead students to embark on new adventures.

One of the joys of teaching writing is how many different forms we can use with students. Even with traditional assignments such as research papers and poems, there is room to bring compositions to life as writers decide how they will organize and deliver their ideas. For example, a research product in a high school classroom might take the form of a podcast, a short film, an animated work, or a scholarly article with supporting images and charts. A poem might take the form of a song, a performance piece, an art installation, or an advertisement. When teachers expand their ideas about what counts as writing and give students opportunities to work with many different forms, students gain valuable tools, strategies, and attitudes they can apply to any number of rhetorical situations that may come their way in the future. They develop creativity and flexibility through these experiences.

As I explain in the introduction, this book recommends that teachers use six strategies to mentor youth writers (see Figure 1.1). This chapter focuses on the first of those strategies: how to use a wide range of writing forms and modes with students.

All six chapters follow a similar format: The first section shares research and theory so teachers can justify using this strategy in their teaching. The second section details how mentors used the strategy in the Young Authors' Studio program. (As a reminder, the study of that program is explained in Appendix A.) An interview with a

FIGURE 1.1. This chapter focuses on the first strategy for mentoring youth writers.

Six Strategies for Mentoring Youth Writers

1. **<u>Use a wide range of writing forms and modes with students.</u>**
2. Encourage student choice and decision-making.
3. Build a supportive writing community.
4. Honor student knowledge, experience, and interests.
5. Nurture students as writers.
6. Connect writers to opportunities beyond the classroom.

secondary teacher then provides additional guidance and advice from the field. Finally, I provide some ready-to-use assignments to help busy teachers implement these ideas in their classrooms right away. Figure 1.2 highlights a short list of key terms to get us started.

FIGURE 1.2. Useful terms to know for this chapter.

Key Terms

Form: The shape a composition takes (letter, essay, memo, research report, speech, slideshow, short story, novel, picturebook, comic, graphic novel, manga, film, animation, etc.).

Mode: A way of communicating meaning. Some examples of modes are linguistic, visual, auditory, gestural, and spatial (New London Group, 1996).

Multimodal: A combination of two or more modes. Some examples of multimodal compositions are comics, graphic novels, manga, video games, visual novels, picturebooks, films, animation, anime, plays, songs, spoken word poems, podcasts, commercials, advertisements, slideshows, and websites.

Genre: A category of works with shared characteristics and conventions. Some genres of fiction include science fiction, realistic fiction, historical fiction, horror, fantasy, western, comedy, and tragedy.

Justifying This Work

When students write in many different forms and modes, they learn strategies for communicating they can use their entire lives. They cultivate habits of mind that support them as they go on to write in college and careers. These habits include curiosity, openness, engagement, creativity, persistence, responsibility, flexibility, and metacognition (Council of Writing Program Administrators et al., 2011).

The NCTE *Position Statement on Writing Instruction in School* (2022) warns against an overly narrow writing curriculum, urging teachers to teach visual and multimodal forms of composition, to honor students' out-of-school writing, and to encourage frequent writing (see Figure 1.3).

FIGURE 1.3. NCTE position statement connections.

Connections to NCTE's *Position Statement on Writing Instruction in School* (2022)

- "K–12 schools often promote limited and narrow notions of what 'good' writing is. 'Good' or 'legitimate' writing is equated almost exclusively with so-called 'academic' forms of writing (e.g., analytical essays, research papers), which perpetuates harmful ideas about what kinds of writing are useful and valued in the world (Coppola, 2019) and delegitimizes the writing that children and youth engage in outside of school spaces (Haddix, 2018; Skerrett & Bomer, 2013; Weinstein, 2006)."
- "Writing instruction in many English language arts classrooms rarely includes opportunities for children and youth to write often (Gallagher & Kittle, 2018), engage in a variety of writing processes exploring a wide range of forms and modes (Coppola, 2017), write for authentic audiences, or make complex decisions about composition."
- "When students are offered infrequent opportunities to engage in multimodal composition, they experience a disconnect between school-based writing and the kinds of composition that most children and youth engage in outside of school spaces (Coppola, 2019)."
- Educators need to "promote curriculum and instruction that broaden definitions of *writing* to include visual, aural, and multimodal compositions."

Teaching a broad range of writing forms gives students opportunities to write for many different purposes, such as to inform, persuade, entertain, learn, and reflect (NCTE, 2022; Stockman, 2022). This practice also helps to build bridges between students' in-school and out-of-school learning (Morrell & Duncan-Andrade, 2002). After all, many students have interesting writing lives outside of the classroom, composing works such as songs, poems, comics, fan fiction, and novels on their own time. When teachers welcome multimodal composition into the classroom—including culturally relevant forms such as zines, raps, and spoken word poetry—they validate students and increase academic engagement. Beucher and Seglem (2019) point out that "school curriculum must account for [young people's] out-of-school literacy practices and interests in in-school spaces, not simply to sanction these literacies, but to invite direct and meaningful engagement with the texts that students are drawing from to make sense of their lives and their positioning in the world" (p. 60). Their study of Black male students who composed a digital autobiography project shows how important it can be to use modes, forms, and content relevant to students' own lives.

Different kinds of writing each offer unique benefits to writers. For example, "creating comics gives learners the opportunity to be active agents in their understanding. Students who put thought balloons beside their characters and decide where to put panel breaks on the page become stronger storytellers, more critical thinkers, and more effective communicators" (Ryder, 2020). In addition, composing an animated work involves making decisions about narrative, visual design, drama, and music (Burn, 2016). Making a film can help students build creativity, communication, leadership, teamwork, decision-making, and listening skills (Bonnet, 2017). As they write and perform spoken word poetry, students may experience therapeutic benefits and gain self-esteem (Weinstein, 2009; Williams, 2015), and those who are learning English can improve their speaking skills by making podcasts (Yeh et al., 2021). Even composing multimodal games can support engagement, encourage collaboration, and benefit students with special needs (Hughes-Roberts et al., 2020). Writing that makes use of different modes improves student motivation as well (Darrington & Dousay, 2014).

Composing in different forms does not have to be expensive or involve all the latest technologies. Many low-tech options are available. For example, students can draw comics at their desks, write and perform a poem or scene, or compose lyrics for a song. When using technology to compose, much is possible even with a basic school computer in a lab (e.g., creating a website) or with a free app on a smartphone (e.g., making stop-motion animation). We are surrounded by so many different kinds of messages today and have an abundance of options for engaging in visual storytelling and other types of communication (Felten, 2008; George, 2002). Given the multitude of forms of writing that are possible right now—both high-tech and low-tech—this is a particularly exciting time in history to be a writer.

What drives me to use different forms of writing in the classroom is that it makes English more relevant and meaningful for students. As they work with forms that involve drawing, music, film, animation, or performance, students have some freedom to explore their different interests and talents. Being challenged to use different forms of writing also keeps students engaged, invites creative problem-solving, and sparks creativity. Students appreciate variety.

Mentoring in Action: Inside the Young Authors' Studio Program

In the Young Authors' Studio (YAS) program, mentors used a wide range of writing forms and modes with students, demonstrating to them that writing can be interesting and exciting. This section breaks down their five themed workshops: narrative, poetry and music, art and writing, drama and film, and genre study. Each workshop was structured to include time for a journal warm-up, an overview of the day's theme, and a choice of breakout sessions. In addition, each workshop included extended time for writing at a station (brainstorming, writing, polishing, performing/sharing) and closed with team time, which was a chance to reflect, set goals, and share writing with an assigned mentor and other writers. The first workshop (see Figure 1.4) also included time at the beginning for reviewing program expectations, decorating a name card and journal, and completing a writing survey. (Students took the writing survey again during the revision and rehearsal workshop in week six.)

FIGURE 1.4. Mentors welcoming students.

Writing Our Way through Five Themed Workshops

1. The Narrative Workshop

Narrative is a useful category for expanding students' ideas about what counts as writing. After all, storytelling is powerful, and a narrative can take so many shapes. These works can be short or long, real or imagined, and conveyed in various ways (e.g., orally, in print, through visuals, through moving images). The possibilities are endless for teaching narrative to secondary students.

Mentors kicked off the narrative workshop with a scar story journal entry. Mentor Emma introduced this activity to students in the YAS program as follows:

> Go ahead and draw a diagram kind of like this [*drawing an outline of a human figure on the board*]. The prompt is scar stories. Mark places on your drawing [*points to drawing*] where you have scars. They can be physical or emotional. Once you're done marking up all the different scars that you have, you'll want to start writing a story about that. You have about ten minutes to write, and then we'll go across the room and share with one other person.

Drawing is an effective brainstorming technique for inspiring vivid, detail-rich writing. Once students have completed this drawing activity, they can quickly select a memory to write about and can visualize the details of that lived experience. Drawing activities like this one make writing more accessible and less stressful for many students. (For more journaling activities, see Nelson's book, *Writing and Being* [2004].)

After students had a chance to share, Emma defined *narrative*, discussed the difference between fiction and nonfiction, and talked about some of the common features of narrative, including characters, plots/subplots, and forms. She mentioned that narratives can include graphics and drawings as well. At the front of the room, she had set up a table with books representing different kinds of narrative, including manga, graphic novels, picturebooks, young adult fiction, and classic literary works. She referred to these works during their discussion.

In the YAS program, students were able to go to their choice of breakout session on the day's theme; right before these breakout sessions started, four mentors—all but the person who led the journal activity and overview—came up to the front of the room to describe their breakouts in thirty-second pitches. Mentor Nari described her six-word memoir breakout session as follows:

> [One of the best known six-word memoirs is] "For sale: baby shoes, never worn." If you come to my breakout session, you will write a story about yourself or your secrets using just six words, and you will also get to draw along with the six-word memoir you've created. If you're interested, join me!

After listening to the pitches, students chose two twenty-five-minute breakout sessions to attend from the four options available: six-word memoirs, photo-based writing, spooky stories, or novel outlining (see Figure 1.5). These breakouts gave students the opportunity to try their hand at an engaging activity related to the theme.

FIGURE 1.5. Activities used for the narrative workshop.

The Narrative Workshop

Journal (Scar Story): Students draw an outline of a human figure, mark all of the places where they have scars, choose one, and write the story of that scar. Everyone then stands and finds someone across the room to share with.

Workshop Overview: The teacher shows students a book table with examples of different kinds of narratives and engages students in a conversation defining *narrative* and identifying its features. The teacher highlights the range of lengths, forms, and audiences for these works.

Breakout Session Options (choose two activities, 25 minutes each):

1. **Six-word memoir:** Students tell a story in just six words and illustrate the work.
2. **Photo-based writing:** Students choose two photographs from a collection and write a story inspired by them.
3. **Spooky stories:** Students write down an idea for a character, a setting, and an object for a spooky story on three slips of paper (one idea per paper). They put these into the three labeled bags and then draw one slip of paper out of each bag. They use their selected character, setting, and object to write their own spooky story.
4. **Novel outlining:** Students think through their plans for writing a novel. They write down the book's title, a summary, a list of characters, and a table of contents.

As an example of the writing students produced in these breakouts, one student in the photo-based writing group shared the following:

> *I got a potion bottle and old building.*
> Deep in a forest with buildings, the most unusual woman . . . stared out of the window into a sea of people who moved in a slow sleepy sort of silence. Her eyes fell on a bottle that lay on its side on top of a little wooden table. It still rocked. Back and forth. Back and forth. If you looked closely, you could see the slightest amount of blue liquid. It fizzed and sparked. But you wouldn't know it unless you touched it, unless you felt its power. That was why she'd done it, why her beautiful city lay in a trance, because of the power in that blue liquid. If only she could go back and change what she'd done. She would go back. She would. Wouldn't she?

Over in the six-word memoir session, a student shared: "Pass, run, kick, score. Unbelievably happy."

Throughout this workshop, the mentors demonstrated to students that narrative composition can be highly engaging. These works can vary in length, and the visual mode can be used to inspire writing or to reinforce ideas in a piece. In our mentor debrief for this workshop, the mentors expressed how glad they were to use these activities with students. Miranda reflected, "It was cool hearing all their stories." Nari added, "I had a lot of fun. We did so many things."

The journal prompt, workshop overview, and four breakout sessions used for this narrative workshop can easily be integrated into secondary writing instruction (separately or together). These activities require minimal preparation and are easy for even novice teachers to implement. Teachers might select one activity to try out with students or give students a menu of options they can choose from. The reflection questions in Figure 1.6 can help teachers think through how they might use different forms of narrative writing in the classroom.

FIGURE 1.6. Reflection questions for readers.

Put Ideas from the Narrative Workshop into Practice

Examine Your Curriculum: What experiences do your students get to have with narrative throughout the school year? Do they have a chance to read and compose stories that consist of multiple modes (e.g., linguistic, visual, auditory, gestural, spatial)? Do students write in different forms?

Get Inspired: Go back and review the journal prompt, overview, and four breakout session activities from the narrative workshop (see Figure 1.5). Which of these activities could you use in your own teaching context? Would they require some modification to work for your students? Did you come across an idea in this section that inspired you to think differently about how to teach narrative?

2. The Poetry and Music Workshop

The second workshop, which focused on poetry and music, engaged students and challenged them as writers. They could work with forms such as blackout poetry, spoken word poetry, haiku, and songwriting in this workshop (see Figure 1.7).

FIGURE 1.7. Activities used for the poetry and music workshop.

The Poetry and Music Workshop

Journal (Object Poem): Students write a poem about a random object at their desk.

Workshop Overview: The teacher and students define *poetry* together and identify its characteristics. They look at different examples of writing and vote on whether each one is a poem. If time allows, the group could watch the video "What Makes a Poem . . . a Poem?" (Kovacs, 2017).

Breakout Session Options (choose two activities, 25 minutes each):

1. **Blackout poetry:** Students take a page from a discarded book (or a photocopied page from a book) and choose some words on the page to form a poem. They cross out the remaining words with a marker.
2. **Spoken word poetry:** Students brainstorm important moments in their lives and choose one to write about. They practice delivering the piece aloud, with attention to expressions, gestures, volume, and pacing.
3. **Haiku:** Students review the format of this Japanese form of poetry, which often deals with nature. They write a haiku of their own or create a group haiku (a series of haikus on a topic that students link together). If time allows, they could illustrate their work.
4. **Songwriting:** Students listen to beats or other instrumental music and write lyrics to their chosen song. They could be invited to bring music and headphones to class on this day.

Mentor Henry began the poetry and music workshop by asking students to write about objects he had placed at their tables. These objects were toys and other random items he had gathered from his little brother's room and from around their house. Henry clarified, "There aren't any strict rules about what kind of poem you need to make, so just be creative and experiment with different techniques."

Henry then asked the students to tell him what makes a poem (see Figure 1.8). The group discussed characteristics such as messages, lines, stanzas, symbolism, wordplay, rhythm, and focus. When someone mentioned rhyme, Henry asked whether poems had to rhyme, and the group decided they did not. Next, Henry took the group through a slideshow he had put together that included examples from Dr. Seuss, Shel Silverstein, E. E. Cummings, Edgar Allan Poe, and Homer, as well as "Eye of the Tiger" song lyrics, a haiku, a blackout poem, "Time Passes" by Anatol Knotek, and the "i" poem by jwcurry. With each slide, Henry stopped to ask students to raise their hands if they

FIGURE 1.8. Poetry workshop.

thought the material qualified as a poem. The interactive element of voting turned this into a lively and engaging discussion. To reinforce these points about poetry, Henry then showed them the video "What Makes a Poem . . . a Poem?" (Kovacs, 2017), telling them, "A poem doesn't have to be a certain length, and it can take a lot of different forms. That's something we're going to talk about during our breakouts."

After the breakout pitches, students chose two sessions to attend from blackout poetry, spoken word poetry, haiku, or songwriting. In the haiku session, one student wrote, "Snow and winter / like brother and sister / waiting for each other." Over in the spoken word poetry session, where students focused on their first experiences with something, they wrote about encountering snow, going on a boat, meeting someone famous, and so forth.

Miranda, who led the breakout session on songwriting, reflected afterwards, "Today's workshop was so fun to conduct! I asked them to listen to their favorite song and change up the lyrics that went with it. Since I felt this could at times be a little personal, I reassured them that if they were too shy to share, they could keep it to themselves or discuss the topics of their lyrics. Most of them shared what they liked about their favorite song." Secondary teachers could use breakout sessions like these to show students a variety of writing forms and modes, encourage them to draw on their personal experiences and observations, and tap into students' interests, including their love of music. See Figure 1.9 for some reflection questions.

FIGURE 1.9. Reflection questions for readers.

Put Ideas from the Poetry and Music Workshop into Practice

Examine Your Curriculum: What kinds of poetry are students encountering and composing in your classroom? Do you see any places where you could incorporate music, songwriting, or performance?

Get Inspired: Review the journal prompt, overview, and four breakout session activities from the poetry and music workshop (see Figure 1.7). Which of these activities could you use in your own teaching context? Would they require some modification to work for your students? Did you come across an idea in this section that inspired you to think differently about how to teach poetry?

3. The Art and Writing Workshop

The third two-hour YAS workshop was focused on art and writing (see Figure 1.10). Mentors developed activities that engaged students in composing works with images. Teachers could use these types of activities in the secondary classroom, or they could invite students to compose longer works such as picturebooks, graphic novel chapters, or animation.

FIGURE 1.10. Activities used for the art and writing workshop.

The Art and Writing Workshop

Journal (Object Drawing): Students draw an object that reflects their personality and explain their chosen object.

Workshop Overview: The teacher and students define *art* together and consider some of the different forms artwork might take (e.g., painting, sculpture, drawing, animation). If time allows, the class could explore some of the elements of art and their effects (McMahon, 2018).

Breakout Session Options (choose one activity, 40 minutes):

1. **Concrete Poetry:** Students write a poem, carefully arranging the words into meaningful shapes.
2. **Comics:** Students explore comics and graphic novels and compose their own piece.

The mentors decided to offer only two breakout sessions during this workshop to give students time to create their artwork. Students could either make comics or concrete poems during the single extended breakout. Henry explained the comics breakout as follows:

> So our table is going to be doing comic books, graphic novels, and comic strips. We have a lot of different options. We have blank templates if you want to draw your own characters. We have templates with characters already in them, so if you don't feel comfortable with drawing, you can fill in the dialogue boxes. And we also have blank sheets of paper if you just want to do whatever you want.

The students were excited to get to work in this session (see Figure 1.11), and they produced some interesting comics (see Figure 1.12).

FIGURE 1.11. Students at the comics breakout session.

FIGURE 1.12. A student's comic.

FIGURE 1.13. Example of a concrete poem.

During the concrete poetry breakout pitch, Nari said, "Did you know that your words mean something and tell a story, but the shape and the color of your words can also tell a story? If you want to write a concrete poem with us, come to our breakout session." This session resulted in concrete poetry that ranged from simple and straightforward (see Figure 1.13) to more complex and mysterious.

In her concrete poem, one author (see Figure 1.14) created the illusion of wind through her arrangement of the words. She wrote:

> Have you been half asleep? And have you heard voices? I've heard them calling my name. Ribbons and tassels and sweet summer noises. Who is she? She never came. Ladybugs. Grasshoppers. Sweet autumn breeze. The river reminds me of dreams, dreams. Have you been half asleep? Have you heard voices?

This student formed the ground with the words "I've heard them calling your name . . ." (see Figure 1.15).

FIGURE 1.14. A student with her concrete poem.

FIGURE 1.15. Close-up of the poem.

Both options for this forty-minute breakout session dealt with words and images, and they reinforced the idea that design and layout play an important role in communicating meaning. These are great activities for supporting visual literacy. To integrate ideas from this workshop into your teaching, check out Figure 1.16.

FIGURE 1.16. Reflection questions for readers.

Put Ideas from the Art and Writing Workshop into Practice

Examine Your Curriculum: What visual compositions are students encountering and composing in your classroom? Do you see any places where you could incorporate arts-based writing?

Get Inspired: Review the journal prompt, overview, and two breakout session activities from the art and writing workshop (see Figure 1.10). Which of these activities could you use in your own teaching context? Would they require some modification to work for your students? Did you come across an idea in this section that inspired you to think differently about how to teach arts-based writing?

4. The Drama and Film Workshop

Going into the drama and film workshop, some of the more introverted mentors and students were understandably feeling nervous. However, the workshop turned out to be less scary than expected. Most people did step out of their comfort zones that day, but everyone also had a lot of fun as they engaged in multiple ways of communicating: listening, speaking, writing, viewing, and gesturing.

The drama and film workshop was structured a bit differently because the mentor leading it, Nari, was a graduate student in theater education. She brought a unique expertise to the group, and the mentors wanted to give her more time to engage students in a sequence of drama activities. As students arrived, Nari asked them to sit at the tables with butcher paper and to brainstorm ideas around words that were written in the center of each table, words such as *mythology, solar eclipse,* and *lullaby.* As it turned out, these words were related to the story to come, "The Legend of Bakunawa" (Clark, 2016), a Philippine myth about a dragon trying to eat the moon. After students had a chance to record their ideas, Nari had them move to an area of the classroom that had been cleared of its desks and chairs, where students produced a soundscape as an icebreaker activity. A soundscape involves "passing" a sound around a circle by stomping, snapping, clapping, rubbing hands together, and so forth.

Next, Nari read part of the myth of Bakunawa and had students write a letter to one of the characters. One student wrote:

> Dear Bakunawa,
> Don't eat the moons! Keeping them all to yourself is selfish. Humans need the moon to light up the night sky. They love the moon as much as you. And what would you look up at when you're down beneath the sea? There would not be anything to look at. Just dark, empty sky.

Students then wrote to another character in the story. After hearing the entire folktale read aloud to them, students made tableaux (frozen scenes) of moments in the story with their group members. As they shared these, the remaining students walked around to study the group's scene.

FIGURE 1.17. Activities used for the drama and film workshop.

The Drama and Film Workshop

Workshop Overview: Students brainstorm ideas on butcher paper and explore drama through a soundscape, passing sounds around a circle (stomping, clapping, snapping, etc.). They explore the story "The Legend of Bakunawa" (Clark, 2016), stopping periodically for listening, writing, and speaking activities. Then they make tableaux in groups to capture a moment from the story.

Journal (Letter to a Character): Students write a letter to one of the characters in the story.

Breakout Session Options (choose two activities, 25 minutes each):

1. **Writing scenes:** Students choose a situation that involves a conflict. They ask questions to try to dig deeper into the conflict and the characters' perceptions before incorporating their ideas into a script.
2. **Six-sentence outlines:** Students follow this model (attributed to Pixar) to outline their play or film: "Once upon a time there was ____. Every day, ____. One day ____. Because of that, ____. Because of that, ____. Until finally ____." (Bunting, n.d.)
3. **Screenplays:** Students explore screenplays of various films and talk about how these works are formatted. Then they write their own scene in this format.
4. **Dialogue writing:** Students watch a muted excerpt from a film and imagine what the characters are saying to each other.

Students chose two breakouts from the four available this day: writing scenes in response to a conflict, making a six-sentence outline for a movie or animated work, exploring screenplays, or writing dialogue for film scenes (see Figure 1.17). These breakout sessions guided students to think more deeply about the structure and content of plays and movies; the sessions also appealed to their interest in popular entertainment. The screenplay breakout session included examples from series such as Star Wars, Harry Potter, Pirates of the Caribbean, Batman, Toy Story, and more. In this breakout, the mentor explained how screenplays are formatted and focused on the conventions of this form:

> I have these handouts. It basically shows you how you make a script. It's kind of complicated, but you don't have to follow it exactly. The main thing is you have scene descriptions written out normally. But character dialogue, you don't do it in quotes like you do when you're writing a story. In scripts, you have the character's name at the top and then you write out the dialogue underneath that. You can also put in parentheses how they talk, their tone of voice, or if they make any noises, like laughter. You put that in parentheses to indicate that. For scripts, you also write out the place of the scene, the setting. Here it is: "ext." That's [an] exterior [scene]. You can put the time of day.

Over in the session on writing a scene in response to a given conflict, Miranda provided a choice of scenarios, such as this one: "Lee builds a rocket in the family garage. What happens when it is stolen? Who stole it?"

Most of the mentors had been apprehensive heading into this workshop because they were nervous about their acting abilities and theater knowledge. However, they commented later that they were pleasantly surprised by how well their activities went and how much students enjoyed working with dramatic forms of expression. Henry wrote in his reflection:

> I thought that the day was successful. I like how every workshop has brought something a little different to the table and that students never have to write just one thing throughout the entire program. The acting portion of this week's workshop was well done, and I'm surprised at how easy it was to perform alongside the students. The tableaux portion of the overview was especially fun. I didn't really have to prompt my students to come up with ideas. One of them immediately came up with something funny and unique, and we just did it. Even if I personally don't have a lot of confidence in my acting ability, it was great to see that the students brought plenty of their own confidence.

In her reflection, Emma wrote:

> Watching Nari present the overview showed me that I already use aspects of drama when I speak in front of others. [Teachers should] not be afraid to incorporate student movement and drama into a classroom. . . . Students of any age need to move. . . . Of course, setting rules and noise levels is also extremely important, especially if there is concern other classes might be disturbed, but [drama has potential] to make a classroom stronger and much more exciting for students.

I think it helped that Nari's overview consisted of several different types of activities, and then the breakouts offered variety as well. The more reserved students were able to find some opportunities for quieter contemplation throughout the day. Figure 1.18 provides some reflection questions to help teachers integrate drama and film into their writing classes.

FIGURE 1.18. Reflection questions for readers.

Put Ideas from the Drama and Film Workshop into Practice

Examine Your Curriculum: Do students have opportunities to engage with drama or film in your classroom? Do you see any places where you could incorporate these experiences?

Get Inspired: Review the journal prompt, overview, and four breakout session activities from the drama and film workshop (see Figure 1.17). Which of these activities could you use in your own teaching context? Would they require some modification to work for your students? Did you come across an idea in this section that inspired you to think differently about how to teach drama and film?

5. The Genre Study Workshop

The fifth themed writing workshop in YAS dealt with genres. Miranda began by reviewing genres (e.g., categories of works such as mystery, sci-fi, fantasy, action, historical fiction). Then she prompted the students to write a story that made use of the conventions of the genre they selected. Miranda explained:

> I'm going to give you a really vague sentence, and I want you to tell me a story about it. [Decide on] the genre. It could be any of the ones we talked

> about. [Think about the] main characters, the time period, and the setting. "You have just crash landed . . ." I'm not going to tell you where, who, or how. I want you to tell me all those things, and I want you to utilize these categories.

The versatility of this crash-landing prompt worked well because students could make it work for any number of genres, such as sci-fi, horror, fantasy, romance, mystery, and more. For example, a student shared a fantasy story that began: "We have just crashed into Banana Island. We look around and see no people, no animals . . . we only see black, like midnight. We see towering gray pillars."

After this activity, students attended two of the four breakout sessions. One of the options was to write in response to a clip from *Zathura: A Space Adventure.* In other breakouts, students could make use of sensory language in their realistic fiction, use their phones to conduct research on a historical period, or roll dice to create a character using a template from a fantasy role-playing game (see Figure 1.19).

FIGURE 1.19. Activities used for the genre study workshop.

The Genre Study Workshop

Workshop Overview: The teacher engages students in a conversation about different genres of stories (fantasy, science fiction, mystery, historical fiction, etc.).

Journal (Crash Landing): Students are told that they have just crash-landed. They need to choose a genre and tell their story, drawing on the conventions of that genre.

Breakout Session Options (choose two activities, 25 minutes each):

1. **Realistic fiction:** Students create a short, realistic story that uses all five senses.
2. **Action-adventure:** Students watch a short film clip up to the climax and write the resolution.
3. **Historical fiction:** Students research a time period on their phone and write a story with this setting.
4. **Sci-fi/fantasy:** Students create a character using a Dungeons and Dragons–style character template.

Mentor Henry explained to students how to fill out the character template for his breakout:

> At the top of your character sheet, you have a spot for character name, class and level (e.g., bounty hunter, wizard, spaceship pilot), race, personality traits, ideals, bonds (e.g., personal connections to people or places), flaws, attacks/spell casting (e.g., weapons, spells, magical powers), equipment (e.g., suit of armor, personal robot, first-aid kit), features/traits, age, height, weight, and eye color. Write a description of what your character looks like or draw a portrait right there in the box. The rest is pretty self-explanatory. You fill in your character's backstory and that kind of thing. One more thing you can do if you are interested is calculate your character's ability scores. It's a way to conceptualize what characters are good at. If you're interested, I have some dice.

Many students were familiar with Dungeons & Dragons from TV's *Stranger Things*. In fact, this session turned out to be so popular that students had to pull up a second table. The sound of rolling dice filled the room.

In the historical fiction breakout, a student shared, "I'm writing about a girl who is a nurse, but she wants to be a fighter pilot. And the two guys are fighter pilots in WWII, and the girl is trying to convince the guys to let her onto their plane, and she can help them as they fly around." Other students were writing about ancient Greece and Rome or 9/11.

These breakouts showed students a variety of ways to engage in writing, and they tapped into students' interests. We found that because genres tend to abide by particular conventions and tropes, they are useful for simultaneously focusing and awakening students' creative energy. The reflection questions in Figure 1.20 can help teachers think more about how they might incorporate genre study into their writing instruction.

FIGURE 1.20. Reflection questions for readers.

Put Ideas from the Genre Study Workshop into Practice

Examine Your Curriculum: Do students have opportunities to read or compose works in different genres in your classroom? Do you see any places where you could incorporate these experiences?

Get Inspired: Review the journal prompt, overview, and four breakout session activities from the genre study workshop (see Figure 1.19). Which of these activities could you use in your own teaching context? Would they require some modification to work for your students? Did you come across an idea in this section that inspired you to think differently about how to teach genres?

Encouraging Experimentation and Play

Teachers can use short activities like those described in this chapter to quickly immerse students in different forms of writing. In the YAS program, the breakout choices were typically offered simultaneously and repeated once, which allowed students to attend two sessions. One mentor was assigned to each breakout, and in just twenty-five minutes that person would introduce the activity, share examples, and lead students through brainstorming, writing, and optional sharing. It is important to note that mentors did not expect students to produce perfect, polished pieces in twenty-five minutes. Instead, these sessions provided opportunities to learn about different kinds of writing and to play and experiment with them—like a child entering a playground at recess and seeing all of the fun equipment they can run around and try out. They choose one and spend some time with it. Writers had the option of continuing to work on their pieces during the extended writing time, taking them home to finish, or abandoning them.

Over the years, we have offered YAS in various formats, including weekly programs, Zoom workshops, and in-person public events. Regardless of the format, the emphasis has always been on giving students the opportunity to experiment with different forms of writing. Even at an in-person YAS event that involved ASU student and professor volunteers leading short breakout sessions for the community on one day only, mentors were able to quickly grasp what they needed to accomplish in their allotted time, offer a variety of types of writing, connect with participants, and get them excited to write. In other words, the work of running a breakout session is not difficult or onerous; even those with no teaching experience can do it, and it can work as part of a stand-alone event.

Our work in the YAS program suggests that it is not necessary to always think of writing outcomes in terms of weeks or months. A twenty-five-minute experience with a new form of writing is sometimes just the right amount of time to spark student creativity and interest in that form and to introduce some of the norms guiding composition. Perhaps we have been thinking about time wrong in education. And perhaps we need to be more open to the idea that students should not always have to finish everything they start. I am not suggesting throwing out units or long pieces of writing. However, I do think we need to make more time for experimentation and play in secondary English classrooms. The study of the YAS program showed that participants benefited from opportunities to try out different modes and forms of writing for the pleasure of it, without fear of punishment or failure. Writing confidence grows out of these moments.

It is worth sitting down to reflect on the experiences with writing that students are having over an entire course or program. If there is little variety in our curriculum or if we are starting to see students disengaging right in front of us, the problem may be that we are thinking about writing in much too narrow terms.

Using Mentor Texts and Props

Another useful observation for teachers to consider is that across this program, *mentor texts* were used to show students examples of writing. Some of these exemplars were professionally produced (e.g., published stories, books), pieces found online, or works mentors composed specifically for their breakout sessions. Part of the reason mentors were successful in quickly acclimating students to new forms of writing was that they provided clear examples of the types of writing students were being asked to do.

In addition, mentors brought in props at every opportunity to engage and inspire students. They used objects for poetry writing, had students roll dice when filling out Dungeons & Dragons–style character sheets, and had students draw idea slips from a bag. In other years of the program, I saw mentors bring in pieces of evidence for a mystery writing activity, use board games, and distribute photographs of characters to activate student imaginations. This kind of visual and tactile engagement is underused in writing education—especially with older students—but it can be an excellent way to build interest and excitement around whatever type of writing is being explored.

Appreciating Writing in Different Forms

In a survey at the end of the YAS program, I found that the one feature adolescents valued the most was engaging in different kinds of writing. They commented:

- "I like how YAS shows us a little bit of everything, letting us choose our favorites and develop our work."
- "The Young Authors' Studio was a wonderful experience! It helped me explore different ways to write."
- "I think of myself as a person who is willing to write almost anything."
- "I love all genres."
- "I learned that there are different forms of writing (not just books and poems and dramas) . . . [and] that I already write a lot."

Students appreciate writing instruction that challenges them to think in different ways. Writing in multiple forms and modes can be empowering, inspiring, and engaging for students. Additional ideas for doing this work can be found in Figure 1.21.

FIGURE 1.21. Additional ideas to inspire creative expression.

More Ideas to Inspire Writers

Here are some additional ideas to inspire youth writers that we used in other years of the YAS program:

- Create a **found poem** with images, using unwanted items (e.g., empty cereal boxes, magazines, old books).
- Take a **photograph** that tells a story.
- Draw a **storyboard** for a scene from a movie you would like to make.
- Make a **round robin zine or short story** (i.e., compose one section and pass it along to others to add to it).
- Write **poetry inspired by a photograph** (in your brainstorming, be sure to include your thoughts about what is *not* pictured in the image).
- Research a problem, write a **monologue**, and perform it.
- Make a **movie trailer** for a book you love.
- Write a **letter** to no one.
- Listen to music and make **graffiti art**.
- Compose a **personal visual narrative** (e.g., animated work, short film, comic, video game).
- Write a **story of a limited length** (e.g., 300 words or 120 characters).
- Choreograph a **dance routine** to convey an emotion and write about it.
- Make **collage poetry** that brings together words, images, and other materials.

Pause and Reflect

Using a variety of writing forms and modes is an important mentoring strategy because it helps students develop flexibility and creativity. These skills are necessary as communication is changing at a fast pace, thanks to advancements in new technologies.

This chapter shows how YAS mentors invited students to write in a wide variety of forms and modes through workshops focused on narrative writing, poetry and music, art, drama and film, and genre study. When considering how to vary the writing that secondary students get to work with in the classroom, these five YAS workshops can provide teachers with a road map for getting started, down to specific activities that could be used (and that require little preparation, if any). In addition, this chapter reminds us of the value of experimentation and play in the writing classroom, and it argues that mentor texts and props can be powerful learning tools in writing instruction. These are important considerations for classroom teachers.

Before we explore what a secondary teacher has to say about using this first strategy in the classroom to support all students, let's reflect on what this strategy means to you (see Figure 1.22).

FIGURE 1.22. Reflection questions for strategy #1.

Pause and Reflect

Strategy #1: Using a Wide Range of Writing Forms and Modes with Students

- How do you already use this strategy in your teaching?
- What are some new ways you can use this strategy to benefit students?
- How does this strategy help bring out the author (or graphic novelist, filmmaker, songwriter . . .) in every student?

Teacher Interview: Carrie Deahl on Using a Wide Range of Writing Forms and Modes with Students

In some ways, the YAS program was an ideal program, one that existed outside of the confines or restrictions that most teachers regularly face in school. Therefore, to really understand how mentoring writers can look in more traditional school settings, it is necessary to turn to secondary teachers to discover how they are using these strategies with their students.

In this section, we turn to a secondary English teacher who uses a wide range of writing forms and modes in their teaching. Carrie Deahl (see Figure 1.23) is a teacher at Maryvale High School in Phoenix, Arizona. Carrie has been a teacher for twenty-four years, has National Board Certification, and has won the Arizona English Teachers Association Teacher of the Year award and the NCTE High School Teacher of Excellence Award. Carrie identifies as nonbinary, and they enjoy writing and performing spoken word poetry and exploring the outdoors.

FIGURE 1.23. Selfie by Carrie Deahl.

Can you share some examples of how your students write in different forms or modes in your classroom?
My teaching draws a lot from Penny Kittle's book *Write beside Them* (2008). We start with nonfiction personal narrative, write really short pieces called snapshot moments, and expand these into longer personal narratives. From there we move into novel writing. Students also write a "This I Believe" essay and record it (audio or video, whatever they feel comfortable with). Then we work in various forms of poetry, including spoken word. Students compile a poetry anthology during National Poetry Month in April, with four poems written by each student.

My favorite unit of the year is the graphic novel. I found out about this project from an article I read in *English Journal* (Maldonado & DeHart, 2021). We brainstorm social issues that are local, national, or global and pick one to research. It's anything from domestic violence to homelessness to the environment to trans rights, etc. [The students] need at least two or three facts to include. Then they make storyboards and workshop them. The audience [of their peers] will say, "This is what's working well. Have you thought about this? Or what about moving the facts here or changing the order?" Students make revisions, edit, and publish. They can use an app like Pixton or Canva to create a digital graphic novel, or they can hand illustrate it. It's a really beautiful process.

I've also done a unit where students write a one-act play and perform it. They get a kick out of that, especially picking their cast from the class. At the end of the year, they have a big electronic portfolio of all of their work, and they write a letter to themselves, reflecting on their growth, struggles, and next steps. They hate it because it's a lot of work, but it allows them to see, "I am a writer. I have gone through these types of writing and created this body of work."

Why do you think it is important to have students work with different forms?
This is real-world writing. I want to expose them to as much of that as possible. Students have these preconceived notions of "I'm not a writer. I don't see myself as a writer." Or they think that they can't do certain things, and they put these limitations on themselves. And maybe I'm out to prove them wrong, that they *can* write a novel. On their end-of-the-year surveys, some of them will pick these pieces as their favorite things they did over the course of the year. I want to expose kids to as many types of writing as I can because the five-paragraph essay is so boring and outdated. We have to be creative in how we're thinking about teaching writing to kids. If I'm teaching persuasive writing, let's write a public service announcement. Let's create some kind of commercial or something to get people to buy a product or to go somewhere. I want them to see that writing doesn't have to be outdated. It's about proving to them that they have the ability to create in different modes and to push themselves as writers.

What are the benefits of this work?
The number one benefit is it builds their confidence. They take risks, and their confidence skyrockets as a result. They begin to trust themselves and each other as writers. Kids need a safe space to take risks. And I would not just throw something like making a graphic novel at a kid without modeling it first. I wouldn't do that without first being vulnerable and sketching out my graphic novel ideas. Another big benefit is that they're building agency as writers. And some of them will find a form they like and get really excited about it. And then that becomes their interest for the year. It also makes them flexible as writers. They have these

different tools and skills they can take and apply. It makes me flexible as an instructor as well. We don't do enough research in English [classes]. The graphic novel project is one way we can bring in real-world research, facts, and statistics and embed those within a story to teach our audiences, maybe including a domestic violence hotline as a call to action. It's really impressive what they end up creating.

Have you faced any challenges with this work?
I had no idea what I was doing with the graphic novel stuff, and it was a struggle. Students hated it at first because we had not brainstormed social issues. They were like, "What does that even mean? And we have to do research? This sounds like it's not going to be worth my time." I pushed back and said, "Yeah, we're going to. Let's back up and brainstorm some social issues. Let's work on this together." I think I have success with kids because I put myself out there first, and I model what they need along the way, whether it's brainstorming or revising. I will say, "I got stuck there for a second," and show them that struggle is part of the writing process. I struggle with illustrations and use stick figures, so I will say, "You know, my confidence is not great in this area, but I need to do this first to be able to get to the next step." I think teachers need to jump in more often and put themselves out there with their students.

How can teachers get started with this work?
At the beginning of the year, I survey the kids. What are the different types of writing that you know about and are interested in? And I'll give them a list. Have you written any of these? And that'll be based on my curriculum that I created for the year. And then we move into what they feel comfortable with, while I also keep in mind that it's really important to get them out of their comfort zone. Storytelling is such a large part of our histories as individuals. We get stories from our families. So that's why I always start with narrative. It just seems like a natural, easy place to start. I want to ease them into the more difficult writing situations.

What additional advice on this topic do you have for teachers?
We have to think beyond traditional forms of writing that have been around for so long and that bog down teachers. Writing doesn't look the same as it did fifteen or twenty years ago. It is possible to combine different types of writing like expository, narrative, and persuasive.

The National Writing Project allowed me to connect with people beyond my district. I think that's probably what saved me as an educator. Attend conferences. Find a way to get a scholarship to go to NCTE's annual convention if you can't afford it. Make connections with people at the local colleges and universities and with other educators who want to expand what writing looks like in their classrooms. Ask about the kinds of writing they are teaching. I think this is the way to broaden how you think as an English teacher. Also, Readwritethink.org is a great resource.

In addition, teachers need to be vulnerable with their students and take risks. I've been very fortunate to have so many connections in the writing and arts community in this city. That's part of my vulnerability and my willingness to get up and perform and model for kids. I allow kids to see that this is a safe space and taking risks is encouraged. And I have been able to take some of my English department colleagues with me on spoken word poetry field trips.

Do you have any favorite resources on this topic?
I have favorite authors I pay attention to like Kelly Gallagher and Tom Newkirk. I watch what's going on with the local spoken word scene and beyond. I follow poets like Sarah Kay and pay attention to the writing scene beyond my local newspaper. The Poetry Foundation and Poets.org are great websites to pull poetry from. When I'm stuck, I literally type "spoken word and [a topic like environmentalism]" and find YouTube videos out there. I have an outline of what I want my curriculum to be, but I also need to shake things up. Yes, I teach Sarah Kay over and over again, but I want to get different people in there, too. So I try to not get bogged down by traditional English curriculum. Who's the "Poe" now? Who's doing horror now? What's contemporary? I think there is a time and place for classics. Absolutely. But there's so much good contemporary literature that kids need exposure to, and we can use these as mentor texts. We will do an imitation paragraph when they're playing with forms, and that's how I get comfortable. "Okay, I don't know how to teach it, so I'm going to play with writing one." I did this with pantoum, a Malaysian style of poetry that I learned about at a workshop fifteen years ago. The kids love that form because of the repetition. Poets.org explains what it is. That's one of my favorites to use. Keep it fresh for different writers and poets.

Do you have any cautions or warnings for teachers?
Preview everything (videos, literature) you want to use. Sometimes we're in a rush, and we want to grab something, but give yourself the time to look through it first.

Do you have any words of encouragement for teachers as they embark on this kind of work?
Anne Lamott has a great quote: "We write to expose the unexposed." And I think that my philosophy about writing is based on that. Make yourself vulnerable. If you're not willing to be real with your students and show them who you are as a writer, it is hard to get them to buy into writing and push themselves as writers. So put yourself out there. Take some risks.

Now You Try: Bringing Ideas to Life in the Secondary Classroom

Let's be honest. It can feel downright scary to try out something new with students, but these moments sometimes turn out to be the most rewarding learning experiences. My students and I enjoy composing spoken word poems, songs, and comics/graphic narratives. Some tips for using these forms with students follow.

Spoken Word Poetry

Spoken word poems are works written to be performed and are usually about three minutes long. Spoken word poetry has roots in African American cultural practices such as testifying and witnessing, as well as call and response (Smitherman, 1977).

At poetry slams, the audience is expected to respond to poets, snapping and offering supportive comments and utterances during the poem. Several book-length studies of youth poets examine how this form honors students' cultures and experiences, how it can be used to build community in a group, and how young people can use this form to reflect, critique, heal, and advocate (Fisher, 2007; Jocson, 2008; Williams, 2018). Spoken word poetry is very much about speaking one's truth and being emotionally vulnerable with others. The delivery of the words is important as well, with the poet attending to elements such as volume, pacing, pauses, gestures, and expressions. Poems may or may not be memorized. They are typically in free verse, but sometimes they do rhyme. Some tips for teaching spoken word poetry are provided in Figure 1.24.

FIGURE 1.24. Suggestions for teaching spoken word poetry.

Tips for Getting Started with Spoken Word Poetry

Begin with a Poem of Your Own: An ideal way to introduce spoken word poetry is for the teacher to launch into a poem, preferably with no notice—just a cold open right into their piece. Students will see the power of this form to convey their own experiences and understandings.

Explore Examples Together: Spoken word videos are widely available online. Students may already be familiar with Amanda Gorman's (2021) inauguration poem for Joe Biden, "The Hill We Climb." One poem I learned about from scholar Susan Weinstein at a conference years ago is Jamaica Osorio's (2009) "Kumulipo." I appreciate this piece because it helps reinforce to students that their languages and cultures are important.

Honor the Writing Process: Guide students through the work of brainstorming, writing, and polishing their pieces.

Sharing: Teachers could invite students to participate in a class poetry slam. However, please do not force students to read their pieces aloud to the class. Spoken word poems are sometimes incredibly personal and deal with traumatic experiences. Students need to be able to opt out of sharing their writing.

Assessment: Consider rewarding the steps of the writing process rather than assigning a letter grade to the final poem. Some things in life are more important than grades. This is one of them.

Resources: *Brave New Voices: The Youth Speaks Guide to Teaching Spoken Word Poetry* (Weiss & Herndon, 2001) is an excellent resource. The unit I use with my students can be found in the NCTE collection *A Symphony of Possibilities: A Handbook for Arts Integration in Secondary English Language Arts* (Macro & Zoss, 2019).

Songwriting

Songwriting can be used in the English language arts classroom as an activity everyone is doing, or it could be one option on a menu of project choices. Songwriting in an English class could involve writing lyrics to prerecorded music. After all, an array of instrumental music and free beats can be found online with a quick search. However, some of our students do write their own music outside of school and play guitar, piano, or other instruments. In fact, new technologies allow people to compose songs with computer programs—no physical instruments in hand! What it means to write a song today looks very different than it did for young people in garage bands thirty years ago. Some suggestions for teaching songwriting can be found in Figure 1.25.

FIGURE 1.25. Suggestions for teaching songwriting.

Tips for Getting Started with Songwriting

Decide How to Use Songwriting: Will students find their own instrumental song or beats and then write lyrics to these works (perhaps using their phones and headphones in class)? Or will you play a song on a loop and challenge students to write lyrics to it? Will songwriting be one of many creative project options on a list?

Challenge Students to Write for Different Purposes: Songs can be used for almost any purpose, such as to inform, persuade, or entertain. Students could write a song to respond to a book they read (Williams, 2013), advocate for a cause, or share something funny or meaningful.

Sharing: Invite students to share their pieces if they want to. This might take the form of a live performance, a class playlist, or lyrics with accompanying artwork.

Extension Activities: Teachers who have more time to devote to songwriting could have students analyze the lyrics and music of songs they like. Students could spend time considering what makes a song powerful or interesting, what similarities or differences lyrics share with other types of poetry, or why the Nobel Prize in Literature would be awarded to a songwriter.

Resources: For a creative take on using songwriting with students, see the work of Evans and colleagues (2021), who discuss a project in which they combined songwriting with personal narrative writing and podcasting. Also, consider exploring some composing software such as MuseScore and Noteflight.

Comics and Graphic Narratives

Comics can be as short as a single panel (i.e., a box) or a few panels long. Others might go on for an entire comic issue or even a series of issues unfolding over many years. Graphic novels are illustrated books that are typically divided into chapters. Manga is a Japanese form of graphic novel in which material is arranged on the page from right to left, as this is the direction in which Japanese is read; with manga in English, the translations are usually placed into the existing text boxes without adjusting the original layout or orientation of the images. These visual forms are incredibly popular with secondary students. In the YAS program, students enjoyed constructing visual works of their own. Figure 1.26 offers some suggestions for teaching visual composition.

FIGURE 1.26. Suggestions for teaching visual composition.

Tips for Getting Started with Comics and Other Graphic Narratives

Challenge Students to Write for Different Purposes: A comic does not have to be comical. It can be informative or persuasive, explore a traumatic event, or expose historical injustices. Graphic narratives might respond to a reading, recall a personal experience, share research, or comment on current events.

Teach Visual Elements: Teach the language of visual design and ask students to analyze visual narratives before composing works of their own (Williams, 2019). Focusing on a collection of concepts such as line, shape, color, size/scale, position, salience, modality, and typography (Serafini, 2014) can be extremely useful for doing this work.

Practice Drawing Simple Shapes with Big Personalities: A fun exercise is to draw a basic shape several times and add limbs, expressions, and clothing/accessories to each figure to distinguish it from the others. See Lynda Barry's *Making Comics* (2020) and Ivan Brunetti's *Cartooning: Philosophy and Practice* (2011) for drawing activities to use with students.

Embrace the Challenge of Design Work: Since the design of a comic matters (art style, visual elements used, page layout), I recommend steering clear of clip art, comic template programs, and AI when teaching the basics of how to put visual elements to use in an original work. Such tools and programs cheat students out of the most important learning that goes along with this work: design.

Set Clear Assignment Parameters: It helps to assign a minimum number of panels (e.g., twelve) spread out over a minimum number of pages (e.g., three).

Sharing: Students could participate in a gallery walk, leaving supportive comments for one another as they visit different projects in the room. This format also works for feedback on drafts.

Assessment: I ask students to include specific details, a thoughtful background, color, and legible print or typed text in their projects. Along with the project, students submit an artist statement in which they describe the work, visual elements used and their effects, and comments on their process, tools used, and any challenges encountered and how they worked through them. They include at least two photographs documenting their process.

Resources: In addition to the texts mentioned earlier, another recommended resource is Scott McCloud's *Making Comics: Storytelling Secrets of Comics, Manga, and Graphic Novels* (2006).

Final Thoughts

The YAS mentors found that teaching a wide range of writing forms and modes was beneficial to participants in the program. According to Emma, the program gave young people a chance to work with forms they had not "been shown or taught in the past." She added, "Teaching students about different forms of writing that are not focused on in school is essential, as writing is so much more than essays."

Today's students need experiences conveying their ideas across multiple modes and forms of writing so they are prepared to respond to the wide array of rhetorical situations they will face throughout their lives. "Essays are just one way for students to express what they know and think; teachers should encourage and make possible a variety of modes through which students can demonstrate learning creatively" (Lyiscott et al., 2021). While traditional forms of writing (essays, research papers, etc.) still have their place in the secondary ELA classroom, we are shortchanging our students if that is all we offer them. Guiding students through different writing forms and modes gives them a chance to expand their visual and multimodal literacies, try out different writing identities (author, graphic novelist, filmmaker, songwriter, etc.), and learn the conventions of writing as it is used in various careers.

Some teachers may feel uncomfortable wading into new waters and trying out new forms of writing with students. This is understandable. I often feel this way myself. However, when we take time to write alongside our students—to play and experiment with words, images, sounds, and more—we can remember how meaningful and rewarding it can be to write. We, too, can lose ourselves in the joy and challenge of composing a song, a comic, a short film, a horror story, or a work in a form that does not yet exist as I type this sentence. How exciting!

Now that we have explored the importance of using a wide range of writing forms and modes with students, the next step is to combine these in ways that invite student choice and decision-making, the subject of the next chapter.

Chapter Two

Encouraging Student Choice and Decision-Making

A gallery walk is in progress. Students' projects are placed on tables around the room, and the whole class is up and moving, checking out each work and responding with comments. There is a buzz as the students express excitement and take joy in seeing their classmates' projects. Their creativity has come alive.

Every time I assign creative work in my classes at Arizona State University, I look forward to seeing what the students will create. I regularly use a creative project in my on-campus Studio Ghibli films[1] course. I give the students a list of options that includes composing an animated work, picturebook, comic, short story, song, artwork, podcast, and the list goes on.

Students have made websites, video games, animated works, model planes, sculptures, a bee house, cookbooks, songs (e.g., for harp, guitar, trumpet), 3D-printed objects, terrariums, crocheted characters, posters, paintings, podcasts, stories, poems, photo essays, and more. Our gallery walk delights me every time because I see skills and talents I did not even realize the students had.

My students enjoy composing these creative projects because they get to decide which film or character to focus on and which form and tools they will use to best convey their ideas. They get to exercise choice, which makes them take ownership of their piece. They put a lot of effort into these projects because they know others will see them.

Along with the project, they write a reflection documenting their process and explaining any challenges they encountered and how they worked through them. These statements make their hidden labor *visible*. I learn a great deal from this documentation of their behind-the-scenes work, and I am always in awe of the tenacity, creativity, and resourcefulness students display.

Many students enjoy composing works when they are able to have a say in them. Having some space to imagine, plan, and execute ideas is necessary to produce innovative pieces. Writers need the freedom to experiment, fail, reassess, grapple, problem-solve, gather more information, fine-tune, and ultimately try again. They become more confident and independent through these experiences. Teachers can play an important role as writing mentors by encouraging student choice and decision-making in the English language arts classroom. Students develop agency as they try out different forms of writing, take control over their words, and experience success.

This book recommends that teachers use six strategies to mentor youth writers. This chapter focuses on the second strategy, encouraging student choice and decision-making in writing instruction (see Figure 2.1). As in the other chapters of this book, I share some background on the strategy, show how mentors applied it in the Young Authors' Studio program, provide an interview with a secondary teacher, and offer sample activities. Figure 2.2 provides key terms for this chapter.

FIGURE 2.1. This chapter focuses on the second strategy for mentoring youth writers.

Six Strategies for Mentoring Youth Writers

1. Use a wide range of writing forms and modes with students.
2. **Encourage student choice and decision-making.**
3. Build a supportive writing community.
4. Honor student knowledge, experience, and interests.
5. Nurture students as writers.
6. Connect writers to opportunities beyond the classroom.

FIGURE 2.2. Useful terms to know for this chapter.

Key Terms

Agency: A sense of power and control over what one does.

Differentiated Instruction: Instruction that allows for some degree of personalization. For example, students might explore different content, use different processes, or produce different kinds of works.

Self-Efficacy: Believing in one's own abilities to accomplish goals; confidence in being able to succeed at something.

Justifying This Work

According to the NCTE *Position Statement on Writing Instruction in School* (2022), "When students . . . are not invited to make choices about their own writing, they can become disengaged in school-based writing (Behizadeh, 2014)." In fact, the NCTE statement has much to say about the importance of student choice and decision-making in writing instruction (see Figure 2.3).

FIGURE 2.3. NCTE position statement connections.

Connections to NCTE's *Position Statement on Writing Instruction in School* (2022)

- "Writing instruction in many English language arts classrooms rarely includes opportunities for children and youth to . . . make complex decisions about composition."
- "Many professional development opportunities related to teaching writing focus more on the teaching of products and forms—i.e., the writing—than they do on building students' decision-making processes as *writers* (Wahleithner, 2018)."
- "An overly narrow focus on products—and particular types of products—leaves young people underprepared to understand the rhetorical nature of writing, to make decisions about their own writing, and to transfer their writing knowledge to new contexts, especially contexts beyond the classroom."
- We must "advocate for writing instruction that . . . invites students to become writers who . . . make authentic choices about processes and products."
- "Writing is an important form of self-expression and communication as well as a tool for thinking, reflecting, and learning."

Many classroom teachers do create opportunities for their students to make decisions about their own writing:

> Many of us design our courses as writing workshops, so that students make choices about the genres they compose in. We structure writing assignments so that students make choices about topics and organization. We teach students to make choices about sentence structure, syntax, diction,

> and style. We resist teaching models such as five-paragraph themes and so-called power writing, which micromanage decisions and deprive students of the opportunity to learn by making authentic choices about their writing. Choices matter for student writers. (Bush & Zuidema, 2011, p. 86)

Gallagher (2006) acknowledges two immediate benefits that come from building choice into writing instruction:

1. "Choice fosters a feeling of ownership in the writer. When a student develops ownership, she is much more likely not only to start a paper, but to maintain a stronger work ethic while in the drafting process."
2. "Choice drives better revision. . . . A student who cares about her paper is much more likely to closely revise." (p. 91)

At the same time, Gallagher recognizes the real-world challenges teachers face in their jobs, including meeting standards and helping students pass standardized tests. Instead of seeing student choice as working against those goals, he sees it as a necessary way of teaching that helps students fare better with such measures. He argues that having some choice helps students build positive attitudes toward writing: "Until students warm up to writing they will never work hard developing their writing skills" (p. 93). Giving students some freedom to make decisions about their writing not only impacts them at that moment, but it is also a long-term investment in their writing lives.

Despite what some textbook companies, politicians, and school administrators would have teachers believe, the Common Core State Standards (2010) document does not dictate the forms that secondary students' compositions must take. Consider the following anchor standards for writing:

- "Write arguments to support claims in an analysis of substantive topics or texts using valid reasoning and relevant and sufficient evidence."
- "Write informative/explanatory texts to examine and convey complex ideas and information clearly and accurately through the effective selection, organization, and analysis of content."
- "Write narratives to develop real or imagined experiences or events using effective technique, well-chosen details, and well-structured event sequences."
- "Produce clear and coherent writing in which the development, organization, and style are appropriate to task, purpose, and audience."
- "Develop and strengthen writing as needed by planning, revising, editing, rewriting, or trying a new approach."
- "Conduct short as well as more sustained research projects based on focused questions, demonstrating understanding of the subject under investigation."

- "Write routinely over extended time frames (time for research, reflection, and revision) and shorter time frames (a single sitting or a day or two) for a range of tasks, purposes, and audiences." (CCSS.ELA-LITERACY.CCRA.W.1–5, 7, 10)

There is no reason, then, why a persuasive piece cannot take the form of a commercial, an advertisement, a short film, or an animated work. Likewise, a narrative assignment could take the form of a graphic novel, a picturebook, or a spoken word poem. Unfortunately, standards have often been interpreted in extremely narrow ways that harm both students and teachers.

Teachers can build choice into their writing instruction through "choice boards." Suh et al. (2022) explain that "choice boards allow students to engage their strengths and pursue one assignment or project in depth" (p. 90). To illustrate, when exploring a theme like "home" as a class, they recommend providing multiple project options for students, such as a letter, song, fictional story, comparative analysis, poem, essay, script, or description of a place. They point out that using choice boards can be beneficial to all students, especially bilingual and multilingual youth.

Furthermore, providing students with a menu of options does not have to be limited to one assignment. Sandven and colleagues (2023) describe an innovative graduate-level course in which preservice teachers had a full menu of assignments (with different point values) to choose from. Due dates were spread throughout the course. Students could even come up with their own assignment options. Students engaged in a wide range of activities, including dances, short films, graphic novels, songs, podcasts, scripts, photo essays, and more. The authors found that using this style of teaching enabled the students to "activate their interests and personal stories . . . and express their learning in ways that featured their talents and skills" (p. 53).

Having some choice can be motivating for students (Iyengar & Lepper, 2000; Patall et al., 2008; Patall et al., 2010). At the same time, "too much choice can actually lead to decreased motivation and satisfaction," claims Robinson (n.d.), who recommends that teachers provide a limited number of options (three to five choices). She also suggests that teachers plan structured opportunities to help students make appropriate choices. This involves giving students time to research topics and make personal connections. Boscolo and Gelati (2007) caution that choice of topic alone will not guarantee increased motivation. Although "an interesting topic is a good starting point, . . . what can motivate students to write is the awareness that writing on that topic is worthwhile" (p. 208).

Teachers can help students generate ideas for writing through practices such as making lists or clustering ideas (Blasingame & Bushman, 2005), identifying writing territories (Atwell, 1998), meeting with a peer to come up with questions about a topic (Robb, 2010), using freewriting diaries (Elbow, 1998), doing quick writes (Kittle, 2008), and more. To assist writers in exploring the different facets of their topic, a "1 Topic = 18 Topics Chart" can be useful; this organizer helps students break down a topic, revealing nuances that students might not have previously considered (Gallagher, 2011, p. 13).

Writers need time for ideas to percolate. Romano (1987) explains, "Percolating prepares writers to write. They talk to friends about their ideas, mentally rehearse lines, read, lie on the couch or stare out the window and think. Idea and image incubate in the writer" (p. 55). Romano points out that percolation is an ongoing mental process that continues while writing, revising, sharing, and reflecting on a work. Dean (2017) recommends providing students with "strategies to help them learn how to come to know enough about their topic so they can write interestingly and knowledgeably about it" (p. 20). Depending on what students still need to know, they might go to a particular place, make a timeline, do an interview, watch videos, read, outline, and so forth.

Writing is an intellectual act. It is thinking manifested in a physical form. We know from experience that writers must make a whole series of decisions during the writing process, including selecting a topic and form for the work as well as generating ideas. "Making these individual choices can be challenging. It requires you to write and re-write until you feel you have expressed your idea clearly" (UNC Writing Center, 2023). In addition, writers must make decisions at multiple levels, including the levels of the argument, paragraph, sentence, and word. "As you write, you constantly choose, sometimes intuitively, but sometimes painstakingly, which idea, phrase, or word should come next as you lead your reader down the page" (UNC Writing Center, 2023). Formatting matters, too. Writers make a variety of choices about how their pieces are physically constructed. Bush and Zuidema (2011) recommend explicitly teaching students design principles so they can learn to effectively communicate through visual elements. Every layout and design choice conveys meaning to readers and viewers of that work.

One practice that teachers can use to draw attention to students' decision-making is to ask them to annotate their pieces with comments. Sanchez et al. (2019) recommend using "comment bubbles" in the margins of papers to make student thinking visible. This can be done with comment boxes in a typed word document or handwritten comments in the margins of lined paper. They found that "students used . . . comment bubbles to react to research they read in journal articles, elaborate on their writing choices, share their personal experiences, and reflect on their future career interests. [This practice] facilitates student self-expression, self-reflection, and critical thinking" (p. 463). Some other ways to inspire and illuminate student decision-making include using reflections and conferences, which I discuss at the end of this chapter.

Mentoring in Action: Inside the Young Authors' Studio Program

It is Saturday and the adolescents are eager to write. They bustle around the room, heading to their choice of breakouts:

Nari: Six-word memoirs are over here!

Amir: Spooky stories!

Miranda: Photo narratives!

Henry: Novels over here!

Emma: If there aren't enough chairs at the table you want, just pull another chair over.

As they write, the students in the YAS program chat away cheerfully. They all stop to listen when someone shares their writing, and they respond with statements like "Nice," "Cool," and "That's wonderful!" Then they fall silent for a while as everyone gets back to working on their pieces.

This section shares findings about how choice and decision-making were encouraged in the YAS program. In addition, the section discusses the importance of giving students the option to share their writing, considers the role of structure and choice in inspiring creativity, and argues that teachers need to be trusted to make instructional decisions.

Offering a Choice of Activities and Paths

Breakout sessions were a significant way for mentors to offer students choice in the YAS program. The idea for breakout sessions was modeled after professional conferences, where participants move around to attend sessions on topics of interest to them. This format can encourage the formation of "micro communities of practice within a single classroom space" (Williams, 2018, p. 156). In these groups, members gather around a common interest instead of being randomly combined because of their age or grade level. Using breakout sessions like this in the classroom can be a great way to differentiate instruction. Students are free to pursue the topics and forms of writing that speak to them, physically moving to an area of the classroom where they can interact with others who share that common interest.

As readers will recall from Chapter 1, mentors offered students five writing workshops over the course of the YAS program: narrative, poetry and music, art and writing, drama and film, and genre study. The mentors typically offered four breakout sessions during each workshop, and students chose just two breakout sessions to attend each day. (The art and writing workshop was the exception: students were offered two choices and attended one breakout session for an extended period.) In other words, student choice was already built into the program structure. As Mentor Amir observed, students quickly figured out the structure of the program and were always trying to "choose the most exciting session" to attend.

Because the program was open to students in grades 5–12, the mentors knew they needed to design breakouts that would appeal to a wide range of ages. For example, the concrete poetry session was a breakout geared toward a younger audience, while the novel planning session was geared toward older students. However, the youth writers did not always make the choices we predicted they would make. As it turned out, sixth graders jumped at the chance to work on long, difficult projects such as novels, whereas some eleventh graders really enjoyed concrete poetry, a form of writing they remembered fondly from their youth. We viewed both kinds of moves by learners, whether they were precociously stretching forward or nostalgically looking back, as legitimate ways to participate in writing in this space.

Offering choice in activities can get students excited to write. In a weekly mentor reflection, Nari wrote, "I was glad that we had a variety of breakout sessions to choose from. Young authors could explore various types of writing [and] find what [they] enjoy." She added that giving students choices supported their development as writers with unique voices. Similarly, Henry observed that the breakouts were an important part of the program because "they allow[ed] us to provide a wide breadth of curriculum in a short amount of time and give the students options to pick and choose from." Figure 2.4 provides some suggestions for using breakout sessions in the ELA classroom.

Mentors not only gave the youth writers opportunities to choose their breakout sessions, but they also provided options within many of these sessions. In the six-word memoir breakout, for example, students could decide whether they wanted to decorate their memoir with cutouts from a magazine, draw an original illustration, or use creative lettering. In the novel planning breakout session, students could outline their original novel using the mentor-provided guide, or they could brainstorm in their journals in their own unique ways. In the short story breakout session, the students were asked to select two images from a larger bank of available photographs and bring them together in a narrative. For the haiku breakout, they could write a poem individually or contribute to a themed group haiku. In one breakout, students chose an object from those available and described it using the five senses. In a breakout session on concrete poetry, students were told they could start writing, or they could draw first to brainstorm some ideas. Structuring activities in these flexible ways fostered student confidence, agency, and positive associations with writing.

Students in the program were encouraged to speak up, and at times they determined the course of the breakout session. To illustrate, during the genre workshop,

FIGURE 2.4. Teaching suggestions for using breakout sessions.

Using Breakout Sessions in ELA Classrooms

The breakout session model can be adjusted for the ELA classroom depending on what teachers need for their specific contexts. One approach is to provide different options for extension activities, and those who choose the same activity could gather to do their work side by side. Alternatively, for teachers using YAS-style breakouts, visitors—perhaps parents/guardians, college students, or older students at the school—could come in and serve as writing mentors (one mentor per table or group). Perhaps students in the class could take turns assuming the role of writing mentor, designing and running breakout sessions on different days. The real-world skills involved with running a breakout—research, organization, communication, flexibility, time management, leadership—are valuable for students of all ages to cultivate because they are needed in a wide variety of careers.

Choosing Activities: We found that it helped when mentors chose a short, high-interest writing activity. The teacher should look across all of the proposed sessions in advance to make sure there is enough variety.

Preparation: Mentors need to know how much time they have for their activity and what kinds of things should be done in that time frame. For example, in most YAS breakout sessions, the twenty-five minutes included a short overview, access to examples, brainstorming, writing, and optional sharing. Whenever possible, mentors should use visuals, props, manipulatives, or other objects to bring their concept to life for students. In addition, providing examples (i.e., mentor texts) quickly makes the goals of the session clear to attendees. These models can be published works, examples found online, or pieces written by the mentor. It is really important to make sure that diverse authors, characters, and forms are represented as well.

Descriptions: If many breakouts are happening simultaneously in a large space like a cafeteria or multipurpose room, put the breakout name, table number, and a short description in an event program and place signs on each table. It is also helpful to have mentors quickly stand up and give a one-sentence description of their session—or even do a thirty-second pitch to attract attendees.

Miranda led a breakout session on writing scenes. She provided students with a choice of scenarios that involved a conflict of some kind, and they developed scenes for these situations. When it came time to share, Miranda let the small group decide which scenario they would address first:

(*Timer goes off.*)

Student: I did both of them.

Miranda: Which one do you want to talk about first?

Student: The genie has granted three wishes and one of them brings misfortune. That one.

Similarly, Nari told her group, "We have a couple of options, and I want you to tell me what you want to do."

When mentors integrated choice into their sessions, they supported learners by allowing them to select their entry point for an activity. In a songwriting breakout session, students had the option to replace the lyrics of an existing song with their own lyrics, write lyrics to go with an instrumental song, or compose lyrics independent of any music. In a comics breakout session, students could compose text for provided images, create both text and art in preformatted boxes, or take a blank sheet of paper and fill it with their own panels, art, and text. In the extended time for writing, students often returned to their favorite works to expand on them (see Figure 2.5).

FIGURE 2.5. Writing in YAS.

Throughout the program, students were able to make use of various materials and tools, including items brought from home. In the songwriting breakout, for instance, students were using their own headphones and phones as they listened to their choice of songs. This session tapped into their love of music and technology. Students in the program were also encouraged to personalize their journals and use them in ways that were meaningful to them. The program welcomed a wide range of youth literacies, practices, materials, and tools. Teachers who are interested in giving students more control over their learning might consider the approaches to differentiating instruction listed in Figure 2.6.

FIGURE 2.6. Some ways to differentiate writing instruction to encourage student choice.

Differentiating Writing Instruction

For teachers wondering where to get started with differentiating writing instruction, one option is to take an existing assignment and offer choice in one or more of the following areas:

- Topic
- Writing form or mode
- Materials, tools, or programs
- Mentor texts (perhaps students can be asked to find examples to share)
- Drafting method (e.g., voice memos)
- Audience or venue (e.g., contest, publication, open mic)

Letting Students Decide What Work Is Needed on a Piece

Another way in which mentors worked student choice into the YAS program was the use of writing stations. These were inspired by Nancie Atwell's (1998) work. Initially, students had unstructured writing and revision time immediately after the breakout session rotations. They could expand on or refine a piece they had started that day or work on something they had brought from home. However, we found that students needed a bit more structure than that, so we created four stations. In our main room, we offered a "Brainstorm" station, a "Polish" station, and a "Perform" station, each overseen by one mentor. In the room across the breezeway from the main classroom, two mentors supervised the "Write" station. The youth writers were encouraged to move between these four stations (two rooms) as their pieces evolved; however, in practice, they never did. They seemed resistant to moving once they had settled into a station.

To illustrate how these writing stations worked, during one workshop, several students were at the brainstorming station. Someone asked a writer, "Why was he [the main character] kidnapped?" and the writer responded, "I'm not sure yet." Over at the polishing station, a student was working on a concrete poem and asked the mentor for some advice on how to turn it into a spoken word poem. Students at the performance/ sharing station were reading pieces they had written during the art and writing workshop, and two students shared excerpts from works they had previously composed at home (a play and a novel accessed from their phones). Across the breezeway in the writing room, students were actively writing and drawing. However, the space was not entirely quiet. Every now and then, students would stop to confer with each other. These different stations gave students opportunities to think about what help they still needed to keep moving forward with a piece.

Sometimes the students interpreted the writing stations in ways we had not expected. For example, a youth writer who had already self-published went to the brainstorming station to get ideas on how to market and sell his how-to book. This provided an opportunity for other students to learn about self-publishing, and they gave this young author some validation, as well as practical tips for getting his work into readers' hands. This experience was also a good reminder for all of us that writing is not a linear path from brainstorming to writing to polishing to performing.

These stations provided all writers with support regardless of how developed their pieces were, enabling "legitimate peripheral participation" (Lave & Wenger, 1991). These stations also gave students opportunities to make decisions about their own writing. The stations were yet another way that mentors differentiated instruction for learners, ensuring that their individual needs were addressed instead of providing one-size-fits-all instruction. Perhaps classroom teachers could similarly group or pair students according to their stage in the writing process, or they could use writing stations in some other way to support students (see Figure 2.7).

FIGURE 2.7. Reflecting on writing stations.

Writing Stations

How could you use the concept of writing stations in your own classroom? What would you need to adjust or consider for your particular teaching context?

Providing the Option to Share, or Not

One of the guiding principles of the YAS program was that sharing was optional. Mentors allowed students to decide for themselves whether they would read their work aloud to others, provide a brief summary of the piece, or opt out of sharing entirely (see Figure 2.8). Being able to opt out of sharing respects students' privacy and different comfort levels. Mentors occasionally read their own pieces to break the ice, or they asked if the students wanted to tell each other about pieces they had written. The mentors found that it was sometimes easier for students to summarize their work for a classmate than to read it verbatim (see Figure 2.9).

FIGURE 2.8. Journal sharing.

FIGURE 2.9. Reflecting on sharing.

To Share or Not to Share?

Are your students able to opt out of sharing personal writing? What does that look like in your classroom? Do you have any scaffolds in place for students who are interested in sharing but are shy to do so?

Inspiring Creativity through Structure and Choice

Having too little choice can be oppressive and stifling for students. On the other hand, having too much choice can be overwhelming and stop some students in their tracks. Therefore, it can be useful for teachers to reflect on the balance of structure and choice available to students. For example, in the YAS program, a breakout session asked students to create original characters, but students were able to do this work with the support of an organizer that guided them through thinking about the character's different features. The fantasy genre itself helped limit what students created while also allowing for some variation. Students had room to be creative within this structure. As we learned, a balance of choice and structure can inspire creativity (see Figure 2.10).

FIGURE 2.10. Reflecting on the balance of structure and choice.

Balancing Structure and Choice

Think of a writing activity you use that inspires students to be creative. What is the structure, or what are the parameters, of that assignment? How does student choice figure into the assignment? What ideas do you have for balancing structure and choice?

Making Choices Is Not Just for Students

When thinking about choice in the classroom, it is important to remember that teachers matter, too! In the YAS program, mentors engaged in quite a bit of decision-making during their internship. As fellow writers in the program, they had to make decisions about the pieces they wrote. As instructional leaders, they needed to decide on the workshop topics, design and lead breakouts, and make adjustments as necessary (sometimes on the spot).

Just as it is oppressive for a student to be subjected to rote learning or a packaged curriculum day after day, it is oppressive to tell teachers they must all teach the same way. We must have the space to make choices, to try things out, and to adjust—to draw on our pedagogical and content knowledge to meet the needs of the students sitting right in front of us. Teacher agency and creativity help drive student success.

Pause and Reflect

When teachers build student choice into their curriculum, they are also building in opportunities to increase student engagement. However, the usefulness of this mentoring strategy goes far beyond the writing classroom. Being able to take control over their own learning supports adolescents on their path toward becoming confident adults. Teachers play a vital role in this work.

This chapter focuses on some of the ways the YAS mentors encouraged student choice and decision-making. Secondary teachers can implement these techniques as well. They can give students multiple options for assignments and nurture student agency by giving students opportunities to brainstorm, compose, and share in ways that are personally meaningful to them. Some ambitious teachers may be interested in organizing a version of the YAS program, complete with breakout sessions and writing stations. More important, teachers can actively look for ways to support student choice and decision-making throughout the year.

Before turning to a secondary teacher to learn how he uses this second strategy to mentor youth writers, let's reflect on what this strategy means to you (see Figure 2.11).

FIGURE 2.11. Reflection questions for strategy #2.

Pause and Reflect

Strategy #2: Encouraging Student Choice and Decision-Making

- How do you already use this strategy in your teaching?
- What are some new ways you can use this strategy to benefit students?
- How does this strategy help bring out the author (or graphic novelist, filmmaker, songwriter . . .) in every student?

Teacher Interview: Scott Wade on Encouraging Student Choice and Decision-Making

Student choice and decision-making are possible in all of our classrooms, not just in the setting of the YAS program. In this section, a secondary teacher shows us how he uses this mentoring strategy with students. Scott Wade (see Figure 2.12) has taught at Newcomer Academy in Louisville, Kentucky, since 2015. The Newcomer Academy is a school for immigrants and refugees who arrive with no English background from nearly fifty different countries. During our interview, this teacher explained to me that Louisville is a refugee hub for the State Department because of Newcomer Academy and the many agencies located there (e.g., Catholic Charities, Kentucky Refugee Ministries, Red Cross). Scott has been an ESL teacher for twenty-two years, and before

FIGURE 2.12. Selfie by Scott Wade.

that he was a news reporter for sixteen years. He is a National Board Certified Teacher and mentor, a finalist for Kentucky Teacher of the Year, and a district ExCEL Award winner. He speaks Mandarin and loves cycling, astronomy, and international travel.

Can you share some examples of how you support student choice in your classroom?
The project that students just completed was six Google slides. They had to imagine they were sixty years old, which is my age, [and visualize what] they had . . . accomplished and explored: Where do you want to go? What do you want to do? What do you want to learn? Kids had answers that surprised me: "I really don't understand what a galaxy is." "I want to learn about artificial intelligence." "I want to learn about human evolution." "How did mountains get there?" "What's a rainbow?" For the final question, "What do I want to contribute in life?," a few kids would say, "I want to be a millionaire and have a big house." Other kids would say, "I want to start a hospital in the refugee camp where I was born." The students chose the content, the design, whether to work in groups, and who to work with.

In January or February, they write persuasive arguments. They have learned to find, summarize, and organize research. Now, there's no doubt that everyone has to write a five-paragraph essay. They have to understand concepts like main idea and supporting evidence; that's standard number one in Kentucky and my district. But how are you going to present your argument? And that's where choice boards come in. They could give a speech. They could make a newscast. For example, "I am here in Japan, where we just had an earthquake," and either a video or an image on the screen could be beside them. "And you can see here, this building just tumbled down." They could work together in a group to make a little play. They could even construct a diorama. So you begin [by] saying, "This is the minimum, and when you have turned in a solid draft of the five-paragraph essay, then you move onto the next one." Choice boards can include various forms of writing: nonfiction, poetry, narrative, memoir, or even a letter to my grandmother trying to explain this complicated thing. It could be a Google Slides presentation with images or videos. It could be using Screencastify to create a newscast that will be projected on the screen of the classroom.

Why do you think it's important to encourage student choice?
We find out about skills and talents that were buried. We have teachers who allow students to express themselves through art. Holy cow! We had this one kid who sang an opera. He ended up performing in front of 15,000 students at the superintendent's opening day speech because that superintendent happened to be coming through when that kid was performing a project. We have drawings on our wall. It's like, "Wow, *Mona Lisa* looks kind of pale compared to that one," but I don't know. It's just giving them their moment to shine.

A project that offers choice helps a teacher get into the mind of the kid. If you do that early in the year, within the first six weeks, you really get a handle on how they learn, what they love to learn, what they already know, what they don't know, and what really turns them up.

I'm a parent, and I can see individuality among young people. I know that if students love it, they will work harder. And if students work harder, they will hit maximum performance. And so you have that joy in the classroom because each person is doing things their own way.

What are the benefits of encouraging student choice in the classroom?
So a kid goes through the day to math, science, and history. My students often work at nighttime. When that

alarm goes off at six o'clock [a.m.], what motivates [the student] to say, "All right, I'm going to school" or "No, I can't even do this. Who cares?" What's the turning point? "I'm in the middle of a project. I've never done anything like this. I didn't know I could do this. This is cool. And I'm on a team. My team needs me. I like this. I'm getting up." And that can be a turning point in life, that decision each morning to get up. I think choice is the motivation.

I want kids to love school. I want them to love coming here. That increases attendance and focus and decreases behavioral problems.

Have you faced any challenges with this practice in your teaching?
It's a lot of work. If you have a team, then you can divide the work, the rubrics, the sequencing, the options, the choice boards. If it comes down to just one person trying to pull that off, a lot of people won't go that far. However, on the positive side, once you get through that process, and once you've created the project and the choice boards and the rubrics and the sequencing and the timeline, that is a staple that can be modified a little each year and improved upon.

Every option has to have limits, and no work can be so easy that everybody does it. So it is really about creating variety and making each possibility attractive to someone in the room. In creating it, you might have four or five choices, but you think of those three or four kids, and there's just nothing in there for them, so you add another option this year. And that becomes part of the arsenal.

How can teachers get started with this work?
During the year, you're gaining all that knowledge of their learning styles, whether they like to be in groups or not, special talents, etc. In the meantime, there are standards to reach (e.g., personal narrative, informative writing, argument, analysis). By the time you get to argument and analysis, you should have knowledge of those students that allows you to build a choice board to reach that standard. But you have to have knowledge of those students first. Imagine if a coach drew up the plays before [knowing] who was on the team. "You're going to go after a pass. Oh, I see. You can't run. Well, that's not going to work." The first time around, give two choices. And then go to three choices next year. Then four.

What additional advice on this topic do you have for teachers?

There has to be a written component. If they performed a two-person play, there would be a written script. If they performed a song, there has to be written lyrics.

Do you have any cautions or warnings for teachers?
The structure has to be scaffolded and customized to individual students in the class. As you move them toward the mandated standards, it cannot be cookie cutter. It cannot be, "Oh, I do this project every year. I have it ready to go."

The structure has to be organized in a time period. There's got to be deadlines, and the train has to keep moving. And I just think that's a huge lesson in life. I want them to understand that good things come through an intentional sequential process with deadlines.

Do you have any words of encouragement for teachers as they embark on this work?
Ultimately, students take joy in the process and complete something they didn't think they could do, which is a lesson in life. When you first think, "I can never do that" and then you do it, the next time something comes around, you think, "Oh, last time I said I couldn't do it. I did it."

Now You Try: Bringing Ideas to Life in the Secondary Classroom

Teachers can foster student choice and decision-making through activities such as creative projects, reflections, and conferences.

Creative Projects

Creative projects can be implemented in a variety of situations: as beginning-of-the-year introductions, as responses to literature, as extensions of research reports, and so on. When I taught high school, I often had students engage in a creative project that responded to a class novel or book of choice. These days I use creative projects in most undergraduate courses I teach (see Figure 2.13). These assignments can be adjusted to fit many different disciplines, units of study, and academic levels. At the secondary level, I recommend scaffolding creative projects. Students could first write a proposal and then have some time to work on the project in class. Teachers could do progress check-ins to help students navigate their way through larger projects.

Reflections

Writing a reflection provides an opportunity for students to comment on work they have produced. A reflection could be a handwritten note on the back of a printed final paper, annotations written in the margins, or a separate document. Reflections are important metacognitive tools because they ask students to stop to think about their thinking. They foster agency and self-efficacy by encouraging students to take control over their learning and their growth as writers.

Reflections highlight important cognitive work that may otherwise go unseen in classrooms (see Figure 2.14). As a teacher, I appreciate opportunities to learn about the challenges that students faced with an assignment and how they used their creativity and resourcefulness to overcome obstacles. I can use this information to refine my teaching, too.

FIGURE 2.13. Creative project suggestions.

Sample Creative Project Assignment

Assignment: Respond to a [book/film/character/theme/etc.] through an original creative project. Document your process in an artist statement.

Time Commitment: Project: 4+ hours; Artist statement: 1 hour

Project Ideas

- Create an animated work (15+ seconds, depending on complexity).
- Make a short film (30+ seconds, depending on complexity).
- Write and illustrate a picturebook (8+ pages)—Do *not* use a template/program.
- Write and illustrate a comic book (10+ panels)—Do *not* use a template/program.
- Write a short story (8+ double-spaced pages).
- Write a series of poems (4+ single-spaced pages).
- Compose a song (2+ minutes).
- Build something (4+ hours of work).
- Repurpose/upcycle/transform materials into something (4+ hours of work).
- Create art (4+ hours of work).
- Make a webpage (4+ hours of work).
- Create a podcast (4+ minutes).
- Design a unit for a class (8+ double-spaced pages).
- Other: If you have another idea, check with me before you start working on it.

Artist Statement Requirements

Reflect on your project in 500 words or more. This document must have four sections labeled as follows:

1. **Description:** Briefly describe your creative project. What is it?
2. **Influences:** Explain how [the book/film/character/theme/etc.] influenced this project. Point to specific examples in the work.
3. **Process & Tools:** Discuss your process and tools used (e.g., programs, supplies, materials).
4. **Photos (2):** Include two captioned photos that capture the project in stages *earlier* than the final draft (plans, outlines, drafts, scripts, sketches, screenshots, etc.). Show the project's evolution and prove it is yours.

Grading (14 points possible)

___/5 How deeply does the project engage with course content?

___/5 Is it a complete and satisfying project, showing an investment of time and effort?

___/4 Is the artist statement complete, specific, and thoughtful? Does it have the four required sections? Is it at least 500 words?

FIGURE 2.14. Examples of reflection questions.

Sample Reflection Questions

Below are some examples of reflection questions, but I recommend using only a few questions at a time:

- What are you most proud of in this piece?
- What would you change if you had more time?
- How did you come up with the idea for this piece?
- Identify your favorite sentence (or favorite feature of the work).
- Describe your process, including any materials and tools used.
- What challenges did you face? How did you overcome them?
- How does this piece fit into your larger body of work? Compare it to other works you have produced. What is familiar? What did you do here that is new for you as a writer? In what ways does this piece represent a moment in your evolution as a writer?
- What did you learn from composing this piece?

Conferences

There are so many wonderful ways to use conferences in writing instruction. Traditionally, conferences occur between a teacher and student in a physical space like a classroom, but that doesn't have to be the case. Conferences might involve a group of students meeting with a teacher or the class splitting off into pairs. Conferences can happen virtually as well, thanks to new technologies.

Conferences do not need to be limited to feedback on drafts either. They can occur at any stage of the writing process (see Figure 2.15). Talking about a work is valuable during prewriting, when ideas are first percolating in the writer's mind, but they can also be used to help students come up with a plan for gathering or organizing information. Like written reflections, conferences can be used as a way for students to point to particular spots in a work and say more about them or to ask for help. Robb (2010) does an excellent job of showing teachers the potential that conferences have, and her book includes sample videos of conferences in action.

In the YAS program, building a space focused on writing—as well as arranging tables to allow for small groups—created opportunities for students to regularly have informal conferences with writing mentors and fellow students. Being able to talk about their writing with others, regardless of where they were with a particular piece, gave students focus, reassurance, validation, confidence, and inspiration.

FIGURE 2.15. Some ways to organize writing conferences.

Using Different Types of Conferences

The teacher does not need to run every conference. Here are some other configurations to consider:

- Students could meet in pairs to respond to an assignment when it is first introduced. They could ask each other about their initial impressions of the assignment, concerns they have, their plans for structuring time, ways they could make the assignment personally meaningful, etc.
- Students who have decided on what kind of project they are going to make could form groups according to the type of composition they have chosen (comic, song, short film, etc.). As they work alongside each other in these groups, they can engage in informal conferences, stopping and getting ideas or feedback as needed.
- Students could meet in pairs with a completed draft of an assignment. The listener could hear the piece read out loud and then ask the writer questions about the work. The listener could also take notes about the discussion and provide this document to the writer.

Final Thoughts

Professional authors are making decisions all the time. For example, novelists invent characters and settings, determine storylines, consider the audience, and carefully choose their words. It is probably no wonder that many students are similarly interested in composing works all their own in their lives outside of school. Adolescence can be a scary and uncertain time. Being able to take control over a piece can be reassuring, a way to have some agency amidst uncertainty. In addition, having some freedom to make decisions about their writing encourages independence as students mature.

Providing opportunities for choice and decision-making in the classroom can help students build positive associations with writing and give them a chance to try out different writing identities (e.g., author, graphic novelist, filmmaker, songwriter . . .). This work sparks creativity, too. I love watching my students get excited about their pieces and seeing them grow into more confident writers right before my eyes. This happens when students have some say over their own learning.

Of course, students are not making choices and working through pieces in isolation. Learning happens with others. The sense of community established in the writing classroom is of utmost importance. This subject is taken up in the next chapter.

Note

1. Studio Ghibli is a world-famous animation studio based in Japan. Directors Hayao Miyazaki, Isao Takahata, and others have created numerous feature-length films known for their stunning artwork, compelling stories, beautiful music, and strong female protagonists. Some of the studio's films include *Spirited Away, My Neighbor Totoro, Howl's Moving Castle, The Secret World of Arrietty,* and *The Tale of the Princess Kaguya.* These works have wonderful potential in secondary and university-level courses (Williams, 2020).

Chapter Three

Building a Supportive Writing Community

Once a month, adolescents from across the Phoenix metropolitan area would meet in a public library for a free writing workshop and spoken word poetry slam. I spent a year investigating this "community of practice" (Wenger, 2008; Williams, 2018), learning about the poets' practices and attitudes. I loved seeing how the adolescent poets, adult teaching artists, and guests interacted. The community was friendly and welcoming. It was clear to me that they enjoyed spending their Saturdays writing together. At the same time, serious work was in progress. Their poems sometimes dealt with difficult topics such as grief, racism, or sexism. One member wrote about living through abuse. Another wrote about police brutality.

Although these youth poets displayed obvious creativity, intelligence, and brilliance with language, that didn't necessarily match to their experiences of school. One member told me about failing English. Another talked about dropping out of high school. Nonetheless, there they were, showing up voluntarily on their Saturdays, choosing to spend their free time writing and performing. They composed beautiful and powerful works and enjoyed being in the space because there they were nurtured as writers and as people.

The teaching artists in the group employed practices that secondary teachers could implement as well to build a supportive community in the classroom. These adult poets shared their poems with the adolescents, sat at eye level with them in a large circle, and used a lot of language focused on safe space and community. They set nurturing ground rules: (1) be brave; (2) be respectful; and (3) your voice matters. They gave positive feedback and encouragement, and they were open to receiving feedback on their writing from the youth poets (Williams, 2015, 2018).

These teaching artists showed me a glimpse of a new model for writing instruction, one in which the teacher shifts from being the all-knowing expert standing at the front of the room before rows of students to instead being a mentor guiding fellow writers. They actively worked to establish and maintain a space in which adolescent writers felt safe and supported.

Building a supportive writing community in the classroom is important. When students feel safe at school, they are more likely to engage with material, take risks, and challenge themselves. They may open up, composing and sharing pieces that are personally meaningful. Writing in a supportive community can be incredibly motivating for students because as these writers interact, they are learning from each other. The good news is that anyone can use the strategies outlined in this book to help build a nurturing space for writers in school.

This book recommends that teachers use six strategies to mentor youth writers (see Figure 3.1). This chapter focuses on the third of those strategies: how to build a supportive writing community.

FIGURE 3.1. This chapter focuses on the third strategy for mentoring youth writers.

Six Strategies for Mentoring Youth Writers

1. Use a wide range of writing forms and modes with students.
2. Encourage student choice and decision-making.
3. **Build a supportive writing community.**
4. Honor student knowledge, experience, and interests.
5. Nurture students as writers.
6. Connect writers to opportunities beyond the classroom.

Like the others, this chapter shares research and theory, shows how the strategy was used in the Young Authors' Studio program, provides an interview with a classroom teacher, and offers sample activities. Key terms are listed in Figure 3.2.

FIGURE 3.2. Useful terms to know for this chapter.

Key Terms

Community of Practice: A community of practice is a group of people gathered around a common interest or practice (e.g., dance studios, karate organizations, online fan groups, writing groups). These communities put members in touch with experts, provide opportunities to build and share knowledge, and make use of certain language and tools. Typically, different kinds of participation are available, members are exposed to multiple possible identities, and they travel on trajectories toward greater or lesser participation (Wenger, 2008).

Vulnerability: Emotional vulnerability involves being honest and open with others and oneself, and there is some risk-taking involved. For example, making friends, getting up on stage to perform, or writing honestly about a personal experience require a certain degree of emotional vulnerability.

Zone of Proximal Development: When learners work with someone more advanced than they are at something, the experienced person can push the learner to learn more than they could alone. Vygotsky (1978) refers to this optimal window for learning as the "zone of proximal development."

Justifying This Work

Teachers can do a lot to help foster a supportive community in the secondary English classroom. To start with, as the NCTE *Position Statement on Writing Instruction in School* (2022) suggests, we can make sure that students connect with fellow writers (see Figure 3.3). This section explores key concepts related to learning and writing with others.

FIGURE 3.3. NCTE position statement connection.

Connection to NCTE's *Position Statement on Writing Instruction in School* (2022)

- Students need "opportunities . . . to engage in complex writing processes within communities of other writers."

Sociocultural theory (Prior, 2006) emphasizes that learning happens with others. Our social and cultural communities contribute to our understanding of the world and influence how we communicate, including how we learn and use language (Bakhtin, 1986; Vološinov, 1973). In the writing classroom, students are influenced not only by the teacher, other students, audiences they are writing for, and even texts they are reading, but also by all the experiences that led them to that moment (Prior, 2006). Even when writing appears to be happening in isolation, it is not. Social and cultural influences are ever present in the ways we communicate and move through the world.

When it comes to mentoring youth writers in the secondary classroom, Vygotsky's (1978) notion of a "zone of proximal development" (ZPD) is particularly useful. ZPD is essentially the gap between where students are and where they can go with help (i.e., what they are capable of learning). To illustrate, I play cello. During the times in my life I have played (in elementary school and now as an adult), I was able to get to a certain point on my own, and then my progress halted. I could not move myself forward. I needed a more experienced player who could identify what I needed to learn and how to get me there. In the classroom, teachers work within the ZPD when they mentor youth writers. Their expertise allows them to identify what a student needs to learn and how to guide that person forward. Coaches, bosses, parents, siblings, fellow students, and others guide learners forward as well.

At the same time, it is worth mentioning that mentoring is not necessarily unidirectional. Often students ask questions or have insights that push teachers forward, too. When thinking about building a community of writers in school, the concept of ZPD is important because every student is bringing valuable skills, experiences, and "ways with words" (Heath, 1983) with them into the classroom. Communities flourish when members have a chance to interact, support one another, and offer feedback that makes members better. In a writing community, having opportunities to engage with other writers, experts, texts, and audiences can help people grow, especially when these interactions occur within students' optimal learning zones. Student learning communities (Fisher et al., 2020) and online writing communities (Bacalja, 2020) can be used to support students as well.

Diversity and inclusion go hand in hand with this work, of course. There is no community if members' cultures, languages, and other aspects of their lives (gender, sexuality, religion, etc.) are disrespected or if members are held back from full participation or from reaching their full potential. All students deserve to be valued members of a classroom writing community.

In a "community of practice" (Wenger, 2008) or an "affinity space" or group (Gee, 2004, 2018), members gather around a shared practice, interest, or goal. The spoken word poetry group I mentioned at the beginning of this chapter, for example, functioned as a community of practice. That is, members had access to experts, learned from each other, had access to tools, and engaged in communication that supported their identities as spoken word poets. There were differing levels of commitment among the members, lots of ways to participate in the practice, and participants were on inbound or outbound trajectories (Wenger, 2008). That is, some of the youth poets were moving into deeper participation, performing in a greater number of slams and taking on leadership roles in the group, while others seemed to be on their way out as they left for college or careers (Williams, 2018).

Of course, one of the dangers of applying community-of-practice or affinity-group theory to school contexts is that for students in school, attendance is compulsory. Participating in a voluntary writing program like Young Authors' Studio or a spoken word poetry group that meets monthly in a library is very different from being forced together with thirty to forty students of the same age in a course the student might not even like and with a teacher the student did not get to choose. Despite such differences, we can learn a lot from out-of-school writing group models. Many community-of-practice principles can be integrated into secondary education to benefit students. For example, teachers can offer multiple entry points for participation, access to experts, and tools and practices that support learning.

For years the National Writing Project (NWP) has been immersing teachers in communities of fellow teacher-writers and modeling effective writing pedagogy. Participants leave these institutes understanding the importance of seeing themselves as writers. The principles espoused by NWP are essential for nurturing a supportive community of writers in the classroom. Practices such as writing alongside students, using mentor texts, encouraging students to give one another feedback, and providing opportunities for writers to share their work and perform their identities as writers can transform a space from a writing classroom into an authentic community of engaged writers. Everyone within a space must work together to "build a worthwhile place and community" (Graves, 1994, p. 124).

Students in writing classrooms need opportunities to engage in collaborative learning (Kagan & Kagan, 2009). Being able to interact—even just a one-minute idea exchange with someone the student has never worked with before—goes a long way toward creating a more cohesive and supportive community of writers in the classroom. In addition, really short, focused lessons can be a useful structure for building community in the classroom: "Minilessons are the ritual that bring us together as a community of writers and readers at the start of each workshop, when we come in from the rest of our lives . . . and put on the cloaks of writers and readers" (Atwell, 1998, p. 150).

It helps if the space is physically arranged to encourage conversations about writing. Graves (1994) argues that when students are able to say to each other, "'Listen to this; tell me what you think of it,' . . . they gradually gain sophistication in helping each other to look at their writing from different points of view" (p. 229). Furthermore, when students have a chance to interact with one another in a supportive community, the classroom can become a "space for wounds to be exposed and healed through the acts of co-signing and challenging," as students affirm each other's stories and offer alternative perspectives (Hill, 2009, p. 71).

Mentoring in Action: Inside the Young Authors' Studio Program

The study of the YAS program found that mentors cared about fostering a supportive community of writers. They built meaningful relationships with students and one another. The strategies they used to foster community are easily transferable to K–12 settings as well.

Establishing Trust

From the beginning of YAS, the mentors worked hard to build trust with students and to make them feel safe. When students did not feel like sharing, Emma asked, "Can you tell me one thing about it?" Sometimes the students were more comfortable talking about their writing than reading the words out loud. Nari had a similar strategy, asking a student if she would like to read a piece very quietly:

> I asked if she wanted to read her piece out loud and said that it would help her spot her mistakes. She was hesitant because she tended to keep her writing to herself and generally avoided performing in front of people. I told her that she could read it in a small voice so that only I could hear. She then agreed to read it to me. As soon as she read it aloud, she recognized the mistakes and was able to fix them on her own.

Nari provided a personalized scaffold to help this student with editing. The student found the courage to share the piece with Nari, and the technique of reading the work aloud helped her identify the issues with it.

Emma told the other mentors, "If [the students] trust you, it makes it a hundred times better. They need to trust their peers, but if they have trust in the [mentor] who is leading [the session, they] will share way more." She pointed out that students need to feel comfortable in order to open up and share their writing, adding, "That's really important, to make that a space in which they feel comfortable sharing." Similarly, Henry noticed that after a while, the students started opening up and showing him that they were writing books and other works.

The students warmed up to these mentors as the program progressed over the weeks. Near the end of the program, Emma commented, "There were students at the beginning of the program who were very shy, hesitant, and/or did not like writing, and it seems to me that each of them has had an attitude change. They are coming out of their shells. . . . It has been an incredible thing to watch and is an honor to be part of." By the second workshop, I was commenting in my field notes that the mentors had made significant strides toward fostering a supportive community of writers. I wrote that "community within the group happened fast," and the mentors had "built a safe and warm space. It feels like a community." Students seemed to feel safe in the space and were quick to share with the mentors and each other (see Figure 3.4).

FIGURE 3.4. Students in a breakout session.

So how did the mentors build trust with students so quickly? One way was by writing alongside the students. I modeled this practice in our first planning session, emphasizing that it was crucial to "sit down with the kids and start writing." I told the mentors, "They love this because they can see that the work is important enough for the mentor to do it. They care about that."

While some mentors did need reminders in the first week or two to write with students, as the program moved along, this became a more natural practice for them. Miranda wrote in a reflection that she wanted to "connect to the students" and "found that writing alongside them made them feel comfortable." Similarly, Nari wrote, "During the exercise, I also wrote my own poem. Looking back at the experience of writing together, it allowed us to be in a truly non-hierarchical and supportive collaborator relationship." She added, "I read aloud my poem about homesickness, which took courage. This exchange happened naturally, and I learned that the young authors and I were all writers who allowed ourselves to be vulnerable."

Students used the mentors' writing for inspiration and asked them for revision suggestions as fellow writers they could trust. The mentors continued to show students their vulnerability all the way up to the final performance (more on this in Chapter 6), when Emma kicked off the event by reading a piece she had written. Nari observed that "Emma . . . allowed herself to be vulnerable, [demonstrating] that sharing one's work in public is scary but also a fun and rewarding experience." The ways that mentors modeled vulnerability and built trust with students can be used in secondary classrooms as well (see Figure 3.5).

FIGURE 3.5. Some ways to build trust with students.

Building Trust and Embracing Vulnerability with Students

Sit at Eye Level: Sitting with students at eye level helps build trust and levels the playing field a bit. Desks can be arranged in a circle or another formation that allows students to see one another. If students are writing in a group, teachers can bring over a chair and sit beside them while checking in.

Write with Students: Nothing says that writing is important like a teacher doing it. Teachers can project their writing in real time on a screen or sit and write alongside students. It is important for students to see us stop, hesitate, go back, reread, cross things out, and write things in. I try to convey through my expressions how I am feeling about my piece (frustrated, amused, confused, excited, etc.).

Volunteer to Share: When teachers share their writing with students, they are demonstrating that they are writers, too! A rough, unpolished piece written while students are also writing is the perfect kind of work to share. After all, students need to see the writing process in all of its messiness. Let's embrace that and the vulnerability that comes with being brave and sharing our work. Leading by example is powerful and a key part of being a writing mentor.

Supporting One Another

Students and mentors were willing to help one another in the YAS space. For example, when students needed help with spelling, they would turn and ask the writer next to them. Other times, they would provide suggestions for titles or ask questions about their pieces. Mentors like Amir noticed that students often asked each other for help or shared with each other before approaching the mentors. One youth writer wrote in a workshop reflection, "I've learned it helps to collaborate with others on different ideas." These exchanges can be really helpful during the writing process, and they are worth encouraging in school (see Figure 3.6).

FIGURE 3.6. Getting students to turn to each other for feedback.

Encouraging Students to Help Each Other

Authors Asking Questions: Ask students to bring a short piece of writing and a question (something they actually want help with) to their small group. Then students take turns sharing their pieces and their question. Providing safe opportunities for students to talk about their writing can lead to them engaging in this sort of behavior spontaneously. This is a practice that professional writers use all the time, turning to a trusted colleague with a concern. Teachers can model this practice by saying, "I am wondering how I can make this piece more exciting. Can you give me some ideas? Let me read it to you."

In the YAS program, mentors not only assisted students but they helped each other, too. They volunteered to bring materials for each other's breakout sessions and offered ideas and advice. One mentor brought pages of a discarded library book for another mentor's breakout session on blackout poetry. Someone else brought another mentor a book about cartooning. Getting together each week to plan and debrief helped build the mentor community. Sitting around a table together (at eye level) helped reinforce the idea that each mentor deserved to be there, and they each had important contributions to make to the team. During workshops, I noticed that whenever a mentor was in a bind, the others would do what they could to help out, whether it was solving technology problems or writing the day's agenda on the board when someone else forgot. These positive attitudes toward each other radiated outward, affecting the students' attitudes as well.

Validating Writers

The program included many opportunities for the youth writers to receive validation. Often this could be seen happening during breakout sessions and team meetings. In addition, the final performance (again, more on this in Chapter 6) served as a validating event, with people of all ages coming out to support the youth writers.

Mentors validated the youth writers by taking their work seriously and offering suggestions. Nari recalled:

> [A student] wrote a concrete poem about spiders. [See Figure 1.13 in Chapter 1.] He said he didn't like it. I then asked him what he did not like about it, to which he said, "I don't know. It's childish." I told him, "You might think it's childish, but other people might not." Then I shared what I noticed about his poem, which was that the shape of the spider made the experience of reading the poem like solving a riddle. Also, despite his comment that the poem was childish, I talked about the simplicity of it that makes a reader feel, "I can read this poem and actually understand what the poet is talking about."

The mentor saw the strengths of the piece even when the writer could not. This kind of support can be crucial to adolescents in particular, who are in a stage of life that often involves experiencing a lot of self-doubt. When teachers validate students in this way, they are doing important work in mentoring youth writers.

Team meetings in YAS provided opportunities to give students validation for their efforts. Nari found these end-of-workshop check-ins "a valuable time to learn about each student's personal and individual interests in writing." The mentors also had many opportunities to check in with students during breakout sessions. Across these different interactions, the mentors played an important role as they put students at ease, helped them develop confidence as writers, and validated them. The following exchange exemplifies what these interactions sometimes looked like:

Emma: How is your novel coming? Have you been working on it this week?

Student: Yeah, I try to write something each day.

Emma: That's good. How many chapters do you have so far?

Student: Seven.

Emma: Wow. That's really coming along.

Student: Have I showed it to you yet?

Emma: I read Chapter 2, I think, last week. It was really good. You're doing a good job. How many chapters do you think it's going to be?

Student: However many it takes to convey the story.

Emma: How far along are you in it? Are you in the beginning?

Student: Yeah, I'm kind of in the beginning still. So I'm guessing maybe thirty chapters.

Emma: I saw on the sheet that you want to finish it by your next birthday. When's your birthday?

Student: [summer]

Emma: I think you can do that. You have seven months.

Student: Yeah, more than half a year.

Emma: . . . eight months.

Student: That's two-thirds of a year. . . . I've only been writing for about two months now.

Emma: Wow. To get seven chapters in two months, that's incredible.

Student: But this is my rough draft. I'm going to have to take some time to type it up and maybe publish it online if I want to, and then maybe it will get the attention of a real publisher. And then I'll get myself a published book and I'll get rich and famous.

Emma: That would be awesome. Well, keep working and maybe one of these days I will see your name. I work in libraries, so maybe I'll see your name on a book someday. That would be cool.

Student: This is actually my fourth attempt at writing a book. First one didn't go so well. The second one, I managed to get part of the way through and then got stuck. I knew where the ending was going to be, but I didn't know how to get from where I was to where I needed to be. The third attempt, I didn't even get a chapter done.

Emma: I've had those. . . . I had one I wrote in ninth grade-ish, and I haven't worked on it for three or four years. I spent some time on it. I'd like to eventually go back and look at it. Some day you might be able to go back to that one, the second one you were doing, and figure it out.

Students in YAS were taken seriously as writers. The mentors acted as writing guides who encouraged the students and sometimes referred to their own struggles with writing. While YAS offered a unique space, classroom teachers can also validate and support writers in these ways, communicating to students that they are not alone in facing challenges with writing.

The writing gallery served as a validating event in the YAS program. Students set up their work at different stations around a large room, and family members and friends circulated, reading the pieces and leaving supportive comments behind for the writer on sticky notes. Nari noticed that the youth writers appreciated receiving written comments on their pieces: "A student in my group expressed how grateful he was for the Post-it notes I left. It is so valuable for a young author to experience that his or her writing has power to affect [others]."

It is worth pointing out that not all of the validation students received was specific. Sometimes mentors made general statements in response to pieces students shared:

(*Students are sharing.*)

Amir: That's amazing. I like it a lot.

(*A student reads a poem out loud about a balloon.*)

Amir: That's interesting.

(*A student reads his spider poem to Amir.*)

Amir: That's amazing.

The writers did not seem to mind the absence of specific feedback on their work in these cases and were eager to share their pieces nonetheless. It was as if they simply wanted a chance to be heard. This type of general feedback is similar to what I observed in the spoken word poetry group I studied. Those teaching artists would often respond in an informal, general way like this. These moments were more about validating the poets' bravery for sharing rather than providing feedback on specific aspects of the piece (Williams, 2018). Sometimes teachers think they have to break out the red pen and give specific comments on everything students write, but often what students need is just to be heard.

The mentors understood that they played a valuable role in validating the youth writers. In a letter to future mentors, Emma wrote about how YAS can help students see that they are "great writers, even though the world often tells them they are 'too young.'" She also addressed the importance of mentors validating students by being a sounding board for their work. Emma advised future mentors, "If they want to share a novel with you that they wrote in their free time, take the time to listen." Figure 3.7 provides some additional recommendations for supporting youth writers.

As it turned out, validation worked both ways in this program. The mentors also received validation from the youth writers. After the performance at the end of the semester, the mentors and I stayed for a post-event debrief. We went through the comment cards from the program participants, which the mentors enjoyed reading. It is important for teachers to receive validation for their work, too. (See more on the comment cards later in this chapter.)

FIGURE 3.7. Suggestions for making writers feel validated in school.

Validating Writers

There are many ways to build a supportive writing community in the classroom. Providing writers with validation is a crucial part of this work.

Favorite Quotes: One high school teacher I know likes to take her favorite lines from students' writing and post them anonymously on a bulletin board in her classroom. She doesn't say why the lines are important but lets the students try to figure it out.

Displaying Work: Teachers can set aside some space in the classroom for students to post their work for others to read. This sharing can take place on a physical bulletin board; online, it could take place in a classroom management system like Canvas.

Grouping Students to Promote Interaction

One of the best ways to build community in the classroom is to give students many opportunities to work together in different configurations (pairs, groups of three or four, quick exchanges, extended conversations, working on a team or group project, giving advice on individual projects, etc.). During each YAS workshop, students had opportunities to meet fellow writers and achieve many tasks. Mixing up the group in these ways encouraged students to interact, which helped build community.

Most workshops began with students sitting at any of the tables for the opening journal activity and workshop overview. Mentors invited them to get up and share their journal responses in pairs with someone from across the room (see Figure 3.8).

FIGURE 3.8. A structure to quickly group students in pairs.

Partner Sharing

"Stand up, hand up, pair up" is a cooperative learning strategy (Kagan & Kagan, 2009) in which students move around the room and find different students to share with. A raised hand is the signal that someone is looking for a partner; this helps people find a partner quickly. (They give a high five and put their hands down when actually paired up and talking.) When done sharing, they can then walk around and find someone else to share with. Having frequent low-risk opportunities to interact builds connections between students and fosters a sense of belonging. As this activity is repeated over time, students start to feel more comfortable seeking out people in class they have not talked to before.

As an example of what different grouping configurations looked like in YAS, during the drama workshop, students gathered in groups around pieces of butcher paper, and then all came together to form one circle for a soundscape and other activities. To write a letter to a character, each student sat facing away from the circle. They were in groups for tableaux and then moved around to see what the other groups had created. When it came time for breakouts, they moved around the room and sat at their choice of table, guided by their interests. For the extended time to write, students moved to writing stations that reflected the current stage of their writing (brainstorming, writing, polishing, performing). At the end of the workshop, they moved into a set team, where they shared work, reflected on the day, and set goals as writers. Moving frequently like this within a two-hour period gave students a chance to burn off some energy, interact with many different people, form groups with others according to their needs and interests, and have some stability by checking in with a set group at the end of the day.

It is hard to form a community if students are sitting quietly in rows. Grouping students in different configurations frequently—and for different purposes—adds variety and interest to the day and encourages social interaction. As students mix, they have a chance to get to know each other and become more invested in each other. Changing group configurations often was one of the ways mentors facilitated a sense of community in the YAS space. This is a technique that teachers can use in their classrooms as well.

Putting the youth writers into small groups and pairs also made it easier for them to share their writing with each other; they didn't have to deal with the stress of reading something they wrote in front of the whole class, which can be intimidating. I wrote in my field notes:

> I think it's important that the mentors sit at eye level with the students during breakouts. The physical setup of these tables and everyone gathered around them seems to help foster small communities where students want to interact with each other and the mentor. This seems more democratic than the overviews, in which the mentor typically teaches from the front of the room with a PowerPoint.

In a small group, every member can be seen and heard. This configuration fosters engagement because students can't just disappear into a crowd.

The team meetings that ended each workshop involved a set group of three or four youth writers meeting with an assigned mentor. This team time was reserved for writers to check in, reflect, give updates, share writing, and set goals. Mentor Henry said of these team meetings, "I'm not the best at conversations, so it was great to see everybody interacting so well." Ending each workshop with the same familiar group provided some consistency from week to week. These team affiliations persisted all the way to the final performances, when mentors handed out certificates to their team members, and they posed for team photographs together. Teachers who are interested in using team check-ins could do this with groups of students, and if older students from another class are available, they could come in to serve as writing mentors who lead these groups.

Maintaining a Positive Atmosphere

Establishing a positive atmosphere begins with caring about the people in the room and being excited about the content we are teaching. As teachers we should not be shy about conveying this enthusiasm to students. Throughout the program, I observed the students' and mentors' enthusiasm as they worked together (see Figure 3.9). My video notes included observations like these:

- "The parents and kids look happy as they leave. They are smiling."
- "Students are sharing their object poems. They look happy. The room seems animated."
- "[Henry] talks about his D&D activity, and students audibly gasp (one student's jaw drops and she looks around) when he announces the topic; at one point he holds up an example of a character sheet. So many students head over to the Dungeons & Dragons station that they need another table."

FIGURE 3.9. Students sharing.

There seemed to be a lot of focused energy in the room during the program (see Figure 3.10). Amir noticed, "Shy [students have] become more comfortable and confident than previous sessions. They share their stories and talk a lot and [provide help] to their classmate[s] when they need help, which [is] good."

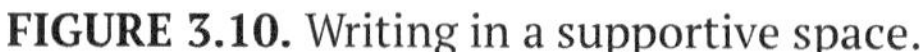

FIGURE 3.10. Writing in a supportive space.

At the writing gallery at the end of the program, families and youth writers buzzed around the room, commenting on the students' writing. Even writers who were not able to be there because of a prior commitment asked that their work be included in the event. As I circled the space, I made a point to find each mentor and say, "Look around. *You* built this!"

The youth writers filled out comment cards that day (see Figure 3.11), and many of them spoke to the positive atmosphere:

- "This is a good space to write."
- "[I learned] that more people like my writing than I thought."
- "I will miss coming here."
- "My mentors were very kind and helpful."

- "This has been one of the best things to happen to me. I grew here, I made friends here, and most importantly, I learned here."
- "The Young Authors' Studio was a wonderful experience! Collaborating with other authors was helpful and really fun. I made new friends and had new ideas. It was amazing."

We had expected to have some program attrition since YAS was free and voluntary, and families are often busy with other commitments on Saturday mornings. As it turned out, not one student dropped out of the program. Together, the mentors and students had created a positive, supportive space worth coming back to each week.

FIGURE 3.11. Suggestions for requesting feedback from students.

Asking Students for Feedback

In the YAS program, we used comment cards and surveys along with informal conversations to get a sense of how students were feeling in the space. Students can be incredibly observant and thoughtful about what is working and what isn't in a classroom. Even when I think a class or program is going well and there is a great sense of community, I like to check in with students to see how they are feeling. At secondary and postsecondary levels, I have used formal surveys and informal check-ins (e.g., "Take a moment to tell me how this course is going for you."), and I have given students the option to submit these anonymously or to opt out. I let them know that I take their feedback seriously, and I give them some examples of times I have made changes in my courses based on students' recommendations.

Pause and Reflect

Building a supportive writing community is an essential mentoring strategy. In a safe space, students are going to be more willing to experiment with writing and help each other when they face challenges. Such spaces can give students confidence as writers and speakers and teach them empathy as they work with others, all of which are useful skills for the world beyond our classrooms as well.

The techniques the mentors used to build community in YAS are also appropriate for secondary classrooms. Teachers can similarly establish trust, make students feel safe, and model honesty and vulnerability with their students. They can create a space in which writers are eager to share their work and help each other. Teachers play an incredibly important role in building community in schools.

The next section shares how a secondary teacher builds a supportive writing community in her classroom. Before we move onto that, let's reflect on what this third mentoring strategy means to you (see Figure 3.12).

FIGURE 3.12. Reflection questions for strategy #3.

Pause and Reflect

Strategy #3: Building a Supportive Writing Community

- How do you already use this strategy in your teaching?
- What are some new ways you can use this strategy to benefit students?
- How does this strategy help bring out the author (or graphic novelist, filmmaker, songwriter . . .) in every student?

Teacher Interview: Kimiko Warner-Turner on Building a Supportive Writing Community

It can be useful to see how a secondary teacher uses this mentoring strategy in the classroom. For the last five years, Kimiko Warner-Turner (see Figure 3.13) has been a teacher at Los Angeles County High School of the Arts, where she teaches ninth grade. In addition, Kimiko works with students in grades K–12 at The Music Center, a performing arts center in Los Angeles. She is a master teaching artist who helps teachers with arts integration, and she co-directs Shakespeare Center, Los Angeles's Shakespeare Social Justice Program, developing Shakespeare curricula for teachers. Some of her other interests include tap dancing, gourmet cooking, and travel.

FIGURE 3.13. Selfie by Kimiko Warner-Turner.

Can you share some examples of how you build a supportive community in the classroom?

On the first day, I have students gather around questions written on big boards: "Who are you? What's your favorite food? What's your favorite play? Where do you see yourself in four years when you graduate?" It's a way of opening up and focusing the class's attention on topics without looking at a person's back. In many traditional classrooms, you face the back of everyone's heads in front of you, and then you raise your hand. It can be a struggle for classes to get to know each other. I have come into classrooms in the spring where students still don't know each other's names.

We allow people to talk without interruption. Students are so accustomed to immediately commenting on things. I want students to just listen and take in the information. That's all. And that's hard because everyone wants to snap their fingers or clap. They want to agree. There's always a moment where we want to support each other and connect, but at the very beginning, it's just about listening, taking in what is shared, and being respectful. Then, during reflection, they're allowed to respectfully share whatever they want. The protocols are to just say something constructive and respectful to prompts like, "What did you see? What did you notice? What did you find most interesting? What was new?" The students acknowledge responses and can correct or add to the information. Then they journal and hand [that] in. So you begin to build a safe space to listen and respond to each other's contributions.

Why do you think it's important to build community in the classroom?
Building community in the classroom allows you to respect each other's identities and be kind. We hold each other up. We eliminate disrespect. My students say to me all the time, "I got you, Ms. Kimiko. I got you." We've taken that and created a community saying, "We've got each other."

What are the benefits of building community?
I think that when you build a community, you build a better society. I am hopeful that the students I teach will be able to impart their knowledge in a way they can be heard, and people will listen to what they have to say, which builds self-confidence. This helps students navigate the world. We can never dictate how another person reacts to what we tell them. After all, we can only control ourselves. So I think that is really important, to understand where you need to control yourself within the community in order to listen and to be heard. Students write more authentically and are able to express their own opinions when their ideas and talents are praised. This helps me, too, as a teacher because they support me. I mean, it's a mutual respect that we gain.

Have you faced any challenges with building a community in the classroom?
A beautiful cacophony of noise comes with people working together. You need to relax into the chaos. I allow them to work on the floor, on the tables, outside, or in the hallway as long as they stay on task. I frequently change the composition of teams [and do] check-ins.

I think chaos is really controlled by giving clear instructions at the beginning of a class period. If it's a multi-day project, then I explain the expectations for [each day]. I think the more the students understand the reasons why they're doing an assignment, then the easier it is to control the chaos. I also use clapping together to get their attention. ("Clap twice if you hear me.") This encourages self-monitoring.

How can teachers get started with community building in the classroom?
Set clear expectations, get parent buy-in, and build trust. Try some community-building activities and see which ones stick. [See the recommended books below.] If one works well, students will ask to play it over and over again. You can reuse it or modify it when you begin a new unit of study. Creating moments of laughter and joy in the classroom goes a long way.

Go for depth over breadth. It's a style of learning strategies we've designed in [the] Shakespeare and Social Justice curriculum. I've had students come to me and say, "Do you know what *Romeo and Juliet* is about? We just read it, and then the teacher said we didn't have time to do anything with it." The student is already frustrated and lost. Instead, they could explore act 1, scene 1, when youth fight in the streets of Verona, compare Verona's community to theirs, [and] take it a step further to create a scene about what they would like their community to be. Write it, perform it, and reflect on what they created. That's depth to me versus reading the whole play because it's [a] required text. If they haven't explored the setting or the words, they don't know what you're saying. They lose interest and say, "I don't want to do it."

Also, let activities be led by the students. They have so many great ideas. Don't think you have to take it on yourself. Ask, "What do you think?" "What do you want to do?" Trust your students. They will give you such great ideas and then get into it. That frees you up to circulate and coach [students], making sure they're on the right track.

What additional advice on community building do you have for teachers?
If you're going to build community, don't be the "sage on the stage." Become more of a facilitator. As a teacher, you must accept that sometimes your goal will change [in response to] student voice. They come with an idea, and I try to incorporate it into their work. Empower them to come up with ideas.

Do you have any favorite resources on community building?

- Augusto Boal's (2021) *Games for Actors and Non-Actors*: This book sets up scenarios that a community is eager to address. The audience (spect-actors) act out solutions to help the protagonist solve problems.
- Michael Rohd's (1998) *Theatre for Community, Conflict, and Dialogue: The Hope Is Vital Training Manual*
- Viola Spolin's (1986) *Theater Games for the Classroom: A Teacher's Handbook*
- [The] Shakespeare and Social Justice [curriculum] encourages and supports students in artistic action against bias. Written by Peter Howard, Marina Oliva, Jon Royal, Laura Turchi, and myself.

Do you have any cautions or warnings for teachers?
I ask myself and teachers not to compromise. If you don't understand what's been written or performed, ask students to clarify their ideas. Be honest. What we want is to develop writers and speakers who can effectively convey a message to others. And if it's not clear, if you compromise, giving too high a praise when it's not great, they'll never know what the goal really is. So the goal is always to express yourself in a way that you can be heard. I don't think students need to hear that they're perfect. I believe that students need to understand that you've witnessed a change and [know] they are doing the best work they can do at any given moment.

Do you have any words of encouragement for teachers as they try to build community in their classrooms?
Breathe! You can do this while having fun. When fostering a safe community, academic achievement will soar. Appreciate the small accomplishments. Don't give up.

Now You Try: Bringing Ideas to Life in the Secondary Classroom

Teachers can strengthen classroom community through their selection of activities. Drama activities, such as tableaux and scene writing, are especially useful for encouraging students to work together. In addition, obstacle courses challenge students to move through a series of tasks together while also drawing on one another's expertise. To facilitate bonds between students, it is helpful to get these writers out of their seats, out of their comfort zones, and working together toward a common goal.

Tableaux

Using drama activities in the English classroom may seem scary to teachers who do not have acting experience. One activity that is fairly easy to use and adaptable to a wide range of content is making tableaux (see Figure 3.14). Tableaux (plural; *tableau* singular) are living pictures, physical depictions of something that require people's bodies and sometimes props to convey information to an audience. Students can create a snapshot of a moment in a scene by freezing in place and holding that position so the audience can take in the entire composition. The activity requires students to work together in a group to coordinate their positions. It can provide a bonding experience and get students excited to get out of their seats.

FIGURE 3.14. Suggestions for using tableaux in the classroom.

Decide How to Use Tableaux: Teachers will need to decide where an activity like this makes sense in their curriculum. You might, for example, use it to introduce a writing activity. When studying literary genres, perhaps students could form teams to create tableaux representing different kinds of stories (e.g., fantasy, sci-fi, mystery, horror). After presenting and discussing these, students could craft a short piece of their own in one of these genres.

Set Clear Assignment Parameters: Using time limits, assigned groups, and cards with tableaux ideas can help students focus on what they need to accomplish.

Sharing: Be sure to take time for each group to present and the audience to ask questions and comment.

Extension Activities: Afterward, students could write a piece exploring one character in the scene, events that preceded or followed this moment, or an alternative reality in which this moment took a different form.

Scene Writing

A great way to build community in the classroom is to have students write and enact a scene in a small group. This writing-based activity helps build community because students have to interact and problem-solve together. They must use their voices and bodies to bring their writing to life, which can demonstrate the power of language and reenergize the class. Figure 3.15 provides some suggestions for scene writing.

FIGURE 3.15. Suggestions for using scene writing in the classroom.

Tips for Getting Started with Scene Writing

Decide How to Use Scene Writing: This could be a stand-alone activity. Alternatively, students could write scenes in response to literature they have just read or a formal piece of writing they have just crafted (e.g., a narrative, an informative or persuasive essay, or a research project).

Set Clear Assignment Parameters: Provide clear guidance about how students need to use the time (i.e., what they need to accomplish and by when) and the expectations for participation (i.e., everyone needs to try to involve everyone else). If the group is crafting the scene together from scratch, provide a choice of themes or situations for those who need assistance getting started.

Sharing: Give groups an opportunity to perform their scenes for the class. They could get feedback from the other groups on staging and then come back and perform the revised scene to see if the changes made a difference.

Extension Activities: Students could write the next scene individually after performing. Group members could then come back together to share these scenes with each other and see the different directions each person took.

Obstacle Courses

A fun way to build community and reinforce learning is to set up an academic obstacle course that asks students to engage with course content in different ways. For this kind of obstacle course (see Figure 3.16), students move in pairs or in a group to different stations around the room in a predetermined sequence to complete different tasks. I have used obstacle courses with students for unit review, to peruse potential books of choice for independent reading, to deconstruct mentor texts, to do different poetry-related activities, and more. One folder or envelope per station could contain the materials needed for that station, such as directions and examples. Objects could also be left at these stations if needed to spark student creativity. I would recommend that students carry their own writing utensil around the room with them. In addition, a handout with an organizer could provide space for them to write in their responses to challenges or questions posed at the stations.

FIGURE 3.16. Suggestions for using academic obstacle courses in the classroom.

Tips for Getting Started with Obstacle Courses

Decide How to Use the Obstacle Course: The first step is to determine how the obstacle course will be used. For secondary students, an academic obstacle course might be used to review course content, to practice applying different critical lenses (i.e., schools of literary criticism) to texts, for peer review, to spark creativity, etc. A poetry obstacle course is a fun way to examine different poetic forms, have students write poems about objects, or have them experiment with different kinds of figurative language.

Prepare the Obstacle Course: After determining the group size and number of stations, move the desks or tables into these configurations. Prepare any props, directions for each station, and handouts or examples needed. Also, determine the path students will use to move through the room and how long groups will have at each station. Will a timer be used?

Accountability: I give students a form with a box for each station they will visit. Each box has enough room to write, make lists, draw, or do anything else required at the station. They turn these in at the end of the period.

Extension Activities: After completing the obstacle course, students could be asked to choose one of the ideas they encountered and use that as the spark to compose a piece of writing.

Final Thoughts

For those of us who were perfectly comfortable staying silent in class and sitting in organized rows of desks year after year as students ourselves, community building may sound scary at first. However, this chapter digs into this abstract concept and shows how anyone—even more reserved teachers or less experienced ones—can take steps toward building a more supportive learning community for students. We have looked at some features of community in YAS and noticed how mentors supported each other, validated students, encouraged them to interact with one another, and more.

Teachers can similarly play an important role in establishing and maintaining a sense of community in their classrooms.

Implementing this mentoring strategy in schools can make learning more exciting, connected, and meaningful for students. It can give writers the security to lean into the writing identities they care about (e.g., novelist, spoken word poet, songwriter, graphic novelist, filmmaker, animator, and so forth). When youth writers work with others in different configurations regularly throughout the year, they are more likely to ask each other for help when they need it, tackle difficult material together, and listen to each other with compassion. In these spaces, teachers and students practice empathy—something we need a lot more of in our world today.

Teachers set the tone of a space and make writers feel welcomed, inspired, and connected. Getting to know the actual individuals within a community—their interests and expertise—also matters. This subject is taken up in the next chapter.

Chapter Four

Honoring Student Knowledge, Experience, and Interests

Recently I developed and taught a course on food writing at my university, and the students composed meaningful and vivid food narratives. They explored joyful memories of family, customs, and culture. Other stories were painful, dealing with loss and regret. Some students chose to write about humorous or awkward moments in their lives that involved food. Others reflected on food insecurity or overcoming eating disorders.

One memorable piece was set at a Marine Corps boot camp. The story explained the Meals, Ready-to-Eat (MRE) that recruits are given and how these individuals are put through grueling challenges during a period known as "the Crucible" at the end of their training. The details this veteran selected revealed his unique expertise, and his story transported me into a world that he knows really well and I know almost nothing about.

All of our students, regardless of grade level or age, have expertise and insider knowledge. They know languages. They have cultural knowledge. They have hobbies and interests. It does not matter if the student is five, fifteen, or fifty. During their lives, all students are accruing valuable assets that come along with them when they enter a classroom. Honoring student knowledge, experience, and interests is important because it validates the student and encourages personal growth. In addition, it benefits everyone in the room to learn from each other, contributing to a more caring world.

What I have learned from this experience, and many others along my journey as a teacher, is this: One of the most important roles of the writing mentor in the classroom is to engineer opportunities for students to tap into their unique knowledge, experience, and interests.

As you will recall, teachers can use six strategies to mentor youth writers (see Figure 4.1). This chapter focuses on the fourth of those strategies, honoring student knowledge, experience, and interests.

FIGURE 4.1. This chapter focuses on the fourth strategy for mentoring youth writers.

Six Strategies for Mentoring Youth Writers

1. Use a wide range of writing forms and modes with students.
2. Encourage student choice and decision-making.
3. Build a supportive writing community.
4. **Honor student knowledge, experience, and interests.**
5. Nurture students as writers.
6. Connect writers to opportunities beyond the classroom.

As in the other chapters, this chapter shares background, shows the strategy at work in the Young Authors' Studio program, provides an interview with a teacher, and offers sample assignments. Let's get started with some key terms (see Figure 4.2).

FIGURE 4.2. Useful terms to know for this chapter.

Key Terms

Culturally Sustaining Pedagogy: Curriculum and instruction that sustains students' cultures, languages, and literacies. All students benefit through this work (Paris, 2012).

Funds of Knowledge: The assets that students have developed in their homes and communities, including linguistic and cultural knowledge (Moll et al., 1992).

Justifying This Work

Students need opportunities to draw on their "funds of knowledge," the culturally and linguistically rooted knowledge they have acquired in their homes and communities (Moll et al., 1992). Historically, the funds of knowledge that students of color bring to their learning have largely been ignored or even actively suppressed (Baker-Bell, 2020). Paris (2012) has argued for a culturally sustaining approach to pedagogy that honors all students. In writing instruction, this includes opportunities for students to work with personally and culturally meaningful forms such as spoken word poetry (Fisher, 2007).

The NCTE *Position Statement on Writing Instruction in School* (2022) "advocates for writing instruction that builds on students' strengths, that values their many ways of using language, that promotes a broad view of what constitutes 'text,' and that promotes young people's voices and purposes for writing within authentic contexts" (see Figure 4.3).

FIGURE 4.3. NCTE position statement connections.

Connections to NCTE's *Position Statement on Writing Instruction in School* (2022)

- The policy statement warns, "Writing instruction and assessments . . . serve as gatekeeping devices when they are built around deficit notions surrounding students' languages and literacies."
- Teachers can "*actively cultivate* young writers' efficacy and engagement . . . [by building] on students' racial, cultural, social, and linguistic resources [and providing] opportunities for students to engage in complex writing processes within communities of other writers."
- Teachers must allow for "diverse perspectives, voices, experiences, and linguistic practices."

Heath (1983) demonstrated decades ago that schools reward certain kinds of cultural knowledge, habits, and "ways with words." Similarly, Anyon's (1980) research revealed that schools are structured in ways that reinforce class, and they prepare students for certain kinds of futures. Teachers have important work to do to break these cycles and ensure that all students are valued and have opportunities to draw on their many strengths in instruction, including the unique set of knowledge, experience, and interests each student brings to the classroom. Teachers can use culturally sustaining pedagogies to ensure that all students have "access to power in a changing nation"; it is essential that teachers "honor, value, and center the rich and varied practices of communities of color" (Alim & Paris, 2017, p. 6).

Eisner (2002) argues that it is the responsibility of the teacher to design "situations that will . . . create an appetite to learn. These situations will contain tasks and materials that will engage students in meaningful learning" (p. 47). Part of this work involves appreciating the unique qualities that every student brings to their learning, including their preferences regarding self-expression (working with art, music, language, graphs, etc.).

Muhammad (2023) reflects, "I have never met a child without genius" (p. 15). She explains that students of color too often are labeled as not meeting proficiency benchmarks on assessments, and she questions the system itself for failing to recognize students' intelligence. Muhammad continues, "It is not the child who needs the intervention or remediation. It is the system and the curriculum that needs reparations. There needs to be a dismantling of systems and curricula and a (re)building of them that is grounded in the genius of our teachers and our students" (p. 16). Students' different ways of knowing need to be seen as assets in education, and students of color need to stop being punished for "failing" to meet narrow standards for proficiency.

Furthermore, students need opportunities to see how their in-school learning is connected to their out-of-school lives (Beach, 2022). They need to be able to delve into their own interests and passions in school and to imagine possibilities for future careers (Robinson, 2011). "Too many students pass through education and have their natural talents marginalized or ignored" (Robinson, 2009, p. 247). In fact,

> People succeed best when they have others who understand their talents, challenges, and abilities. This is why mentoring is such a helpful force in so many people's lives. Great teachers have always understood that [their] real role is not to teach subjects but to teach students. Mentoring and coaching is the vital pulse of a living system of education. (p. 249)

An important part of mentoring youth writers in the classroom, then, involves tapping into students' knowledge, experiences, and interests.

Mentoring in Action: Inside the Young Authors' Studio Program

The study of YAS showed that the mentors attended to the youth writers' different interests, experiences, and knowledge (see Figure 4.4). Importantly, they recognized these differences as strengths.

FIGURE 4.4. Songwriting breakout session.

Creating a List of Guiding Principles

Even before we started curriculum planning, I asked the mentors to join me in coming up with a list of guiding principles for the YAS program. I wanted to set the right tone toward students, draw attention to the many assets students bring with them to the classroom, and highlight some of the ways we could set students up for success. Our program's guiding principles evolved into the following list:

1. We are a community of writers.
2. We honor diversity and encourage writers to draw on their languages and experiences.
3. Bringing writers of different ages together creates new learning opportunities. The youngest writer has something to teach the oldest writer in the group.
4. Young people engage in legitimate forms of writing outside of school (e.g., blogs, diaries, comics, videos, etc.) that support personal and academic growth.
5. Authentic audiences matter. We write to be heard. We have important ideas and stories to communicate.
6. Writers have the right to opt out of sharing their work.
7. We celebrate youth voices in a safe, supportive space.
8. We must do no harm. We will be positive, caring forces in writers' lives.
9. As writers ourselves, we can empathize with the challenges students face when writing.

10. Writing is fun!
11. Writing should be meaningful.
12. Writers make choices (Williams & Reid, 2019).

We found that taking the time to articulate our guiding principles together helped us all get on the same page and approach planning and instruction with similar aims. We also shared these principles with the youth writers and their parents so that everyone was clear about what we were trying to accomplish in the space. Teachers can formulate their own list of guiding principles as well (see Figure 4.5).

FIGURE 4.5. Design your own list of guiding principles.

Guiding Principles

What principles guide your teaching of writing? What kind of space do you want your classroom to be? Take a look at our list of guiding principles. Then make your own list. As you do this, don't forget that students bring many strengths with them to the classroom (e.g., cultural and linguistic knowledge, experiences, talents, interests, etc.). Since many students write in their lives outside of the classroom, how will you acknowledge that? Share your list of guiding principles with students, parents, and colleagues, and ask for their feedback. Revisit your list over time and refine it based on your evolving knowledge of teaching and learning.

Learning about Students

Mentors learned about students in the YAS program through conversations, writing activities, and various forms that students filled out during the program. We found that students in the YAS program were a diverse group. They ranged in age from eleven to seventeen, were enrolled in grades 6–11, and were familiar with a wide range of languages: Spanish (9), German (2), Hindi (1), Urdu (1), and Dutch (1). The students identified as follows: Caucasian or white (8), Hispanic or Latinx (4), African American or Black (2), Asian Caucasian (2), Asian Indian (1), and Caucasian Hispanic (1).

The youth writers also disclosed to us many interests and hobbies:

- writing
- reading, manga, webtoons, fantasy
- movies, films, animation, anime
- music, playing instruments, ukulele, singing

- art, sketching, drawing, coloring, photography, design, crafts
- games, gaming, video games, computers
- chemistry, science, history, math
- dancing, sports, basketball, baseball, soccer, figure skating, swimming, fishing, martial arts
- drama, acting, cosplay, musicals, Broadway
- makeup, sewing, fashion, designing clothes
- travel, road trips
- sleeping

Teachers can support such varied interests in the writing classroom in a variety of ways. They can introduce students to multiple forms of composition, such as research reports, process essays, presentations, plays, songs, stories, films, animated works, video game design, comics, and more. Chapter 1 goes into detail about using a wide range of forms and modes.

Learning about students' interests in different subjects can lead to fascinating discussions about writing across the curriculum, such as the conventions involved with writing a lab report. Perhaps students who are interested in sports or musicals could explore different kinds of journalism, crafting articles for a school paper. Perhaps those who enjoy traveling could write a travel blog. In other words, finding out students' interests can open up new worlds of writing that are exciting for students. These different types of writing can prompt students to tap into the strengths they already bring with them to the classroom.

Teachers should also draw on students' cultural and linguistic resources. Specifically, writing activities such as neighborhood maps and heart stories (Nelson, 2004), family member interviews, and food memory narratives invite students to draw on their unique languages, cultures, and histories, paving the way for authentic reflection and sharing.

Some teachers give students a short survey at the beginning of the year so they can get to know them right away. In addition, icebreaker activities like scavenger hunts get students up and moving and interacting. I try to learn as much as I can about my students as early as possible because it helps me connect with students and better tailor instruction to them, whether this means adding more options for creative projects, selecting particular books for book talks, or inviting student expertise into our discussions. Some teachers have students share information about themselves in an author bio (see Figure 4.6).

FIGURE 4.6. Tips for using author bios.

Author Bio Assignment

Invite students to craft an author bio at the beginning of the year. This autobiographical work could include details such as their hometown, interests, attitudes toward writing, or aspirations. Students could include a photo for this write-up and then post these around the room. In Fleischer and Andrew-Vaughan's (2009) *Writing outside Your Comfort Zone*, the authors discuss how to teach the genre of "author blurb" writing (pp. 33–42). They help break down this type of writing for teachers and students, pointing out that author blurbs are often characterized by simple sentences and third-person point of view. These blurbs might include a favorite quote, other works by the student, awards received, etc. Fleischer and Andrew-Vaughan include examples, rubrics, and more to make their author blurb assignment an easy-to-use and meaningful project in the English classroom.

Honoring Languages and Cultures

Our students have rich cultural and linguistic knowledge. In the YAS program, we wanted to encourage students to draw on these assets in their writing. I reminded the mentors, "With spoken word poetry, you need to use your language, your experiences, and your culture. We should all be encouraging students to do that. I know that sometimes students are writing pure fiction, but the more they can draw on their own experiences, the better."

Nari talked about how students she was working with knew Urdu, Hindi, Spanish, and English. I reminded her that as a multilingual writer herself, she could model how to make use of more than one language in a piece. I said, "*You* have multiple languages, so there may be a place in the poem where you think, 'This word says it better. I don't want to translate this. They have to hear it like this.'" I recommended that she consider showing the students Jamaica Osorio's White House Poetry Jam video, "Kumulipo" (2009). In this beautiful bilingual piece, the poet makes a powerful argument for not forgetting one's cultures and languages.

We were fortunate to have two mentors who were international students. In their bios, they introduced themselves as follows:

> **Amir:** I am a senior. My major is information technology. I was born and raised in Riyadh, the capital city of Saudi Arabia. I'm the youngest member of my family. I like to do meditation and exercise in the

park during the weekend. My first study abroad was in New York City. When I graduated from high school, that was the first time I took an English course. I decided to take this course because I like to give my knowledge to young people. I'm planning to open my own business when I graduate from the university. I speak three languages: Arabic, English, and French.

Nari: [Nari] is a second-year graduate student in the MFA Theatre for Youth program. She is originally from South Korea and has lived in United Arab Emirates, India, and United Kingdom. She joined Young Authors' Studio as a mentor because she is passionate about creating spaces for young people to find and strengthen their voice as writers. She enjoys writing travel stories, letters, memoirs, performative poems, and persuasive essays. In her spare time, she likes to visit art museums, practice yoga, and make Korean food with her friends. One item from her bucket list is to write and illustrate a picturebook for children.

The mentors' cultures and languages were assets they brought with them into the YAS space. We saw this when Nari was writing a piece in Korean about homesickness during one of the workshops. Her work included the words, "Home is far away, and I am an island. I called a name once, twice, and some more. Tears sent me to bed." I noticed that as she was writing, students had gathered around her, curious and eager for her to share her writing with them, asking about the language system she was using.

The exchanges went in both directions in this program, with the mentors sometimes curious to learn more about the students' cultures and traditions. During team time at the end of a workshop, I overheard a conversation between Amir and the students. He was asking them about the differences between Halloween and Thanksgiving: "So, Thanksgiving, the situation is different right?" A student replied, "From Halloween? Yes!" Amir followed up, "You eat turkey, right?" The group continued to talk about holidays for several minutes. It can be so useful for students of different ages and cultures to have opportunities for these kinds of informal exchanges (see Figure 4.7).

In the writing classroom, teachers can design assignments that invite students to reflect on their experiences, cultures, and identities. One poetry assignment that exemplifies this concept is the "I am from . . ." poem (see Figure 4.8). Students learn a lot about themselves and others as they write and share these poems.

FIGURE 4.7. A student and a mentor.

FIGURE 4.8. Tips for using the "I am from . . . " poem.

Inviting Students to Write about Their Cultures

Teachers can support students by honoring their cultural and linguistic resources and by using assignments that celebrate where students come from. Christensen (2000) explains that she came up with the idea for the "I am from . . . " poem—an assignment still popular among English teachers today—from a piece she read by George Ella Lyon that used this repeating pattern. Christensen used that poem as a model for students and had them brainstorm lists that captured some of their own experiences and memories (e.g., items in their homes, yards, and neighborhoods; people; sayings; food; places). Her students used those ideas to formulate list-like poems that began with the words "I am from . . . " and that "sound[ed] like home" (p. 20).

Another way teachers can honor language and culture in the writing classroom is by putting students in touch with the work of a wide range of writers, including authors from a variety of cultural and linguistic backgrounds. Their works can serve as mentor texts that exemplify the craft of writing while also teaching readers about different cultural experiences. While short works and excerpts may fit best for twenty-five-minute breakout sessions like ours, students can explore longer works when given more time.

In one of the later iterations of YAS, the program secured a grant that enabled us to give each student a book from a culturally diverse list of authors (see Figure 4.9). To introduce each book, I guided students through a short writing activity specific to that book. These prompts helped the students get excited to read and showed them how all texts can be used as springboards for writing. These sorts of writing prompts grounded in young adult (YA) literature are useful for honoring multiple experiences and cultures in the writing classroom.

Teachers can demonstrate that all languages and cultures are welcome in writing instruction by putting students in touch with a variety of authors. If funds are available, the author could be invited to come to campus or deliver an online talk, like the one on visual storytelling that YA author Xavier Garza (2023) did for us. (We also had local author Tom Leveen [2023] present on publishing.) In fact, a wide array of author talks can be found online with a simple search, and these can be a nice way for students to learn from an expert at no cost.

Encouraging Writing from Experience

The mentors in the YAS program invited students to draw on their experiences. Sometimes mentors encouraged simple personal connections. "I want you to think of your favorite color and three adjectives [describing] why this color is your favorite," Nari told one group in a warm-up activity. This mentor also led a poetry breakout session that asked students to write about first-time experiences (e.g., the first time they ate ice cream, were poked by a cactus, etc.). One student responded by writing about her first time experiencing snow:

> I looked out of the car and fell into the pile of shredded ice. Standing up, freezing cold, waddling the best I could. Wee! Yet scared to make a snow angel. But it was love at first sight. My pink coat cradled me as I got carried into the car. The memory soaked into my soul. The snow trickled off of me.

FIGURE 4.9. Mentor texts can be springboards for creative writing.

Using Mentor Texts to Spark Creative Writing

Writers can learn a lot about their craft from reading works by published authors. Below are some YA-based writing prompts used with students in a later iteration of the YAS program.

- **Prompt #1. *Maximilian and the Mystery of the Guardian Angel* by Xavier Garza (2011):** What are your hobbies, skills, and languages? What "insider knowledge" do you have that others might like to read about?
- **Prompt #2. *Brown Girl Dreaming* by Jacqueline Woodson (2016):** Read the poem "Gifted" in this book. How are you similar to or different from someone you care about? Write a few lines of poetry highlighting differences or similarities.
- **Prompt #3. *Sick* by Tom Leveen (2013):** What if something completely bizarre happened at your school or workplace? Explain the scenario.
- **Prompt #4. *Ninth Ward* by Jewell Parker Rhodes (2012):** If you were going to write a work of historical fiction, which moment or figure from history would you focus on? Why?
- **Prompt #5. *The Arrival* by Shaun Tan (2007):** Imagine life in a world unlike our own. Draw a fantastical pet for your protagonist.
- **Prompt #6. *The First Rule of Punk* by Celia C. Pérez (2018) or *The Invention of Hugo Cabret* by Brian Selznick (2007):** How comfortable are you with visual storytelling? Do you like to draw? Paint? Make collages? Take photographs? Make short films?
- **Prompt #7. *American Born Chinese* by Gene Luen Yang (2021) or *Anya's Ghost* by Vera Brosgol (2011):** Share a defining moment from your childhood or adolescence through a three-panel comic. Feel free to mix realism and fantasy. You don't have to portray the moment exactly as it happened.

Students in this session wrote about meeting a movie star, getting hooked on anime, playing basketball, traveling on a boat, and going to the dentist. During the comic book/graphic novel breakout session, Miranda noticed that students "were drawing things from their personal life, rather than making stories about fantastical things." She concluded that for students, "drawing realistic things may be easier to connect to versus alien creatures."

Throughout the program, the mentors used journal prompts that asked students to tap into their experiences. To get students started with the work of brainstorming, they sometimes asked students to draw something first (e.g., a human figure, a neighborhood map, a heart) and to fill that shape with memories. For one prompt, students drew a heart in their journal and filled it with family, friends, pets, objects, hobbies, holidays, and "anything [else] that is close to your heart." Then they selected one of these things to write about. The mentors encouraged and praised the youth writers for sharing their stories. Nari told the students, "Thank you for sharing your words. You are all very brave to share your personal stories. And you can keep working on this during your writing time after the breakouts. I'm so excited to hear all of your stories!" (For more of these multimodal journaling activities, including neighborhood maps and scar stories, see G. Lynn Nelson's *Writing and Being* [1994].)

At times I observed a disconnect between students' experiences and what they were being asked to write about. For example, in one breakout session students were working on a series of haikus about winter. One student quietly objected, "It's never winter in Arizona," but the mentor didn't seem to hear. It can be challenging for kids in Arizona to write about the stereotypical winter scene because our winters are mild. In a desert where saguaros grow and winter days are often in the sixties to seventies (sometimes even in the eighties!), we do not have many of the visual cues, like snow, that signal winter for most people around the world. Teachers can be sensitive by writing their prompts in a way that allows the writing to reflect a wide variety of experiences. I also recommend that teachers solicit ideas from students, trusting them as experts who are capable of coming up with topics to write about, too.

In the YAS program, students sometimes drew on experiences from their recent past. These moments were still vivid in the students' minds, and they wanted to talk or write about them to process their feelings. One student wrote a story about a world being flipped upside down; that author had just been watching the show *Stranger Things*. Someone else wrote a piece about two men taking all of the candy from a bowl on their porch at Halloween. The student was annoyed that the men didn't even bother to wear costumes or bring any kids with them. Ultimately, the student decided to craft a piece that fictionalized the ending and punished the culprits:

> Jack the Lantern was told by his carver, "Stand gourd for me, Jack. Let only the worthy take a treat and give all of the others a trick." And so the

> pumpkin stood, watching the little children come by gleefully, taking a candy each. So Jack waited . . . "Aha! What scallywags! What phonies! What horrible monsters!" A pair of men not even with a proper costume or children of their own dared to set foot upon Jack's porch. They poured each morsel left straight into their greedy mouths. "How dare you take what is unjustly yours. You shall trick or treat no more." Jack rose from his table, ready for action, glowering at the startled men, his toothy smile turning into a terrifying frown. He glowered at the now trembling duo with crowds of amazed children cheering him on. He belted, "You have failed to do the simple task of containing your own greed. You will now become something that no man has ever been." Bang! Boom. Swirl. . . . The . . . men became robbed of their forms. Orange pumpkins. Jack stopped. He smiled. He gave a great jolly laugh, and he said, "Happy Halloween," before nestling back onto his little table, sure that his master would be proud.

Writing allowed this adolescent to take control of a situation that disturbed her, and she was able to imagine the scene playing out a different way. Sometimes small talk in the form of "How was your holiday?" or "Have you watched any good shows lately?" can give us insight into students' worlds, but they also remind students of material they already have to work with (and experiences they can work *through*) in pieces of their own. By frequently checking in with students about their day-to-day lives and giving them a lot of different ways to write, the mentors helped students see that they actually had quite a lot they could write about if they just drew on their experience, knowledge, and interests. In fact, students can keep track of great ideas for future pieces by charting out their "writing territories" (Atwell, 1998) in a journal (see Figure 4.10).

FIGURE 4.10. Keeping track of areas of expertise for writing.

Writing Territories

Students know so much that they can draw on in their writing. Nancie Atwell (1998) asks students to come up with a list of writing territories they can revisit throughout the year as they need ideas for their writing. These categories might include memories, passions, sorrows, fantasies, hobbies, places, people, things, and more. It helps if students have a set amount of time to brainstorm within a category (e.g., make a list of all the places you are familiar with in a two-minute period). They can then take those lists, choose one idea, and write about it in detail. Keeping these lists in a journal means that students always have an abundance of ideas they can come back to.

Connecting to Art, Music, and Film

Another way the mentors honored students was by integrating the arts (including music, art, and film) into their breakout sessions. Too often the models of good writing that teachers offer in English classrooms are strictly text-based. In such environments, it is no wonder that students disconnect and disengage, not caring about the content and not seeing themselves as writers or readers. In their out-of-school lives, students are composing comics, watching shows, making short films and animated works, writing songs, and playing video games. The more that teachers can tap into students' interests in visual and multimodal forms, the better.

Having a workshop devoted to art and writing gave the youth writers a chance to look at examples of comics and graphic novels and then craft comics of their own. At the same time, art was not limited to this workshop. Mentors looked for ways to bring in visual elements to other workshops as well. As mentioned in Chapter 1, for example, the poetry workshop included a blackout poetry option, a form that can involve illustration and design.

During the songwriting breakout, students had a chance to talk about songs they liked. Some of the artists they mentioned included Kendrick Lamar, Imogen Heap, and Vance Joy. One student said, "I think music is my favorite form of writing. I love to sing." She talked about how her school does not have a choir, but she planned to participate in the school talent show that year. Her brother added that she sings at 10:00 p.m., and because of the way their home is laid out, she wakes them all up. Other students in this breakout added that they enjoyed playing piano and guitar.

Miranda noticed that students in this session wanted to keep working on their songs even after the breakout session had ended. In addition, a student who was "hard to reach the week prior was much more talkative and wanted to speak to the group about the music he preferred." The workshops on art and music truly spoke to him and led to a change in his attitude toward writing.

It was common practice in this program to bring in examples of writing that students could relate to. When Henry led a screenwriting breakout, he brought in scripts for the *Pirates of the Caribbean*, *Harry Potter*, *Star Wars*, *Batman*, and *Toy Story* films. Later, he told us in the workshop debrief, "There were two girls who got really excited when they saw the *Harry Potter* script I had." Nari similarly tapped into students' interest in animation by using a Pixar story template (Bunting, n.d.) in her breakout session. Making connections between writing and film/animation can help students see that writing actually plays a crucial role in the forms of entertainment they enjoy in their out-of-school lives.

When I taught at the secondary level, I wanted students to have frequent encounters with film, art, and poetry, so I made time for students to engage with these works during some of our class warm-up activities. A framework (see Figure 4.11) helped them analyze different kinds of creative pieces and move from simple description into higher levels of thinking.

FIGURE 4.11. A "Describe, Analyze, Connect, and Evaluate" framework for interpreting film, art, and poetry.

A Framework for Interpreting Film, Art, and Poetry

Arts integration can take many forms in the English classroom, from exploring pieces as mentor texts (e.g., studying a screenplay to write a screenplay) to reacting to a work through an artistic form (e.g., writing a song in response to a class novel studied) to "transmediating" or adapting a work into another medium (e.g., taking a short story and putting it into the form of a comic). When I taught at the high school level, I kept a collection of laminated artwork that students could pick up on their way into the classroom, a list of film/animation clips I could pull up on the screen, and a collection of different poems students could choose from. On days when we worked with film, art, or poetry for bell work, we used the following Describe, Analyze, Connect, and Evaluate framework:

1. **Describe:** What do you see? Spend some time thinking about the piece. What is the title? What seems to be happening? What are possible meanings? Look and/or listen carefully. Figure out as much as you can from the clues you are given.
2. **Analyze:** Pay attention to the construction of the work. What are the basic elements or parts? How do they communicate information? What does the work mean?
    - Film elements: sound, lighting, setting, costumes, camera angles, shots, etc.
    - Art elements: medium, color, line, shape, position, symbols, etc.
    - Poetry elements: figurative language, word choice, line breaks, etc.
3. **Connect:** What other works does this piece remind you of? Can you make a personal connection? Can you connect it to something you learned about in another class?
4. **Evaluate:** What is your opinion of this piece? Why? Point to specific details to support your conclusions.

Valuing Teacher Knowledge, Experience, and Interests

Of course, teachers have important knowledge, experience, and interests, too. These assets shape how and what is taught. In the YAS program, I often saw examples of the mentors' lives influencing their teaching. Amir said he chose to lead the overview on art because he loves art, and he goes to museums whenever he travels. He had students draw objects that reflected their personalities and was excited to find that students shared his passion for art. Henry had taken an introduction to poetry course, so it is no wonder that he revisited his class files for sample poems when it came time for him to prepare a workshop overview on poetry for YAS students. Also, since Henry was a Dungeons & Dragons fan, he devised a character-building activity based on that game. Miranda, who designed a songwriting breakout, talked about how she had worked at a radio station for a while. Nari, a graduate student in a theater-for-youth program, took the lead for our drama workshop. She did a fantastic job running that workshop, and we all benefited from her expertise. As Nari herself pointed out about the program, "What makes [YAS] unique is the diverse interests and experiences that each mentor brings."

As teachers, we don't just forget who we are when we develop curricula and interact with our students. Our knowledge, experience, and interests help drive the work we do in education. These parts of ourselves can help us recognize gaps and opportunities in English education—including ways to push our field forward. These qualities also enable us to make authentic connections with student writers. Have you stopped to think about the ways your interests and experiences have influenced your teaching (see Figure 4.12)?

FIGURE 4.12. Teachers' interests, experiences, and knowledge matter.

Teachers, Who Are You Outside of Your Teaching Lives?

Reflect on your own life outside of teaching. What experiences have shaped you? What special knowledge do you have? What interests and hobbies excite you? Your interests can spark new ideas for teaching and help students relate to you. You also need those parts of yourself as you decompress from a difficult week of teaching. Some of my interests (e.g., film, art, music, gardening, cooking) have surfaced in my teaching in ways that have surprised me; they also give me an outlet and allow me to come back to teaching refreshed. Teachers, your interests and experiences and the vast knowledge you possess are incredible assets that you bring with you to the classroom every day of the school year. Don't forget that.

Pause and Reflect

Honoring student knowledge, experience, and interests is one of the most important strategies for mentoring youth writers because it involves valuing the assets students bring with them to the classroom, including the forms of writing they enjoy and identify with. Not only can students tap into these resources when they are tasked with writing, but they can also learn from the wealth of knowledge and experience that others around them bring to the space. It is vital that we send students out into the world with a strong sense of themselves and a willingness to continue to learn.

This chapter shows how the YAS mentors honored student knowledge, experiences, and interests. The ways they did this are applicable to the secondary classroom as well. Specifically, teachers can learn about students and find ways to build on their interests in art, music, and film. They can honor students' languages and cultures and invite them to write from experience.

Before we see what a secondary teacher has to say about the importance of this fourth strategy for mentoring youth writers, again let's reflect on what this strategy means to you (see Figure 4.13).

FIGURE 4.13. Reflection questions for strategy #4.

Pause and Reflect

Strategy #4: Honoring Student Knowledge, Experience, and Interests

- How do you already use this strategy in your teaching?
- What are some new ways you can use this strategy to benefit students?
- How does this strategy help bring out the author (or graphic novelist, filmmaker, songwriter . . .) in every student?

Teacher Interview: Matt Hamilton on Honoring Student Knowledge, Experience, and Interests

FIGURE 4.14. Selfie by Matt Hamilton.

It can be useful to explore how a secondary English teacher honors student knowledge, experience, and interests in their teaching. Matt Hamilton (he/they) taught middle school and high school for nine years across private, public, and magnet schools (see Figure 4.14). Currently, they run a statewide education program with PBS called the Michigan Learning Channel and work with families, libraries, community organizations, and teachers in schools to bring that content to students. Matt has done a lot of co-teaching, served many special education students, and done interdisciplinary teaching fusing English and history. They are a National Writing Project teacher consultant with a commitment to social justice and antiracist, culturally responsive teaching. In addition, Matt is passionate about food and runs Masafrenda, which sells fresh masa and homemade tortillas. They also enjoy cooking.

Can you share some examples of how you have honored student knowledge, experience, and interests in the classroom?

I like to leverage as many open-ended prompts and writing opportunities as possible. I have found there's no magic assignment or prompt that's just going to flip the switch for every single student and all of a sudden we're all sharing the deepest parts of ourselves. But if the culture is like, "Oh, it's writing time," or we do a warm-up every day in the writing classroom, and if students recognize that your voice matters and your story matters, you can build that culture and that trust: "When I come to this classroom every day, I am sharing myself." And you actually don't have to share your writing to share yourself. There's trust there. "I'm going to practice writing and know that nobody else has to see it."

Sometimes we have to write an argumentative essay. And there are rubrics and rules around what that looks like, but we can think about ways that invite you to bring yourself into even that. There are things that we have to do, but I think that distinction and comfort and the transparency of "We are in a writing classroom, and we're all writers, and we all have stories to tell" matters. For me, I found success building that culture and inspiring that sense of trust.

I always try to take something, whether it's an argumentative essay or literary analysis or whatever, and make it as authentic as possible. We are all writing a literary analysis, for example, and we might practice by writing about the short stories that we read, but also we all read different things. And analyzing a film might be the thing that brings the fire to you. I might analyze a recipe, or someone else might analyze a Marvel movie or whatever. I try to be flexible and creative myself and open to the different ways that young people are going to write authentically and still meet the criteria and the standards. I would try to always be open-ended not in just the prompts as we're building a writing practice, but also when we get to some of the summative assessments or final projects. What are the ways that one kind of assignment can become a variety of different prompts and invite students to participate in that process?

One thing that drives me and feeds my own cultural knowledge is I really love food, and I learn through food. It has helped me to understand the power of authenticity and story and voice and heritage and culture. I've learned about myself and about the rest of the world through food. I read a lot of cookbooks, I read a lot of recipes, and I especially get interested in heritage cooking and deep ancestral cooking and anticolonial and precolonial cooking. So that's my main hobby, reading cookbooks and practicing recipes. I run a little side business where I make fresh heirloom corn masa and handmade tortillas that we sell locally, which has been really amazing. I have Mexican American heritage.

When you have an opportunity to connect and deepen and tell stories based in your own interests, it can be really empowering for an individual. We did this amazing food project that invited students to take a favorite recipe, whether it be a family recipe or whatever, and trace the origins. And so that was how we did history in a fun way, talking about food and illustrating and thinking about a menu. I've done a lot of recipe writing and food blogging. I mean, everybody loves food. It's a great way to get connected and fuel writing.

We would do a lot of literature circles and jigsaw activities with nonfiction to put different kinds of texts in front of students so they have an opportunity to see different forms of writing and different prompts. And then inviting that reflection. One of my favorite first-day-of-school activities is to put on this TED Talk where someone is telling a story of a scientific discovery. Like when scientists up at the Arctic Center at the North Pole discovered this bone fragment that led to the understanding that camels are arctic creatures. They're not of the desert, even though we all have this image of the camels being desert creatures. And then I put the students into groups, and I give them all names of animals and two different names of places, and they're totally random. They pull them out of a cup, and I'm like, "Tell a story. How did this animal get from this place to this place? What did that evolutionary process look like?" And that's always fun because it's a community-building opportunity. It's a storytelling opportunity. And then we talk about "How were you able to be creative? How did you rely on each other? Did you do some research? Did you just make it up completely?" It's about validating different types of writing that we will work with this year. We're going to talk about forms of writing that are completely oral. We're going to talk about forms of writing that are based on research and driven by nonfiction. We're going to talk about opinion writing. We're going to talk about storytelling that's completely imaginative and fantastical and opportunities to embrace that with creativity. We need all stories. And this includes from a cultural perspective, and recognizing that the stories that you have been told, bring those in. They are worth telling. They are valid. I want to deconstruct the idea that novels are the only stories that matter. What's a short story in the form of a video, a poem, a dance, and all of these different things?

Another favorite thing is inviting students to bring something to class (e.g., an object, a recipe, a dish, a memento, a photo), and I would get these family stories about heirlooms. We did a couple of different iterations of "What's your time capsule or your suitcase that you bring with you?" "What is your life as a museum exhibit?" "Who are you? What are the artifacts that define who you are, where you come from, where you want to go?" And putting writing in the context of an exhibit, a film, those different kinds of forms, helps students to break out of what they think writing is and to have different opportunities to bring themselves into it. It forces creativity that's going to lead to authenticity at some point. You can't make that up. So I really liked what that can bring out of young people.

I care deeply about honoring language. Even though I've not taught in many spaces where a lot of students spoke additional languages, it was always important to talk about the significance of language. So I've had students bring in languages when they're telling stories about their home or telling stories about family members. And we've talked about the significance of the phrase your grandma always says, and including that kind of piece of dialogue in your story or being able to capture and sort of translate. And we've seen that in models and mentor texts.

We've also had a lot of conversations about the English language, recognizing that many students in an English classroom think they're supposed to write in a specific kind of way, even if it's in a variety of the English language. And so I've seen students who write completely differently from how they talk or try to tell stories in this sort of highfalutin way because that's what they think is expected of them. We've had to deconstruct that in some cases. "How can you use language to be authentic and have an impact?" And sometimes that means using keywords and phrases that mean something to you. Sometimes it is pieces of other languages that are relevant. Sometimes it's like slang. Sometimes it's swear words and curse words. They're like, "What do you mean? I can swear in my writing?" And it's like, "Yeah, there are absolutely places where that's super appropriate and super necessary." There's this balance of bringing yourself into your writing and making sure that you're being represented, that you're being thoughtful, and that you're being authentic to your language and who you are. And there's also, "How do you want to have an impact? How do you want your reader to feel? Do you want to make your reader uncomfortable? Do you want to cause your reader to feel angry or feel something?" That's kind of an advanced conversation, but it's something I would talk about with seventh graders, and they would actually get it right away.

There's this series of videos on the TED website called "Small Thing Big Idea." It takes a small thing and in three minutes, it goes through the history and cultural significance. There's one about the jump rope, the hoodie, etc. And that was a really fun opportunity for me to invite students to bring something that they see every day that they care about. And so a lot of students would bring in a basketball if that was a huge part of their life or a pair of shoes that was really important to them. I appreciated that opportunity to learn about students because it disarmed them a little bit. It wasn't like "write about something you care about." I've done that too. "Bring in an object that's meaningful to you." Those are cool opportunities, but this was literally, "Pick a random object and research it, talk about it, and make connections to it." And [students] produced videos as well. They didn't just write about it. They made their own and edited these short videos that always turned out really, really cool. So that was a powerful exercise to get students to talk about things that they cared about.

I did some comic writing. We talked about superheroes, and we would read a lot of stories about superheroes, origin stories, and stuff like that. Bringing in those pieces allowed them to tap into, again, some different kinds of things that they wouldn't necessarily bring up.

Using open-ended prompts and products really helped me to tap into what students were interested in from an "I can write about this" or "I can see writing in my life" kind of perspective. I had students compose documentaries, plays, recipes, newspaper articles, entire websites, Minecraft settings, whole video games, and board games. I was able to tap into student interest by building that trust and inviting them to make anything.

Why do you think it's important to honor student knowledge, experience, and interests in the classroom?
I don't see any reason why you wouldn't. If you are teaching a group of human beings, then you should see

them as human beings. I think our job as educators is not just to take something we know and put it in the people who are in front of us to empower them. It's to help them understand what happens when you learn new things and the power that you have. And I think especially in the English classroom and thinking about writing and communicating, that power can lead to the ability of a young person to reach new goals, be successful, have an impact, be a citizen ultimately. And so I think [teaching this way is] especially activating and empowering [in] a world where statistically more than half of young people in our classrooms are people of color, 10 percent of them are LGBTQ+, and all these statistics that I'm sure you're familiar with. There are so many [times] outside of the classroom where [students are] told that they're not valued or they're not worth it, or their voice doesn't matter. They literally can't vote. They literally don't have a voice in so much of what surrounds them. And so taking every opportunity to say, "That's wrong. You do matter. Your voice matters. Your story matters. And not only should you hold that and know that it matters, but you should bring it, and you should find ways to make sure that you can put it in front of people and you can share it in ways that are meaningful."

What are the benefits of honoring student knowledge, culture, and experience?

I think our students, especially right now, are growing up in a world where there's a lot of looking around and being like, "Well, what does that matter? Because no one's going to listen to me. Nothing's going to change." And the earth is on fire. Everywhere you turn, there's a bleak message. And so I think saying, "Well, first of all, there's a benefit to who you are and just being a part of this." And then second, you can take that and you can turn it into something where they see they can make a difference. So I think that empowering students is really a benefit. We can't have great storytelling unless more people know that they have stories to tell. And I really believe that storytelling is the thing that brings us together, that moves us forward, that helps preserve us. And it's really hard, but convincing young people [of] that is important. They should be preserving their stories, their family stories. They should have opportunities to say, "I'm important because of where I come from," regardless of where you come from and what you're being told about what that means.

We're preparing a generation of young people who are going to bring themselves into what they do. I think we're setting up a future with a Congress that's going to have representatives who think about the humanity of their constituents. We're going to have CEOs who think about the humanity of their staff and the people that they serve, who think about the world around them as an actual community and not just a bottom line, because we're practicing and teaching empathy. We're teaching people to bring their cultural values into a space and to seek them out. We mentioned, "What are your ancestral values or your cultural values?" And they're like, "I don't know. What does that mean? We celebrate Christmas or whatever." And it's like, "No. What are the things that you've been taught, and where does that come from? Go look for it."

Have you faced any challenges with this work?

When you're the teacher doing this work, students recognize it, and they want more of it. I've experienced at several schools that my classroom became the safe space, the club space, and the lunchtime space, and the after-school space. And all of a sudden, those kids are always around and practicing what I've taught them about how to be a good human and care about other humans. Now they want to go to school board meetings and advocate for real change in the community, which is amazing. But it can be precarious as a teacher, as someone in the community. And depending on where the community alignment is, they may be like, "What's going on here?" We've seen that play out at the national level, this "teachers have an agenda" and "teachers are leftist" kind of thing. Where you are, you might have a supportive administration and union, that kind of stuff. The slightly more dangerous piece is adults who don't understand what authentic student voice is, and the fact that young people really do have voices and have things to say and have things they care about. I did have a group of students who were like, "The school we go to is trash. We need a better racial justice policy. It's not diverse. We're not learning the right things." And they wanted to go to the school board. There were a lot of community members who were like, "Their teacher is orchestrating this." I don't really know what it's going to take, but it's convincing other adults that young people do have value and have things to say because when [adults] don't understand that, then that's where it becomes kind of dangerous for teachers.

How can teachers get started with this work?
I think teachers should start with themselves. To be totally honest, I think we need to experience the magic of tapping into our own stories. For me, it was food, it was cooking, and it was learning stories and telling stories through food and discovering more. I think every teacher needs that thing that inspires them to tap into who they are and bring their identity into spaces and figure out what that identity is because we're not encouraged to do it. So starting with that piece, and then I really do think that's probably the biggest thing in terms of just opening [yourself] up to being more creative in the classroom.

The other things are just allowing yourself to be flexible and creative. Take one day and go in and ask students to write about whatever they want, in whatever way they want, and see what happens. It doesn't have to be a whole big project. It doesn't have to be a thing where every student in your classroom makes a multimodal website that has five subpages with video content and poems and journalism. And it can be just a five-minute warm-up at the beginning of class where it's like, "What do you want to write about today?"

And then the thing that I say as often as I can is to be perpetually in awe of the young people in our spaces, practicing that [with intention], being awestruck, being amazed by young people. If we always take that posture, they're going to see it, and they're going to be encouraged by it, and they're going to show up as more and more and more of themselves every day.

What additional advice do you have on this topic for teachers?
Always be a teacher and a learner. Experience the world as someone who is always learning and always being in awe of humanity, and always have that teacher lens of "How can this become a project?" I think it's really very cool that this author, artist, playwright, whatever, did this thing. I bet fifteen-year-olds could do it too.

Do you have any favorite resources on this topic?
Learning for Justice and Facing History [& Ourselves] are the two web-based places where I've gotten a lot of professional learning. Global Oneness Project is a film site. They have mostly short documentary films about identity and culture, and specifically a lot about Indigenous culture and ancient wisdom and things. And so those were really inspirational for me. They have prompts for students that have been really thought-provoking.

And then, TED Talks are everything for me. There tends to be one for pretty much [anything] you're trying to talk about. It's also a really cool space to send students. I've done a number of assignments that have them go to the site and pick a topic. And I think it's also a medium that relies so much on personal storytelling and identity.

Do you have any cautions or warnings for teachers?
Be endlessly creative. Be endlessly in awe. And a huge part of that is not boxing students in. Once they've opened up to you—that point where a student is showing up as their authentic self—you need to realize that's actually in progress. Even as adults, we're never in a place where we are our full selves at any given time. We're building and iterating and creating ourselves, and teenagers are especially in that place. I had a number of students of color in a majority white school who woke up to their own racial identity and came into this wanting to be advocates for racial justice. And I had to remind myself that's also not their whole identity. That's a really exciting identity for them to come into. It's empowering. It's a beautiful thing to see them realize that they can advocate for this thing that's bigger than themselves. And also they like racing cars on the weekend, or they enjoy going to the woodshop class or playing video games and these kinds of things. And so don't box students in. Do not forget that our students contain multitudes. I think as teachers, we can get excited and attached to the thing that is powerful or exciting or flashy. The theater kid who was the star in the musical is also so many other things. Invite students to bring their whole selves into our classroom, which means as they want to show up. We don't get to pick.

Do you have any words of encouragement for teachers as they embark on this work?
If this is a thing you commit yourself to, you are going to be endlessly inspired. You're going to be endlessly energized. We're lucky that we get new students every year because there is that opportunity to meet new, amazing human beings who have things to say and things to share. You'll learn more things about your community. Your eyes will be opened up to so many more things. That's really exciting. It's always going to be fun. It's always going to be different. If you're just asking students to meet the criteria of the classroom, they're going to do the same thing. They might even be beautiful writers, but if you invite them to be themselves, you are going to be surprised over and over again. You're going to be constantly in awe. You're going to be excited about the human beings that are sitting in front of you on a daily basis. And I don't know who wouldn't want that.

Now You Try: Bringing Ideas to Life in the Secondary Classroom

There are many ways that writing teachers can honor student knowledge, experience, and interests in the secondary classroom. As Matt mentioned, using food writing with students can encourage them to reflect on their cultures and traditions. Assignments like how-to demonstrations can give students opportunities to share their unique areas of expertise with others. Stop-motion animation assignments allow students to tell stories with tools and resources on hand. These assignments are discussed in more detail below.

Food Memory Narratives

Food memories are powerful because these experiences are often rooted in multiple senses—taste, touch, sight, smell, and sound. They can create opportunities for our students to draw on their languages and cultures as they write about the people and traditions that are important to them. I use the following assignment in my Writing about Food course at ASU (see Figure 4.15). It can be adapted for any level of learner.

How-to Demonstrations

A how-to demonstration can be a live presentation or a recorded video. These demonstrations may or may not require the student to complete some research beforehand. This assignment (see Figure 4.16) gives students a chance to share information about something they are knowledgeable about, positioning them as the experts in the room.

Stop-Motion Animation

Stop-motion animation is a popular form of animation that does not require any drawing. Photographs are taken and combined to form a larger work. These works can feature actors or objects, and they can make use of a variety of materials. Sound in the form of dialogue, voice-overs, music, or sound effects may be included as well. There is so much potential to tell stories and convey other information through stop-motion animation, but it remains an underused form of composition in ELA classes. Fortunately, getting started with stop-motion animation is easier than most people realize (see Figure 4.17).

FIGURE 4.15. A sample food memory narrative assignment.

Sample Assignment: Food Memory Narrative

Part 1: Brainstorm

Think about the most vivid and important food memories you have. What people, places, traditions, and experiences do you associate with food? Make a list of five to ten ideas. If you are stuck, see Roode's (2020) website for additional brainstorming ideas.

Part 2: Freewrite

Select a food memory (or several connected vignettes) from your list to write about. Your task is to write as much as you can about your food memory. Try to recall everything and immerse us in that moment. Don't worry about spelling and grammar when you are writing a first draft. Instead, concentrate on getting ideas down on the page. Write as much as you can, as fast as you can. You should have several pages by the time you are done with your freewrite.

Part 3: Polish

Type your narrative, polishing the writing as you go. You are welcome to include photographs and recipes. Once you have a full draft, use the following questions to do some additional polishing:

- Where can you add vivid and specific details and language that appeal to all five senses?
- Does your piece contain dialogue?
- Would your narrative benefit from rearranging the order of events? If the story takes a while to get going, try starting with the action and then back up to show us how you got there.
- You can use section headings to help your reader navigate their way through the piece.
- Is anything missing?
- Does your piece sound like you? Does it have your personality? Make sure you use *I* in this personal writing assignment.
- How interesting is the word choice? Are there any places where you could use a more precise word? Any places where the writing is stuffy and in need of an adjustment?
- You are welcome to include terms and phrases from other languages you know if you feel it would give your story more authenticity and make it sound even more like you.
- Look at the first word of each sentence. Do you always start sentences with the same word? If so, add some variation in your sentence openings.
- Look at your sentence lengths and structures. Are they all similar? If so, mix them up.
- Read your piece out loud. Cut any words, sentences, and sections that seem unnecessary or redundant. Add transitions as needed. Make sure the piece flows smoothly.
- Proof your piece for grammar and spelling. Sometimes grammar and spelling checkers are wrong. You have the right to ignore them.

FIGURE 4.16. Tips for using how-to demonstrations with students.

Tips for Getting Started with How-to Demonstrations

Decide How to Use How-to Demonstrations: Will this assignment fulfill a requirement for students to write a process essay? Will you use it at the beginning of the year to learn more about students right away? Will it happen later in the year, perhaps as part of a larger inquiry project?

Set Clear Assignment Parameters: How long should the demonstration be? What kinds of components must be included?

Honor the Writing Process: Guide students through the work of brainstorming, writing, polishing, and presenting. Keep in mind that students may need to prepare a script beforehand or at least come up with bullet points of key ideas to address. If having students make videos, know that this can open up both opportunities and challenges as students select music, record voice-overs, plan different kinds of shots, coordinate multiple people, change locations, and so forth.

Sharing: How will these presentations be shared? What will the audience do while watching or listening?

FIGURE 4.17. Tips for teaching stop-motion animation.

Tips for Getting Started with Stop-Motion Animation

Gather Materials: Students will need to consider their story or message and the materials needed to best convey those ideas through animation. Over the years, I have seen some creative works, from characters on a quest (told using toys and shot at their eye level in the grass) to a shoe looking for its mate (with emotional music and cutaways and images of twins to convey the shoe's inner thoughts). Students may put their friends in their animation, make use of items they have found around the house, or create original backgrounds or sets for these works.

Download an App: Encourage students to find a free stop-motion app such as Stop Motion Studio. An app will simplify the process of taking and assembling the many photographs.

Set Clear Assignment Parameters: I ask my students to compose a work that tells a story, has at least two characters, has sound of some kind, and is thirty seconds long.

Assessment: Along with the project, I ask students to submit an artist statement in which they describe the work; visual elements used and their effects; and comments on their process, tools used, and any challenges encountered and how they worked through them. They include at least two photographs documenting their process as well.

Resources: Many examples of stop-motion can be found with a quick internet search. In addition, check out Claymation films such as *Wallace and Gromit: The Wrong Trousers* and *Coraline*, as well as classic shows from the past like *The Gumby Show*, which is bound to give students a laugh. Also, see the incredible silhouette animation of Lotte Reiniger (BBC Ideas, 2018).

Final Thoughts

It is essential that teachers honor the knowledge, experience, and interests that students bring with them to the classroom. Students' funds of knowledge, including the cultural and linguistic resources they have gained in their homes and communities, deserve a place in literacy learning. In the writing classroom, there are so many opportunities to connect to students, whether we are encouraging them to draw on their personal experiences in writing assignments, learn about different cultures or authors, or share their wisdom with each other.

Here in Arizona, we have seen the harm done to children when they are forced into English-only instruction, punished for speaking their home languages at school, or taught that only formal pieces like the five-paragraph essay or research paper count as legitimate writing. Students need opportunities to see that writing can also be deeply meaningful and personal.

Writing teachers may very well run into obstacles when trying to diversify the curriculum and honor students' communities, especially in the current political climate. However, highlighting a wide range of voices, inviting students to draw on their cultures and languages, and appreciating the numerous skills, talents, and interests that students bring with them to the classroom are important first steps for creating a more inclusive writing space. These changes do not require deep pockets, fancy materials, or a lot of time or energy on the teacher's part. Instead, they require a shift in perspective, seeing the teacher as a mentor to youth writers. Using this mentoring strategy values the different kinds of authors (e.g., songwriter, graphic novelist, filmmaker . . .) our students care about being. Our students have rich imaginations and a lifetime of valuable knowledge to draw upon if we just let them.

The next chapter delves deeper into the role of the writer in writing instruction, considering how teachers can nurture students as writers by taking their writing histories, practices, preferences, and attitudes seriously. Some students already have a strong sense of writing identity and even long-term writing goals, which teachers may or may not be aware of.

Chapter Five

Nurturing Students as Writers

Dillon was a writer who did something few others would dare to do. In November 2021, he walked into his local public library in Boise, Idaho, and stealthily added his own book to the shelf. The librarians then did something equally unexpected. They added Dillon's book to the library catalog and prepared it to be checked out. Within just a short time, well over one hundred readers had reserved the text, creating an estimated wait time of about five years for this title. The book, *The Adventures of Dillon Helbig's Crismis*, is approximately eighty pages, full of typos, and handmade with illustrations by the author. At the time, the author also had a second work, *The Jacket-Eating Closet*, in the planning stages (Lukpat, 2022; Zdanowicz, 2022).

Dillon's story quickly became national news because this writer was only eight years old at the time, and people thought it was cute that a child would sneak into a library to add their own book. Some found humor in the idea that a child would have the audacity to place an amateur work alongside professional authors' books. In an ironic twist, publishers were soon calling with offers to publish this eight-year-old's book (Lukpat, 2022; Zdanowicz, 2022).

Adding his book to the library shelves might simply have been a bold act by a mischievous boy, but I read this story as something more profound: the enactment of writing identity. Of course Dillon's work deserves a place with those other books! Dillon is a real writer, too! This story demonstrates the desire many young people have for their words to be read, for their writing to reach authentic audiences beyond a classroom where a teacher is waiting with red pen in hand, ready to dole out points and criticisms.

It is essential that teachers tap into this love of writing that so many students have. As writing mentors, we need to recognize that students are already writers who have important ideas and experiences to communicate. It is a wonderful thing when students take pride in their writing and feel like real writers. In these moments, they are enacting writing identities.

FIGURE 5.1. This chapter focuses on the fifth strategy for mentoring youth writers.

Six Strategies for Mentoring Youth Writers

1. Use a wide range of writing forms and modes with students.
2. Encourage student choice and decision-making.
3. Build a supportive writing community.
4. Honor student knowledge, experience, and interests.
5. **Nurture students as writers.**
6. Connect writers to opportunities beyond the classroom.

As I reiterate at the beginning of every chapter, this book recommends that teachers use six strategies to mentor youth writers (see Figure 5.1). We are now at the fifth of those strategies, how to nurture students as writers. This chapter shares background on this strategy, looks at how mentors applied it in the Young Authors' Studio program, provides an interview with an English teacher, and offers sample assignments. The key terms to get us started can be found in Figure 5.2.

FIGURE 5.2. Useful terms to know for this chapter.

Key Terms

Metacognition: Being aware of one's thinking. Teachers can foster metacognition by asking students to reflect on their writing and on themselves as writers. Asking students how they did something, what they are proud of, what goals they have, and what they need to reach those goals can help students develop more awareness about how they think, write, and learn.

Identity: According to Muhammad (2023),

> Identity is composed of notions of who we are, who others say we are (in both positive and negative ways), and who we desire to be. There is a complex and dynamic dance between the three toward identity development. Identity isn't static; it is moving and changing. And we don't have just one identity, but layers of them. Identities (cultural and other identities) are constantly being (re)defined and changing. They are fluid, multilayered, and relational, and also shaped by our social and cultural environments, as well as our literacy practices.

> Our identities encompass many facets, including racial, ethnic, cultural, gender, kinship, academic/intellectual, environmental, personal/individual, sexual, and community. (p. 74)

Learning Identity: A sense of oneself as a learner. Learning identity (Wortham, 2006) plays an important role in learning and motivation. How we feel about ourselves in relation to a content area can drive—or limit—what we are willing to learn.

Writing Identity: A sense of oneself as a writer. Writing identity may be general, as in "I am a good writer," or specific, such as "I am a [poet, blogger, novelist, songwriter, researcher, filmmaker, graphic novelist, etc.]." Students already have attitudes toward writing and toward themselves as writers. Writing attitudes and writing identities can change over time.

Justifying This Work

How students feel about writing and about themselves as writers can motivate them to learn or hinder their progress. Wright et al. (2019) point out that "being identified as having underdeveloped skills may place students on a trajectory of specific coursework and lowered expectations" (p. 65). This can lead to the student developing a negative attitude toward course activities, the subject as a whole, or even their sense of self.

The NCTE *Position Statement on Writing Instruction in School* (2022) points out that more attention needs to be paid to writers, not just their writing. In addition, an overly restrictive curriculum can lead to disengagement (see Figure 5.3).

FIGURE 5.3. NCTE position statement connections.

Connections to NCTE's *Position Statement on Writing Instruction in School* (2022)

- Problems can arise when there is too much "focus on the *writing*—the products that are ultimately assessed and evaluated—rather than on the *writers* themselves."
- In addition, some "aspects of classroom writing instruction [such as 'test-driven curriculum, instruction, and assessment'; 'narrow definitions of and limited practices for writing'; and 'dominant ideologies around writing and language'] can lead students to reject identifying as a writer."

Teachers can support students as writers by helping them notice how they feel about writing, the role writing plays in their lives, and to what extent they see themselves as writers. In previous research with adolescent rappers and spoken word poets (Williams, 2013, 2018), I found that students who were writing in their lives outside of school very much saw themselves as real writers with important ideas to communicate to the world. When they were in front of a crowd performing a poem or when they posted songs online, they were enacting specific kinds of identities as writers. They cared about their public personas, daydreamed about being famous, and even studied other writers and their works as a way to improve their pieces. These writers could talk in detail about their writing histories, devoted an incredible amount of time to their craft, had preferences about the tools they used and writing practices they followed, developed strategies for overcoming writing challenges, and imagined their writing futures. In addition, they talked about losing track of time when they wrote, suggesting that they were working in a "flow" state (Csikszentmihalyi, 1990).

Wenger (2008) argues that schools need to give students opportunities to try out various learning identities, noting that having "deep transformative experiences that involve new dimensions of identification . . . even in one specific or narrowly defined domain—[is] likely to be more widely significant in terms of the long-term ramifications of learning than extensive coverage of a broad, but abstractly general, curriculum" (p. 268). Wenger recommends that schools provide opportunities for students to affiliate with (or reject) different identities within a field of study. He cautions that when schools do not do this, they disadvantage students not just in a specific class but also as they move into careers in the world beyond the classroom. He writes, "Identity and learning serve each other" (p. 271). Students draw on their learning identities as they navigate their way through school and the many other spheres of their lives.

Vetter and colleagues (2022) found that students need to feel like they are writers and have support as writers in the classroom. They point out that "one-size-fits-all teaching and assessments of writing negatively [impact] teens' ability to find meaning and satisfaction from writing" (p. 332). Students need "interested peers," "invested teachers," and "meaningful writing tasks"; these contribute to the "interpersonal and intrapersonal spaces [necessary] to . . . feel like a writer" (p. 332). Teachers can support students as writers by building a nurturing community of writers in the classroom and providing an interesting and meaningful curriculum for students, topics already explored in this book.

English teachers should be aware of the construct of writing identity because it can be useful for understanding why students may associate with—or disassociate from—certain writing tasks and projects in school. To better support students as writers, we can look for ways to learn more about and nurture students' out-of-school writing

(Hull & Schultz, 2001). We can also invite students to reflect on their relationship with writing, as well as their feelings about writing in school. Ivanič (1998) argues:

> Discussing the writer's identity places an act of writing in the context of the writer's past history, of their position in relation to their social context, and of their role in possible futures. Bringing identity explicitly onto the agenda in the learning and teaching of writing transforms it from a local "fix-this-essay" undertaking into a much more broadly conceived project. (p. 338)

Moreover, students need "critical awareness of the nature of writer identity, so as to give them maximum control over this important aspect of writing" (Ivanič, 1998, p. 339). Reyes (2006) reinforces writing identity by using titles for students such as "writer" and "poet" to show that they are being taken seriously as writers; this can certainly validate a student's identity as a writer.

Along with inviting adolescents to reflect on their writing lives, teachers can ask them to explore their feelings about writing through the Daly-Miller (1975) writing apprehension survey or other instruments designed to measure attitudes and beliefs about writing (Wright et al., 2019). The survey I used with students in the Young Authors' Studio program can be found on page 139.

Mentoring in Action: Inside the Young Authors' Studio Program

The study of Young Authors' Studio found that mentors nurtured the writers in various ways, providing opportunities to share their out-of-school writing, explore writing identities, build confidence, and set goals. Over the course of the program, the students' attitudes toward writing improved.

Making Space for Out-of-School Writing

Making space for students' out-of-school writing in the classroom takes little time and effort on the teacher's part, but it can make a significant difference to students. This could be something as simple as dedicating time for students to work on their choice of project or to bring in a project they are already working on at home, such as a novel, play, song, etc.

In the YAS program, we let the youth writers know at the first workshop that their out-of-school writing was welcome in the YAS space. I told them to use the extended writing time for these projects:

> You are writers. You know what you need to do. Don't be shy about bringing your writing from outside of school into this space. If you're thinking, "Oh, I'm working on this novel at home," bring it in and work on it in here. You will always have time to do that.

We found that many of the students were already engaging in out-of-school writing and were enthusiastic about these pieces. Consider these examples of projects they told us about:

- A second how-to book (coauthored). The student's first book dealt with how to do various things, such as how to win at tic-tac-toe, how to whistle, how to make a tinfoil top hat, how to write comics, how to make pipe-cleaner monkeys, how to make tiny weapons for a mini-war, how to write amazing songs, how to draw cute eyes, and so forth.
- Novel about a girl who enters an alternate universe.
- Play about Anne Frank.
- Poem called "Tacos" that would become part of a "recipe book of concrete poems about food."
- Story about a past life.
- Story about a group of kids.
- Novel about "different species (vampires, werewolves, humans, dwarves, things like that) at war."
- Two different novels: one about someone in training to protect the world and the other about robots.
- A TV show script.

One student wrote, "I have been working on my book whenever I can." Another student was keeping a list of favorite words, while someone else was working on world-building.

These students saw themselves as writers with important stories to communicate (we saw them that way, too). They enjoyed working on projects on their own, and as they started to trust the mentors, they became eager to share their writing with them (see Figure 5.4). During team time at the end of a workshop, for example, a student brought in his novel. Emma said, "When I asked him what it was about, he turned to the second chapter and handed it to me, asking me to read it." She thought the novel was good and was "thrilled that the student" wanted to share it with her. Similarly, Miranda encouraged a student to bring in her pieces when she discovered that the student was at work on two book projects.

FIGURE 5.4. Students were eager to share.

When teachers are aware of the writing that students are doing in their lives outside of school, they can seek out opportunities to highlight these writers and their pieces throughout the year. One way teachers can make space for students' out-of-school writing—beyond providing them with extended time to write (working on any project) in class—is to invite students to create a display of their best pieces (see Figure 5.5).

FIGURE 5.5. Displaying student work can be validating for students.

Display of Best Pieces

Ask students to bring in copies of three examples of writing they have done that they are proud of (any kind of writing, from any year, on any topic). Invite them to turn these works into displays to be arranged around the classroom, the school library, or another space on campus. On index cards, students could write a short overview of each piece and explain what they are proud of in the work.

Exploring Writing Identity

Another way for teachers to support students is to invite them to reflect on who they are as writers. During weeks one and six of the YAS program, the reflection during team time asked the students, "Who are you as a writer?" Many students responded by commenting on their creativity (e.g., "I am an artist who can make creative concepts come to life."). Others addressed confidence in their ability to write (e.g., "I am a writer who can write anything" and "I can do anything that adults can do, and maybe more"). Some of them envisioned themselves in writing careers such as screenwriter or novelist. One student simply wrote, "I really want to be an author/writer when I grow up. I really want to write."

Their comments addressed their preferences as writers, too. They enjoyed certain genres (e.g., fantasy, science fiction, horror, comedy) and forms (e.g., short stories, poems, songs). Someone appreciated having an assigned topic or other required elements. One student mentioned having problems with spelling, grammar, and editing. One student remarked, "I take writing seriously. I only listen to suggestions if they're good."

When teachers ask students who they are as writers, they will invariably receive a wide array of responses. Students may point to particular forms or genres, assess their confidence levels, share insights about creativity, or imagine writing careers. Simply asking, "Who are you as a writer?" can be useful for students because the question can get them to think more deeply about their preferences and attitudes associated with writing. This question could be answered in writing or communicated in a conversation between two students (see Figure 5.6).

Building Writing Confidence

Teachers can support students as writers by building up their confidence. One way the mentors consistently did this in YAS was by asking students what work they were proud of. Every week, students completed a reflection during team time that included the questions, "What writing have you worked on today (or lately)?" and "What are you proud of in the piece?"

It was interesting to see what students were proud of in their work. Some cared a lot about the length of the piece (e.g., "I am proud of how long the piece is because I usually just write eight-page comic books." Alternatively: "It is so short it is hard to appreciate."). Some comments spoke to their attention to detail or characters they had created. One student wrote, "I got to think about things the character was good at and . . . bad at." Someone else wrote, "I feel like I know the main characters." Students were proud of their descriptions and endings, kingdoms they had created, character names, and their ability to achieve realism, adventure, and tension. They also mentioned being proud of their punctuation, word choice, and use of symbolism, rhyme, and imagery.

FIGURE 5.6. Questions to reflect on one's writing life. (Some questions adapted from Williams [2018, p. 170].)

Questions for Writers

Invite students to reflect on their writing lives. Below is a bank of potential questions to choose from:

- Who are you as a writer?
- What do you like and what do you dislike about writing?
- What are your favorite and your least favorite kinds of writing?
- What is difficult and what is easy for you when it comes to writing?
- Do you like to share your work with others?
- Have you ever been a part of a writing group?
- Who are your writing role models?
- Who has supported your writing?
- What out-of-school writing do you engage in?
- How did you become the writer you are today? What is your writing history?
- How do you feel about writing?
- Why do you write?
- Can you think of a time when you were confronted with a challenge related to writing? What happened? How did you work through it?
- Describe your writing practices. When do you write? How often? Where? With whom? With what sort of tools? On what topics? In what forms?
- What are your writing pet peeves?
- Do you ever lose track of time when writing?
- Do you think that writing will be important to you in the future?

Some students commented that they were fond of their artwork or were happy to have created pieces in different forms, such as scripts or poems. Students were delighted when they produced a work that was unexpected, that turned out better than envisioned, that sprang from a simple drawing, or that had "a good amount of thought put into it." They pointed to particular sections of text and their use of information. One student was pleased with how easy a piece was to write, while another student was pleased that their "book will be sold." One student was satisfied to think that their work might "help another person's life." Someone else was excited to discover that "just by taking out some words, the meaning of the story changes completely." Another writer was proud to have connected two characters "even though they don't know each other."

Some student comments focused on the self (e.g., "It has a piece of me," "I'm proud that my novel is my own idea"). They were proud of their progress and advancements, too, especially having "persevered through challenges." One writer was proud of sharing a work with others, while someone else appreciated the creativity involved.

Expressing pride in their work like this is an important indication of a positive sense of self as writer. As students head into more challenging situations down the road—higher expectations, more challenging material, forms or topics they are less excited about—those with a strong sense of writing identity are going to be able to tap into that sense of writing self to push through new challenges. Giving students opportunities to take joy in their work can support them in building up some strength, resilience, and fortitude, which are critical in so many other parts of life. Teachers can play a crucial role in building students' self-confidence. When students feel good about themselves as writers and the work they have produced, they are going to want to do more of it.

Setting Writing Goals

In the YAS program, the mentors guided students through goal setting each week during team time, asking them to reflect on their writing goals and any assistance they needed to accomplish them. This is a practice that teachers can use in their classrooms as well to support metacognition, learn more about students as writers, and understand how best to support them.

We found that the students had a variety of goals, and the YAS program gave them the space to engage with writing in the ways and to the degree that they felt comfortable. Many students' goals focused on finishing a particular work (a novel, a comic book, a movie adaptation, a song, an essay). Some students aimed to compose a series of books or just a piece of substantial length. We observed that some students wanted to become better writers—specifically, to improve their organization, details, symbolism, rhyming, or character development. Others wanted to become more confident. A handful of responses addressed performance or going public with their work; they wanted to perform plays, to "write poetry that inspires everyone," to enter a short story in a contest, to "perfect [their] poem and perform it," to publish their work, or to turn a TV script into a show. Some students just wanted to get better at writing fiction or brainstorming. One student mentioned wanting to pay off a loan for a self-published book. Another student aspired to "become a successful author."

The mentors asked what they could do in YAS to assist students with achieving their goals. Students indicated that they could use help brainstorming subplots and ideas, polishing and editing their pieces, and "learn[ing] to write better." They found "feedback and ideas" from mentors helpful and asked whether the mentors could help them edit an essay for school or assist with rhyme schemes for an assigned poem. Some students simply asked that mentors continue to nurture them. They wrote, "Tell me to keep writing," and "Continue to encourage me that I can do it."

Although the reflection form asked what assistance students needed, they often concluded that they were the ones who needed to get the work done for themselves:

- "I need to get back to it. Stop procrastinating."
- "[I need to] sit down and start writing."
- "[I] have ideas [and just] need to write."

These writers knew that they were ultimately in control of whether a piece would be written.

We noticed that some students were struggling with their longer projects. One student said, "I've planned out the main plot points, but I don't have the details for the little plot points that can happen. . . . It has a beginning, the end, and there's this thing in the middle, but there are no subplots. I can't come up with anything." Fortunately, fellow students were able to provide this writer with some ideas for subplots: a love triangle, a kidnapping, a case of amnesia, etc.

One of the really exciting things we observed in the YAS program was that many students who took themselves seriously as writers also regulated their own learning, filling in their own knowledge gaps. They seemed to already know what help they needed and were not shy about asking for assistance. To illustrate, a student in the scriptwriting breakout session asked how to format internal monologue. The mentor said to use parentheses and *v.o.* for voice-over, and the student responded, "I needed that. I needed that!" She continued to look through screenplay examples with an excited squeal. She told me, "I write what they're saying, and I put in parentheses what's happening. But now I realize that I'm doing it all wrong." In this session, she also learned how to add song lyrics to her script. Henry told her, "I saw a *Lion King* script, and the way it worked, there's a piece of the song, and it had some description of the scenes it was showing, and then it had another piece of the song and then some more descriptions because the scene is moving along as the song is going. You go back and forth that way." It did not escape our notice that the student was in sixth grade; even young students can be mature about their writing goals. All student writers, including the youngest among us, need to be treated with respect.

Sometimes the youth writers did a great job articulating exactly what help they needed from peers. A student who wanted some help with a story about a spy said,

"They are right now training at the facility, and I have nothing after that." Someone else in the group suggested, "They could go on a mission to see if she's ready." The writer agreed, saying, "I think a cool idea would be there's a surprise mission, and they're not really ready for it yet."

Another student, who was working on his second how-to book, said, "I just need help on one thing. I don't know how to advertise or sell it." The other people in the group suggested putting up posters, trying to get a professional publisher, or selling it at the school's holiday boutique or our final performance. Asking students about their writing goals is a great way to support them as writers (see Figure 5.7).

FIGURE 5.7. Setting goals supports agency.

Setting Goals

Try asking students to answer these questions: "What are your writing goals?" and "How can I help you accomplish those goals?" These questions support metacognition as writers consider where their pieces are, where they need to be, and how they might get them there. These questions also foster student agency and encourage students to advocate for themselves.

Noticing Changes in Attitudes toward Writing

Teachers may notice changes in students' attitudes toward writing if they provide some opportunities for them to reflect on how they feel about it at different times of the year. In YAS we were surprised that students became more positive about writing during such a short program. One student went from feeling like a "wannabe" writer to later stating, "I love writing. I don't know exactly who I am as a writer, but I feel like I'm making progress toward being a writer instead of a wannabe." My favorite set of comments came from a student who, at the beginning of the program, wrote, "I don't enjoy writing. It is one of the last things I would do in my free time." At the end of the program, this student realized, "I'm starting to like writing."

The mentors saw changes in students' attitudes over the course of the program. Emma noticed "growth in students' love of writing." She also observed:

> They are growing and realizing that they are legitimate writers. So many kids, including myself when I was [their age], see themselves as just being kids who don't "really" know how to write. But one of the biggest parts of

> YAS, to me, has succeeded: our goal to help them realize that they are real writers! Several students . . . have mentioned how they appreciate that this program brings together writers that are their age, and [it] helps them feel more confident in their identity as a writer.

I had told the mentors early on in the program:

> You are building positive feelings around writing. They are making this positive association between writing and feeling happy and accepted and listened to. Even if they're not producing a whole lot or it's not the kind of writing you hoped for, you are giving them a space that's dedicated to writing, and you're making them feel a certain way in this space. That's important. And later, they might look back on that, and it might actually mean something. It may change their attitudes about writing in school.

The mentors enjoyed seeing how their work in a college class made a difference in the lives of these younger students. We were all surprised that just a few workshops would be enough to inspire, nurture, and validate these writers. This gives me real hope as a teacher and teacher educator.

In my field notes from the first workshop, I noticed that some students were entering the program feeling low. In the second week, all of the youth writers came back. I wrote in my notes, "This surprised me because I expected that some would not return" due to anticipated program attrition. At the end of the program, many students expressed enthusiasm for writing:

- "I loved it! I learned a lot and I feel more confident about my writing."
- "I really enjoyed the experience of YAS. It was a highlight of my week. . . . I hope this comes back next year."
- "Great opportunity for young authors to work on their works. Really helpful mentors."
- "It was fun. I enjoyed writing for the first time."
- "Young Authors' Studio has helped me learn a lot about writing."

In addition, a youth writer brought us a card on the last day that read:

> To: All of the Young Authors' Studio Teachers
> Thank you so much for teaching me about writing. I think that I'll become a successful author because of you. You taught me that you don't have to be a certain age to write. You showed me other writers that were actually writing books. Thank you so much.

> P.S. My second book is almost done.
> P.P.S. I need to know your addresses, so that I can send it to you.
> P.P.P.S. Thank you for teaching me.
> [He drew his first and second books on this card and noted that the first one was fifty pages and the second one was one hundred pages.]

This enthusiasm, and the evidence of writing identities witnessed across this program, reminds me of the story of Dillon at the beginning of this chapter, the student who received national attention for adding his book to his local library's shelves. There is a special kind of confidence and pride that writers may feel toward their works, especially those longer pieces they voluntarily compose in their lives outside of school.

I did a formal assessment of youth writers' attitudes toward writing through a survey administered at the beginning and again at the end of the YAS program. It revealed some positive shifts in the group's attitudes toward writing over the course of the program (see Figure 5.8). These survey results do have limitations. Even though all youth in the program participated in both surveys (eighteen young people, thirty-six surveys collected total), this is a small cohort.

I am especially interested in the survey items to which some students initially responded negatively, but by the end of the program, no one did. To illustrate, at the beginning of the program some students did not enjoy writing, did not enjoy sharing their writing with others, did not think of themselves as writers, and did not find writing easy. However, by the end of the program, no students selected those options. They were on a new trajectory. The survey found that over the course of the five themed writing workshops (about ten hours of instruction), the group's attitudes toward writing shifted in a positive direction.

To be perfectly honest, I did not expect this survey instrument to pick up on any changes in attitude at all. I figured we were not offering enough contact hours to make a difference. I also assumed that students who came in feeling negative toward writing wouldn't be persuaded out of that mindset. That was not the case at all. It appears that for those who dislike writing, who find it difficult to write, who find it unpleasant to share their writing with others, or who do not see themselves as writers, programs like YAS offer some hope and a way forward.

FIGURE 5.8. YAS survey results showing positive shifts in writing attitude.

Statement	Beginning of YAS	End of YAS
I enjoy writing.	66.7% Agree 16.7% Neutral **16.7% Disagree**	83.3% Agree 16.7% Neutral **0% Disagree**
It is fun to share my writing with others.	27.8% Agree 38.9% Neutral **33.3% Disagree**	44.4% Agree 55.6% Neutral **0% Disagree**
I think of myself as a writer.	44.4% Agree 22.2% Neutral **33.3% Disagree**	55.6% Agree 44.4% Neutral **0% Disagree**
Writing is easy for me.	27.8% Agree 55.6% Neutral **16.7% Disagree**	55.6% Agree 44.4% Neutral **0% Disagree**

Pause and Reflect

Nurturing students as writers is an important mentoring strategy. All students have distinct histories with, attitudes toward, and goals associated with writing, whether we know about these or not. How students feel about writing and about themselves as writers can influence how they respond to writing instruction. Paying attention to writing identity honors the deep connection between learning and identity.

The techniques the mentors used in the YAS program can also be implemented by secondary teachers as they mentor youth writers in schools. Teachers can give students opportunities to pursue their out-of-school writing, explore their writing identities, build their writing confidence, and set writing goals. Through these experiences, students' attitudes toward writing may change as well.

Before turning to a secondary teacher to see how she supports students as writers, let's reflect on what this strategy means to you (see Figure 5.9).

FIGURE 5.9. Reflection questions for strategy #5.

Pause and Reflect

Strategy #5: Nurturing Students as Writers

- How do you already use this strategy in your teaching?
- What are some new ways you can use this strategy to benefit students?
- How does this strategy help bring out the author (or graphic novelist, filmmaker, songwriter . . .) in every student?

Teacher Interview: Andrea Box on Nurturing Students as Writers

FIGURE 5.10. Selfie by Andrea Box.

Andrea Box (see Figure 5.10) is a secondary teacher who nurtures students as writers. She has been an English teacher for twenty-nine years, twenty-six of those years at Westwood High School in Mesa, Arizona. Previously, she was a reporter who was invited to talk to seventh graders on career day and changed jobs when she realized she had more fun in that hour than she did as a reporter. Andrea has also worked as a school counselor helping gang members. These days she teaches senior English, creative writing, and multicultural literature. She has received numerous awards: You Made a Difference district awards, the Martin Luther King Jr. Teacher of the Year award, Teacher of the Month school awards, the Arizona English Teachers Association English Teacher of Excellence Award, the NCTE High School Teacher of Excellence Award nomination, and the Shield Warrior Teacher of the Month. The student body at her school is 10–11 percent Indigenous/Native American, and she has played an important role in developing a Native American literature curriculum at her school (Metzger et al., 2013). She loves hiking, being in nature, and meeting people. She also works with senior citizens as a recreation coordinator. She enjoys talking to people and getting to know their stories.

How do you nurture students as writers?

My students know they're not allowed to leave my class before I ask them, "What is your story?" And they can't leave until they say, "I am worthy." We talk a lot about how every single one of them has a gift, has something to share with the world. We are a Title I school, a minority majority school, and a lot of our kids are from single-parent families, first generation, or undocumented.

The very first week of school, I have them write me a letter telling me about themselves. I do want to kind of see the skill set where they're coming in at, so I know what they need. They know that any time they turn in writing, I will respond. I try and give them that balance of validating their story but, at the same time, giving constructive criticism for how we can up our game a little bit. I never ever grade in red pen. Once they know that their story, who they are, is validated, then they start opening up more and getting more into their identities as writers. And I tend to focus a lot on narrative writing because their stories matter. We do "I am from . . ." poems. It's a lot of introspective writing, and we do a lot of fun activities that are nonthreatening. And I always leave it up to them if they want to share with their partner or not.

We use essential questions and figure out a working draft. I tell the students, "You can doodle, draw pictures, whatever gets you to the next step." I have a timeline, but I tell them, "I will not treat you equally in my class. I'll treat you equitably. So if you need more time in your writing to find your voice, then let's work together." I always try and have that one-on-one with them where we can talk just as individuals.

And I write with them as well. And I show them my rough draft to my final draft. The first time that I do it, they don't know it's my writing, and they just tear it apart. And so then I'm like, "Okay, well that's mine." I am not just a writing teacher. I'm a teacher who writes, but from start to finish there's going to be a whole lot of editing. And so I said, "When you get these edit marks from me and from your writing group, understand we're not trying to knock you down. We just want to know more of your story." And I tell them, "You can start here and end up in a completely different story frame." And the beauty of writing is that I'm not going to force you into a box. What a lot of the kids say is, "We hate writing about things we don't want to write about." Agency is huge in my class. I will always have my idea of what I want the final to be. And then I tell them, "Go through the motions. And if at the end you're just like, 'I don't want anything to do with what Ms. Box wants, I want to write about this,' brilliant. Write about it. Obviously that's something that you're passionate about. Let's write about your passion. Find your voice as a writer in your passion." And so they get such a kick out of it. And they do start seeing themselves as writers as well.

Part of the process is they have to be in writing groups. They give me a rough draft, hard copy. I'll go and make copies for their groups. We've established from day one that this is terrifying for some of your group members. So if you all are kind of scared to share your writing, then you're going to give gentle suggestions to your classmates. They never are in the same group. So that way they hear all the different voices, they write all over, so they have to read their story out loud to their writing groups. And I have kids just bawling and they're trying to get through their writing, and I say, "This is what real writing looks like. This is what real writing feels like." I add, "If you need to pull back, if this is too personal for you or just too hard, you're not ready to write about it, then just put it aside. Maybe think about doing it for something later on." I tell the students, "If you do not want to share your writing at all with your classmates, you and I can work together for this particular project." And again, I still have to set the guidelines if you are letting me know that you're in danger of hurting somebody or yourself. If you're being hurt, by law I have to let somebody know. But other than that, anything is fair game. And just the stuff that they come up with! They identify as writers who have a story, and as they start making connections with people they would've thought they had nothing in common with, they say, "Oh my gosh, my grandma did that too," or whatever. They look forward to those writing days and getting back those papers from each other and then moving that story to the next step until we have that gorgeous final version in our hands.

Then we have what are called "Feather Circles." A lot of this I got from my mentor, G. Lynn Nelson. Feather circles in my class are no bigger than ten [people]. Again, I make copies for everybody, and as the students are reading, I say, "This is a celebration." I read my story first, and we literally have feathers. So as that student's reading, they have the feather and everybody else is celebrating on their piece of paper, highlighting, smiley faces, annotating about how they connect with it, or "Oh my gosh, I'm so sorry." And then they give those papers back to the original author. And we have three writing groups going at the same time. And so one group over here will be laughing, and another group will be crying. So I'm passing out tissues and I'm celebrating with them. And when one group is done, we don't clap. We do snaps, and then they pass the feather. They have to choose three people to write thank-you notes to. Students I had decades ago still have their thank-you notes. I still have my thank-you notes [from] when I took Nelson's class. It's powerful. Instead of seeing that red pen, [they are] seeing that "Thank you. I connected to you as a writer, as a human being." It is something they look forward to. And at the end of the class, they say, "We're writers." And I respond, "You were always writers. You just needed to find what you were passionate to write about."

To manage the feather circles, it's a lot of front-loading your expectations. When they're reading, I walk around, not in a threatening way but so I can hear their voices. They know that there is no messing around. I take these feather circles seriously. When I model the first time, I will take two students and model that with them. I give them something from my writing group, the original rough draft. I have my kids make suggestions on the paper and turn those in. And then I will show them, "Okay, these are suggestions that one of your classmates made, but here are different suggestions." What are the similarities? What are the differences? They know you don't just write things. You have to give solid feedback. And I use Praise Question Polish: (1) What is fabulous about this piece? (2) What are some questions that you feel are not answered? (3) And what are some suggestions that you would give them?

If anyone's off task, they will call each other out and say, "Hey, somebody's reading." It is a lot of trust. It's a lot of modeling. It is trial and error and sometimes failures, but that's how you learn. I perfected it over the years and it comes second nature to me. A lot of my colleagues would like to do what I do, but they say, "Well, that's a lot of work." And I respond, "It is, but look at the payoff. Are you willing to put that time in?" The end product is [the students] see themselves as writers and they see themselves as storytellers. And because we're going to standards-based grades, we feel so confined in what we can do anymore. And I say, "I'm going to do it because I know it works. I'll figure out whatever standards you need, whatever boxes you need me to check. But these kids are learning. They're learning every day, and they're learning to be writers, to be thinkers, to be human beings."

On any given day or any given writing piece, if I know that a student is really struggling, I'll call them up first or I will ask, "Hey, who needs my help?" And so they're my priority for that day. If I just see them kind of staring off into space, then I will call them up and say, "Bring your notepad, bring your computer, whatever it is." I'll often bring up the ones that I'm most concerned [about], but I also need to make sure that I'm not neglecting the ones that this comes second nature to.

Why is it important to nurture students as writers?
Oh my gosh. I just feel like their voices have been taken away by the mass media, by commercials, by ads, by former English teachers and English classes where you have to write about what the author thinks. And it's so important that they see that identity. They see their importance.

What are the benefits of feeling like a real writer?

I love using the word *published.* Let's publish this. I think it gives them authenticity and it gives them the opportunity to see their place in the world through their stories. I had a student who sent this book to me. She started it in my class. Her note says thank you for encouraging my writing seventeen years ago. I made a huge difference. When they hear their voices, when they get that validation from me, from their fellow classmates, from themselves, then they think, "Where can this lead?"

Have you faced any challenges trying to support students as writers?

Some students are just in my class to get the grade. I may get initial pushback from them, but once they realize they're in a safe place to tell their stories, then they start to kind of loosen up. I try and come at it in a nonthreatening way: "Hey, what is your story?" It starts with something as simple as the letter. I want to validate them.

How can teachers get started with this work?

I would just write with them and show them the process for themselves. Have the kids analyze what you as a teacher are writing. Have them write something and maybe self-edit or have somebody else edit. I think the only way kids are going to take you seriously is if you write with them. And that is terrifying for a lot of teachers. But if they know that you're going through the process with them, then they're going to trust the process more, but they're also going to trust what you have to share with them as valid.

What additional advice do you have for teachers on supporting students as writers?

Make it fun. I know that it's hard, especially when we have these standards. Just write and then see what comes from it. Tomorrow we're doing writing prompts where I give them a topic and they have to write for two minutes about that topic. I tell them, "Don't censor yourself. Whatever pops into your head, go with it. Maybe an animal pops into your head that you would connect with. A dolphin. Tell me about your life as a dolphin. Who's your mom, where are you, and are you eating fish?" And they're writing and laughing, and I try and keep it as a quiet activity, and it takes a whole hour, but sometimes kids will finish before others. They kind of get tapped out. I have them sitting in groups, and they'll slide the paper over, and it's just so much fun. I want kids to see writing is not a punishment. It is joy and silliness and spontaneity. I want writing to be a celebration.

Do you have any favorite resources on this topic?

Writing and Being by G. Lynn Nelson (2004).

Do you have any cautions or warnings for teachers?

I always have to tell the kids, "Understand that if you write about hurting yourself, hurting others, or being hurt, by law, we have to then take the next steps."

Do you have any words of encouragement for teachers as they embark on this work?

Have fun. Don't be hard on yourself. We are our own worst critics. Keep some kind of a journal or something about how you do things. Did it work or not? There's so many different ways to approach writing. Be willing to take those risks.

When we finish the class, I have them pick their favorite writing piece, and then I publish it as a book, and I give it to every single student, kind of like *Freedom Writers* (Freedom Writers, 2009). They can choose whether or not to have their names in there. Some kids don't want their names, but they will read it out loud to the class. I also display their zines on the classroom walls.

Just find whatever works. Don't stop yourself from taking those risks, because in the end, you don't know how you will inspire a future author. It's an amazing process, and it's a privilege to be teaching kids how to write and how to find themselves as authors and writers and storytellers.

Now You Try: Bringing Ideas to Life in the Secondary Classroom

We can nurture students as writers in the English classroom through a variety of approaches. For example, completing writing surveys, assembling portfolios, and researching writing careers can be beneficial to students.

Writing Surveys

Teachers can use writing surveys to get a sense of who students are as writers. The survey could be administered at the beginning and the end of the year, and students could reflect on any changes they see. Figure 5.11 is the survey I administered to students in the YAS program.

Portfolios

Portfolios (see Figure 5.12) are a great assignment for prompting students to pause and reflect on their writing. Students could be asked to answer questions about these pieces as they look back on them as more experienced writers. They could also look across their body of work to notice similarities and differences and to appreciate the range of writing they have done.

Career Exploration

Teachers can support students as writers by encouraging them to learn about writing careers (see Figure 5.13). As Wenger (2008) writes, "Students must be enabled to explore who they are, who they are not, [and] who they could be. They must be able to understand where they come from and where they can go" (p. 272). In YAS we had students who wanted to be novelists and scriptwriters, but the truth is, writing is important in a variety of professions.

FIGURE 5.11. Survey used in YAS.

Writing Survey

Directions: Circle *one* answer for each question below.

1. I enjoy writing.	Agree	Neutral	Disagree
2. I have a hard time getting started with my writing.	Agree	Neutral	Disagree
3. I would like to publish or perform my writing.	Agree	Neutral	Disagree
4. I sometimes lose track of time when writing.	Agree	Neutral	Disagree
5. It is fun to share my writing with others.	Agree	Neutral	Disagree
6. I am sometimes scared to write.	Agree	Neutral	Disagree
7. Teachers seem to like the writing that I do.	Agree	Neutral	Disagree
8. I think of myself as a writer.	Agree	Neutral	Disagree
9. I would like to improve as a writer.	Agree	Neutral	Disagree
10. Writing is easy for me.	Agree	Neutral	Disagree
11. The writing we do at my school is fun.	Agree	Neutral	Disagree
12. I am really good at writing.	Agree	Neutral	Disagree
13. I hope to have a career that involves writing.	Agree	Neutral	Disagree

Directions: Please answer each question below.

14. How much time do you spend writing your own pieces (**not** school assigned) each month?

___ 0 hours ___ ½ hour ___ 1 hour ___ 2 hours or more

15. What kinds of pieces do you write outside of school for fun? Please check **all** that apply:

___ Stories ___ Novels ___ Films ___ Diary Entries

___ Poems ___ Graphic Novels ___ Plays ___ Zines

___ Songs ___ Comics ___ Podcasts ___ Letters

___ Other: ______________________________

16. Who are your favorite writers and/or your writing role models?

____

17. Of all your writing, what piece are you most proud of? Please describe it.

____

____

18. If you could change anything about writing in school, what would it be?

____

FIGURE 5.12. Suggestions for using portfolios. (Adapted from Williams [2018, p. 171].)

Tips for Getting Started with Portfolios

Teachers can ask students to assemble their best pieces into a portfolio and reflect on these works. Here are some portfolio questions I like to use with students:

1. Tell me about the piece. What is it? When did you write it? Why did you write it? What audience did you imagine? What about the work are you proud of? Explain any challenges you faced writing it.
2. Tell me about how you wrote it. What was your process? What tools did you use? Did you get help from others?
3. How does this work fit with other writing you have done? Is it typical/atypical of your larger body of work as a writer?
4. Where does this piece show hints of the writer behind it?
5. Looking across the portfolio, how are the works similar? How are they different?

FIGURE 5.13. Suggestions for exploring writing careers.

Tips for Getting Started with Writing Career Exploration

Tapping into Local Expertise: For teachers interested in having students explore writing careers, a good first step is to get a sense of the expertise already available in the school community. Teachers could ask parents and other community members if their jobs involve writing and if so, what that looks like. These experts might then come to class to speak individually, as part of a panel, or in breakout sessions with small groups of students.

Brainstorm: Together, the class comes up with a list of careers that involve writing. Students then choose different careers to research.

Research: Students could research the salary, education required, and opportunities for advancement of various writing jobs. They could learn what the working conditions are like for that job, whether writing happens individually or in teams, and what rules guide that type of writing. If possible, they could gather writing samples and interview workers to learn more. They might also consider the ways that new technologies like AI are expected to impact that job in the future.

Sharing: Students share their research findings with the class in one to three slides.

Final Thoughts

It is worth our time and effort to help students imagine possible selves associated with different areas of study, including potential identities related to writing (e.g., author, graphic novelist, filmmaker, songwriter, etc.). This work supports students' learning and expands their understanding of the many career options available to them. In secondary English classes, it is essential to take students seriously as writers and model possible paths forward.

At the end of the YAS program, a student was half joking when he asked if there would be a math studio. We all laughed, but it was actually a great question. Having opportunities to try on different identities (e.g., mathematician, scientist, historian, athlete) can make learning more relevant and meaningful. I know that my entire physical education experience in school would have been different if I had started from a place of already believing that I was an athlete or had the opportunity to engage in and identify with particular kinds of exercise I enjoy, such as yoga, walking, swimming, or karate. When my teachers limited PE to one team sport after another and treated some children as athletes and others as losers, they failed us because they missed out on powerful opportunities to nurture positive identities associated with exercise that could have sustained us throughout our lives.

It is easy to get hyper-focused on elements such as the assignment, the lesson sequence, time on task, or assessment and forget that students' attitudes toward the subject—and degree of identification with the task at hand—are incredibly important, too. If we want students to learn content and really care about the subject, we must also provide opportunities for them to explore possible identities in our field.

Most students will probably never identify as authors of school essays, but they may see themselves as poets, novelists, graphic novelists, fan fiction writers, filmmakers, web designers, content creators, and so forth. Limiting the curriculum to a narrow view of writing shuts the door on the wide range of exciting writing identities that are available to students in the real world.

Of course, a writing identity is not enacted in isolation. Although we may compose some works just for ourselves, writing for real readers, viewers, and listeners reinforces writing identity. The next chapter looks more closely at how teachers can connect writers to opportunities beyond the classroom.

Chapter Six

Connecting Writers to Opportunities beyond the Classroom

It's a night to celebrate writers. Round tables, covered with tablecloths, are spread around the school library. Pastries and drinks are available. A student jazz band plays tunes in the corner. Students, parents, teachers, and administrators are milling about the room, chatting with one another. Soon the writers come up to the microphone one at a time to share their pieces. The audience will snap at lines they appreciate and erupt in applause when each writer is finished reading their work.

A high school teacher had the great idea to honor the winners of her school's writing contest at a poetry café-style event. The event turned out to be a meaningful way to bring the students' writing to life. As they read their pieces, we could hear their voices, see the people behind the words, and celebrate their writing. This experience also gave the writers a chance to connect to a larger audience for their work. They obtained some real-world experience, as the event mimicked the kind of work that professional writers do as part of their jobs (e.g., giving book talks and readings to promote their work). For those who are interested in holding a café-style event like this, it does not have to be limited to celebrating only the winners of a contest. All students could be invited to share their pieces.

Great mentors actively look for ways to connect their mentees to new learning opportunities that will foster their continued growth. This includes giving students access to new audiences for their work. This chapter focuses on the sixth strategy of mentoring youth writers, connecting writers to opportunities beyond the classroom (see Figure 6.1). This mentoring strategy involves guiding learners into deeper participation in the practice of writing through brokering techniques.

FIGURE 6.1. This chapter focuses on the sixth strategy for mentoring youth writers.

Six Strategies for Mentoring Youth Writers

1. Use a wide range of writing forms and modes with students.
2. Encourage student choice and decision-making.
3. Build a supportive writing community.
4. Honor student knowledge, experience, and interests.
5. Nurture students as writers.
6. **Connect writers to opportunities beyond the classroom.**

This chapter explores why it is necessary to connect writers to opportunities beyond the classroom. It shows the strategy in the Young Authors' Studio program, shares a teacher interview on the topic, and provides teaching suggestions. Figure 6.2 lists a couple of key terms to guide us in this work.

FIGURE 6.2. Useful terms to know for this chapter.

Key Terms

Audience: The readers, listeners, or viewers of a work—either real or imagined.

Brokering: This term is used in business, language education, and community-of-practice theory in slightly different ways. In the context of writing instruction, I define *brokering* as putting writers in contact with an opportunity or audience outside of the classroom to support their development as writers. Examples of brokering could include helping students find new audiences for their work around campus (e.g., pen-pal letters, installations, poetry readings) or making students aware of writing opportunities off campus, whether at the local or national levels or in digital spaces (e.g., National Writing Project summer camps, spoken word poetry slams, writing contests, teen publications).

Justifying This Work

This chapter focuses on connecting writers to opportunities beyond the classroom through the practice of brokering. Let's explore that term a bit. Readers are likely already familiar with the term *brokering* from business, where a broker "facilitates mutual accommodation between different . . . parties (Ng et al., 2004)" (He, 2009, p. 154). In community-of-practice theory, Wenger (2008) associates the term with the practice of traversing the boundaries that separate groups. He writes, "Brokers are able to make new connections across communities of practice, enable coordination, and—if they are good brokers—open up new possibilities for meaning" (p. 109). The term is used in language research as well, where it describes the "bilingual children/persons of immigrant families who translate and interpret for their family members and other individuals (Morales & Hansen, 2005, p. 471)" (He, 2009, p. 154), a definition that assumes anyone can act as a broker, even a child.

Drawing on these different ideas and applying them to writing instruction, I define *brokering* in this book as "putting writers in contact with an opportunity or audience outside of the classroom to support their development as writers." Brokering here still involves permeating, traversing, or breaking through the boundaries that would otherwise confine people to a particular group, but two communities of practice are not required under this definition; instead, brokering involves connecting students to any outside opportunity or audience that supports their writing. For example, teachers are engaging in brokering when they put students in touch with local or national writing contests, publishing opportunities, summer camps, writing groups, author events, library programs, and so forth. This definition also covers the practice of *creating new opportunities* for students to reach different audiences around campus or in the world beyond. Furthermore, anyone can act as a broker, even fellow students. We certainly saw evidence of this in YAS when a young author explained to fellow writers how they could self-publish as he had.

Although brokering is "a situational factor which contributes to learning," that does not mean "learning . . . automatically occur[s]" (He, 2009, p. 163). That is, not everyone is going to take advantage of a brokered opportunity, and even if they do, they will not get the same things out of it. Brokering is an important mentoring strategy because it has the potential to push students to think beyond the confines of their immediate time, place, and situation. It can open up new possibilities and new audiences for writers. In addition, these connections can help to sustain writers when they later move beyond the classroom and travel through the world as adults.

This take on brokering shares some similarities with the concept of "third space," a space that results when two spheres of life, such as school and home or community, overlap to open up new possibilities for learning (Gutiérrez, 2011). The main difference is that a third space blends two worlds to create a hybrid space, whereas brokering involves a push from inside to outside, a redirecting of members' attention to the world beyond the classroom.

Teachers who help connect students to new opportunities for writing and performance put students in touch with authentic outlets for their work, which can be a deeply meaningful experience. If students are limited to writing only for teachers in school (and mainly in traditional forms like essays), they will develop a limited view of why people write in the real world and why they might actually want to do it themselves. These are missed opportunities.

The NCTE *Position Statement on Writing Instruction in School* (2022) contains some ideas that are relevant to this chapter (see Figure 6.3).

FIGURE 6.3. NCTE position statement connections.

Connections to NCTE's *Position Statement on Writing Instruction in School* (2022)

- Students need to be able to "transfer their writing knowledge to new contexts, especially contexts beyond the classroom."
- "Writing instruction in many English language arts classrooms rarely includes opportunities for children and youth to . . . write for authentic audiences."
- "[T]here are ways to . . . *actively cultivate* young writers' efficacy and engagement. This kind of instruction . . . offers frequent opportunities for students to make decisions about composing for authentic purposes and audiences."

Mentoring in Action: Inside the Young Authors' Studio Program

This section shares findings from the Young Authors' Studio study to illustrate how mentors brokered opportunities for writing and performance. Sometimes their brokering involved connecting students to contests, events, or groups. Other times the mentors created opportunities on campus that allowed the youth writers to find a new audience for their work.

Novel Writing Challenge

One way the mentors engaged in brokering was by putting students in touch with materials from a national novel writing challenge. Henry explained in his breakout session pitch, "National Novel Writing Month . . . is this . . . challenge that they do in November. It's going to be really fun and exciting. I know that when you hear the words 'write a novel,' that sounds kind of scary, so this is kind of a cool way to get into it and . . . basically create a plan." His breakout session focused on creating a novel outline using a template that asked for the novel's title, summaries of each chapter, and descriptions of each character.

During the breakout session, Henry elaborated a bit more:

> People try to write an entire novel within one month. . . . Sometimes people get stuck when writing. They think, "Oh, this isn't good. I have to go back and change this." And this challenge is to just encourage people to write, to get words on the page. . . . They have different word goals based on grade and age and that sort of thing. If you don't want to write a whole novel during this month, you don't have to, but it's pretty cool to try. . . . [Today] we're writing the novel outline. If you want, you can take this once it's finished and use that to [write] your book [in November].

Henry set up his session so the youth writers would not only become familiar with this special opportunity but also be well prepared to face it with a novel outline already in hand.

In another workshop, a student said, "At home, I've been writing about all these different species—vampires, werewolves, humans, dwarves, things like that. They're all at war over a single piece of land. Whoever captures it holds the land for one year. They're going to rule the world." Emma said that was "super cool" and asked if it was a novel or short story. When the student replied, "I'm going to make it pretty long," Emma recommended that the student do the novel writing challenge. She said, "It's coming up. You can make a writing goal for a certain number of words. There's an adult one that is 50,000 words, and then there is a kids' one where you can set your own goal. I did the kids' one when I was in ninth grade, and I set my goal for 10,000 words. It was a lot of work, but I was able to get through it. It's kind of a good way to challenge yourself."

Novel writing challenges (see Figure 6.4) give students the experience of what it feels like to be a novelist as they craft an original book-length manuscript of their own. The pride students feel from this work reinforces their writing identity and helps them see they can tackle a really large project if they just break it down into manageable pieces.

FIGURE 6.4. Novel writing challenge.

Writing a Novel in One Month

The challenge to write a novel in one month (either in November or at any other time of the year) can be an exciting way to engage students. Students set a larger word count goal and break it down into smaller daily goals. To learn more about how this can work in the secondary classroom, see Carrie Deahl's article "Bracing for NaNoWriMo" (2020) in *English Journal.*

Events, Programs, and Contests for Writers

Whenever the opportunity arose, mentors brokered connections to local events, programs, and contests. They passed along information about a musical theater songwriting challenge, a citywide writing contest, and a National Writing Project camp for youth. When I heard that a student was interested in spoken word poetry, I told her about the ASU Sparky Slam poetry event I was hosting for adolescents, and I gave her the name of a local spoken word poetry group that offers free workshops and poetry slams.

Take a few minutes to see what writing events, contests, and programs are available near you (see Figure 6.5). A word of caution: When connecting students to opportunities outside of school, involve other stakeholders such as parents and administrators (some districts require that anyway in order to distribute these types of materials to students). In addition, make sure the opportunities are credible. Look at factors such as the professional standing of the organization, years in operation, reviews and results over time, and current operating procedures to keep kids safe.

Many districts offer writing contests, but these are typically limited to specific types of writing (poetry, short story, etc.). We know that students write in a wide variety of forms in and outside of school, so shouldn't writing contests reflect that? If you are hosting a contest (see Figure 6.6), be sure to encourage multimodal forms of writing (film, animation, comics, etc.), including those that have cultural and historical relevance, such as songs, spoken word poetry, and zines.

FIGURE 6.5. Finding writing events, contests, and programs.

Writing Events, Contests, and Programs Near You

Do a quick search for writing events, contests, and programs in your area. Is there a National Writing Project site (www.nwp.org/) near you? Are there any youth spoken word poetry workshops or contests? Do any local libraries or bookstores regularly host author talks, writing workshops, contests, or open mic events? Do local colleges or universities offer any community literacy events or programs? Make sure you know your local professors of English education because many of them organize literacy programs and events for the community or they know others who do. For national contests, be sure to check out the Scholastic Art and Writing Awards (www.artandwriting.org) and NCTE's Promising Young Writers and Achievement Awards in Writing contests (https://ncte.org/awards/student-writing-awards/). In addition, what opportunities can you find for teachers who write? After all, you need to sustain yourself as well.

FIGURE 6.6. Suggestions for starting a writing contest.

Starting a Student Writing Contest

Contest Categories: Writing contests typically have categories such as poetry, fiction, and nonfiction, but we can expand those categories to invite a broader array of forms. I did this when I chaired NCTE's Achievement Awards in Writing Advisory Committee and when I directed the Arizona English Teachers Association's Teachers as Writers Contest. It is not difficult to open up a contest to encourage multimodal composition, which can result in much more interesting pieces to read, view, and listen to. A poetry category could be open to spoken word poetry videos and recorded songs. A fiction category could include short stories, graphic narratives, short films, or animated works. When deciding on the contest categories, think about ways to honor the forms that inspire students in their lives outside of school. I recommend including both a page length and video length maximum for each category. That is, a poetry entry might be limited to three pages or three minutes, depending on the form it takes. A work of fiction might be up to five pages or five minutes.

Judging: Recruit a panel of volunteers to help with judging the entries. Decide whether the entries will be reviewed with author names masked. Will teachers, administrators, parents, students, professors, or other community members be invited to serve as judges? A Google form can be useful for keeping track of scores and justifications.

Recognition and Prizes: Will winners receive a prize, perhaps a gift certificate, books, or something else? Will there be other types of recognition involved, such as publication in a journal, formal announcements, or invited readings? Be sure to mention any prizes or other recognition in the contest announcement.

Publishing Opportunities for Teens

Teachers can broker publishing opportunities for students, even creating journals if necessary. In later iterations of YAS that were conducted online, mentors published an online journal for youth with categories for poetry, fiction, animation, and artwork. Publishing can be a great way to connect students to a larger audience beyond the classroom, assuming permission-to-publish forms from students and their parents are on file. Tips for starting a journal for student writers can be found in Figure 6.7.

In addition, as mentioned elsewhere, we had a sixth grader in YAS who had already navigated the world of self-publishing. He had published a how-to book and was working on a second. Everyone enjoyed learning about his process, and we discovered that his grandfather had given him a small loan that he expected to be repaid through book sales. When the author told the other students about his project and brought his first book for them to see, a fellow writer interjected, "Wait! How old do you have to be to publish something?" Some were shocked to learn that they could get their own work out in the world this way. "I feel like we should all write a book and publish it now. This is a great idea," Nari remarked. Of course, self-publishing is just one way to put writing out into the world, but it doesn't need to incur a cost. These days many students are publishing their writing on their own websites and promoting content through social media.

FIGURE 6.7. Suggestions for starting a journal for student writers.

Starting a Journal for Student Writers

Call for Manuscripts: When organizing a publication, it is important to think about which categories of writing will be accepted and what the length requirements will be. Some advantages to having an online publication are low cost, more flexibility in length, and more variety of media (e.g., video files, audio files, image files).

Permission-to-Publish Form: When we created an online journal for youth writers in later years of the YAS program, the first thing I did was consult my university's legal team to make sure the form I used was one they approved of. For teachers in schools, I highly recommend consulting with school and district administrators. Of course, for a piece to be published online, student and parent consent must be in writing.

Issue Launch Event: Every year when a former ASU colleague of mine released an issue of her student-run literary journal, she held a launch party. This event celebrated the hard work of the students who were involved in reviewing entries, corresponding with authors, editing and laying out the issue, and handling social media. And, of course, it was an opportunity for the published authors and artists to be recognized. This type of event would work in a high school setting as well.

Additional opportunities for publishing include school or district literary magazines and class anthologies of student writing. Alternatively, teachers could put students in touch with venues like *Teen Ink* (see Figure 6.8).

FIGURE 6.8. Publishing in *Teen Ink.*

Teen Ink

Teen Ink (www.teenink.com) is a publication for writers between the ages of thirteen and nineteen that has been around since 1989. I remember when it used to be delivered to classrooms on newsprint; these days, free digital subscriptions are available. This is a wonderful resource for the classroom because it is a forum for students to publish their writing, and students can read the writing of other authors their age.

Writing Gallery

Teachers can broker opportunities for students to connect with larger audiences on campus. In the YAS program, we invited students to participate in two culminating events, a public writing gallery and performance, which were held back-to-back on the same day. We started to tell students about these events from the first week of the program so they could imagine what writing they might put on display and what they might read aloud to a crowd. For the writing gallery, I explained:

> You should be thinking right now, "What am I going to put in the writing gallery? What piece looks really nice and polished, and I want it out on a table for people to see?" And on the revision and rehearsal day, we're going to walk over there during YAS so you can see the space. You'll see where we'll set up the writing gallery and how much space you'll have.

During another workshop, I emphasized:

> When people walk by your table, they're going to be like, "Oh, I'm going to stop here and look at this." [Maybe] you're really proud of the comic you did, or it's your haiku on a nice piece of paper with decoration. It could be the piece you just wrote and maybe you're going to go home and type it up and add images. Your writing gallery piece needs to be interesting enough that people will stop, walk over to it, and read it.

I wanted them to understand that when there is a room full of writing and potential readers milling around, their pieces will have to work to bring people over.

The writers could have multiple pieces at their station in the writing gallery, and they could bring in anything they had written—novels, comics, works written at home or at school. I also told the writers:

> Bring in writing that matters to you. If the essay really matters, then bring that. . . . If you're writing a play and you want to share that with people, put that out there. . . . There will be Post-it notes around. People who come by and read your work are going to leave you little notes. "Oh my gosh, this script looks fantastic! I can't wait to see it." It's your chance to kind of say, "I'm a writer. Check out my stuff."

The students ended up bringing in a wide variety of pieces to the writing gallery, everything from haiku and concrete poems to stories, novels, comics, and essays.

At each station, the writer displayed the name card they created on the first day of the program. Around it, they put any works they wanted to share. We left pads of sticky notes and pens so guests could leave comments for the young authors (see Figure 6.9).

FIGURE 6.9. Writing gallery station with comments.

Some of the mentors set up stations to share their writing as well, and the youth writers enjoyed taking their turn to give their mentors feedback on their writing. After the performance, students went back out to the writing gallery to collect their writing and sticky notes full of comments. A few students who could not attend because of prior commitments gave their writing to friends to display in the gallery (they returned these works and sticky notes to the authors after the event). In this way, even students who were unable to attend the last day of YAS could get encouraging feedback, which was a nice perk.

In a reflection, Amir thought about how the writing gallery worked: "After all [the] parents came in, we started our writing gallery. The work that students produced was really creative, and I [noticed] most parents [were] happy and took pictures of their [children's] work. I was so happy to see how much our students improved their skills and how much thanks we got from the parents. As we saw a work that we [liked], we wrote a comment to praise the person for [their] effort, [reinforcing their] self-confidence."

For teachers who are interested in hosting a writing gallery, Figure 6.10 provides some suggestions.

FIGURE 6.10. Tips for hosting a writing gallery.

Hosting a Writing Gallery

Gallery walks are a great way for students to share their work. Basically, students post their work on the walls around the room or set up pieces at their desks. They then wander around the room and leave comments for the writers/artists. Gallery audiences need not be limited to student audiences. Perhaps students could display their writing for a Meet-the-Teacher Night. (This goes without saying, but pieces in a gallery must not have a grade or teacher feedback on them.)

Determining the Purpose: Often the point of a gallery walk in my class is to appreciate the amazing work students are doing. Other times we use this structure for feedback on a work in progress.

Setting a Path: Devise a logical path people should take through the space to get to each piece easily and communicate that to gallery goers.

Time per Piece: Some teachers use a set amount of time at each station, but I like for people to be able to wander through at their own pace.

Comments: For in-class gallery walks, I talk with students about giving appropriate feedback. As they move around the room, they will leave comments on sticky notes or a piece of paper. In addition to writing comments, they will sign their name in case any follow-up is needed. I also ask the student in the last rotation to read all of the comments at that station and make sure they are appropriate to share with that author/artist before the author returns to their seat.

Public Performance

The second culminating event students participated in as part of the YAS program was a public performance (see Figure 6.11). We prepared students for this event from the first week of the program. I explained:

> You'll have about three minutes to perform, so if you have a longer piece, you'll have to look at it and cut it down. Start thinking about what piece would sound nice if read aloud. You could perform with a group, make a video, or even bring music in. You might just want to get up and read a haiku.

The week before the performance, we walked students over to the small auditorium so they could see the performance space.

FIGURE 6.11. YAS final performance.

During the rehearsal, the writers were invited to read a couple of lines from their performance piece while mentors listened in the back and gave feedback (e.g., "slower," "louder," "look up") (see Figure 6.12). The mentors had some general comments for the students, too. Emma said, "It's better to be too loud than too quiet." I emphasized that slowing down gives the audience time to take in every word. Miranda said that she took voice classes, and her instructor told her to imagine her voice as a laser. I added that their words should reach the back row when they talk. I then talked really quickly for a few sentences so they could hear how strange it sounds when someone speaks too fast. I reminded them, "When you're up here, you have power. If there's a part that's emotional, that you really want to hit them with, slow down. Take your time. Vary your voice, your volume, your pitch, and your speed."

FIGURE 6.12. Mentors listening to rehearsal.

In his reflection for that day, Amir commented that it was important for the youth writers to see the building where they would be performing to prepare them for the "real situation" and so "they [wouldn't] get nervous during the performance." He wrote that the youth writers appreciated this and "no one was afraid or [asked to not participate]." Before the event, the mentors also debated whether they should read their pieces. I reminded them, "We want to show students that this is a safe space where they can take risks, and it doesn't have to be perfect."

At the final performance, Emma shared a piece she had written about her experience in Young Authors' Studio:

> Every Saturday I walk in, more excited yet more emotional than the week before. The tables that wait in rows know that they are about to be moved into six sets of two. They jiggle as we move them across the floor, the metal legs of the chairs clanging against the metal bases of the tables. The writers are going to come soon. The door clicks open right about 9:25, and the room that was only filled with the voices and movements of the mentors [now contains] the voices and the excitement of the writers. Some are wide awake and ready to roll, and others are still half asleep, almost dragging their feet on the floor. Five minutes are over before I know it, and a mentor steps up to the front to lead the journal session. We all journal together, hear about the day's topic for a few minutes, and then hear about the day's breakouts. A sort of controlled chaos arises as everyone moves around to the breakout that they want to go to. And then the room quiets again somewhat as the breakouts start: 6-word memoirs, blackout poetry, comics and graphic novels, writing a play, or character sheets. Which will you choose? Time flies by and it's time to choose another breakout. Some stay put. Some move around. Again, the noise increases. Then quickly decreases. Then it's time for more concentrated writing: brainstorm, quiet writing time, polishing, sharing. Mentors are all around to assist with projects. Pieces worked on during the session. Work started years before. Then we break out into teams, 3–5 writers and a mentor, checking in on projects and how the session went. Before we know it, parents come in to pick up the writers, and soon the room is quiet again. Joy and sadness are overwhelming. Another session completed. Writers have learned and been encouraged, but we are just one week closer to having to say farewell, writers moving onto bigger things and bigger dreams. I'm so grateful to play a part in it.

The crowd cheered. Then the cohosts, Emma and Miranda, thanked the guests for being there. The youth writers came up, one at a time, to read pieces they had written to a room filled with family members and friends.

Most of the students read short pieces. Since the purpose of the event was to encourage the writers to get up and be brave, sharing anything, we judged it a success. Some examples of the writers' performance pieces are highlighted in Figures 6.13–6.15.

FIGURE 6.13. Student performance piece: "No Escape."

No Escape

A boy in ancient Rome was enslaved two years ago. Now he has the biggest risk of his life and [must] escape from his master. He is hiding in a window of a tall building of which his master is right outside. He has commanded his general to search the building for the boy. Did I mention that his master is also the commander of the army? The doomed boy is looking for an escape but despite his keen eyesight and desperation, he can't find one. What's he going to do? The generals are about to find him. They're coming into the room.

FIGURE 6.14. Student performance piece: "The Grand Penumbra."

The Grand Penumbra

Chapter 1. It was the time for the annual moonlight creature welfare meeting. Or as most of the . . . Grand Penumbra called it, the AMCWM. Only the greatest creatures of the kingdom were allowed to go. This year Felix the Fifth . . . was finally invited. The past years had been quite embarrassing because his brother . . . had been invited to go to AMCWM for the past seven years. Not to mention, Cassio was his younger brother. Felix was set to prove that he should have been invited for the past seven years, not his brother. It was [his] time to shine.

FIGURE 6.15. Student performance piece: "Self-Defense in My Experience."

Self-Defense in My Experience

There are those who wish to bully us and even hurt us, so we must defend ourselves. Sometimes with force. I learned this lesson a long time ago when I was in second grade. At the school I went to, there were many mean people who chose to pick on me. Due to the nature of the school, no teacher could help me despite my pleas. This is when I realized I had to stick up for myself. . . . I felt trapped. . . . It was at recess. The sun was pointing at high noon. The field was a grassy template for all sorts of adventures, real or imaginary. Bordered by two sidewalks and a large aspiring building, I stood at the basketball court. Behind me was the gate, an icon representing entrapment but also safety from the murky waters of the canal. I did not expect this day to come. . . . He pushed me . . . but before he could make his next move, I saw a small window of opportunity, and I took it. I lunged at him with all my might.

Before the event started, we had a slideshow running in the background that featured the youth writers and mentors in action during the YAS program. Amir wrote that this made "the performance less [stressful] for the students." After all of the students had performed, the mentors called their teams up and handed out certificates, and each team posed for a picture together.

I noticed that the youth writers exhibited different levels of confidence as they performed, and the oldest writers were not necessarily the most confident. We wondered how the students felt about the experience and asked them to fill out comment cards before they left. They seemed to have appreciated the challenge of performing:

- "The final performance was nerve-wracking but fun."
- "Everyone is supportive when you share your work."
- "It was fun performing. It was a little nerve-wracking. Thank you for hosting this."

Henry reflected on the event, "A cool moment that I had was . . . when [a student] and his mother came over to shake my hand and thank me before leaving. It's awesome to see how excited the students have become about their writing, and I'd like to think that we inspired them to continue writing in the future."

For teachers interested in hosting a performance at their school, these events could take place in a classroom or a larger space on campus like an auditorium. They could be informal or formal events depending on the time and space the teacher would like to devote to them. Figure 6.16 offers some suggestions for hosting a performance.

FIGURE 6.16. Suggestions for hosting a performance.

Hosting a Performance

Planning: Use the following questions to get started with the planning process:

- What is the purpose of the event?
- Who will be invited to attend?
- What are the expectations for pieces? (Maximum length? Forms of writing allowed?)
- How will the order of performance be determined?

Setting the Room: Most classrooms can be set up for a performance without too much hassle. The chairs and desks could be arranged so everyone is facing the front, or the furniture could form a large circle. Alternatively, a larger space on campus could be used if parents or additional students are going to be invited to attend.

The Podium: A podium gives writers a place to set down their writing and provides something to "hide" behind for those who are nervous. Although I do like to encourage students to come out from behind the podium and to use their bodies as they gesture for emphasis, I also recognize that this requires a greater degree of comfort than first-time performers usually feel. It's important that we show empathy as writing mentors. Public speaking is terrifying, and it takes practice to get good at it and to feel comfortable.

No Forced Performances: Please do not force students to share personal writing with others. Being vulnerable in front of teenagers can be traumatic if forced. Instead, teachers can use performance as a carrot, holding it up as something students can do if they are feeling brave.

Benefits in Repeated Events: Host several performance opportunities throughout the year. It can take shy writers several times of watching performances before they feel ready to step up there themselves. There is nothing wrong with that. If this does eventually happen for a student, believe me, it will be worth the wait.

Special Flourishes: Consider whether it makes sense to have prizes, awards, or thank-you cards for authors. Should the space be decorated in a special way? Will there be refreshments? Music? Perhaps a slideshow could run before the start of the event.

Additional Reading: Many publications address the benefits of performance (Kahn et al., 2022; Weinstein, 2009).

Pause and Reflect

Brokering is an important strategy associated with mentoring youth writers because it helps students become aware of wider audiences for their work, larger networks of writers, and the many possibilities for writing in the world beyond the classroom. When we connect students to new experiences, we open up the possibility, too, for their continued, deepening engagement in the practice of writing over the lifespan.

This chapter explores some ways that mentors in YAS connected writers to opportunities beyond the classroom. Teachers in secondary classrooms can also employ these techniques to support students. Specifically, they can put students in touch with events, contests, and publishing outlets. In addition, teachers can organize campus-wide writing galleries and performances to help students take their work to larger audiences.

Before we explore how a teacher connects writers to opportunities beyond the classroom, let's pause to consider what this strategy means to you (see Figure 6.17).

FIGURE 6.17. Reflection questions for strategy #6.

Pause and Reflect

Strategy #6: Connecting Writers to Opportunities beyond the Classroom

- How do you already use this strategy in your teaching?
- What are some new ways you can use this strategy to benefit students?
- How does this strategy help bring out the author (or graphic novelist, filmmaker, songwriter . . .) in every student?

Teacher Interview: April McNary on Connecting Writers to Opportunities beyond the Classroom

It can be useful to explore how an English teacher brokers opportunities for writing and performance. April McNary (see Figure 6.18) has been an educator for sixteen years. She teaches sophomore English at Sunnyslope High School in Phoenix, Arizona. She is a recipient of the Arizona English Teachers Association (AETA) English Teacher of Excellence Award and is a National Writing Project teacher consultant. She has been recognized through the AETA Teachers as Writers contest for her poetry. She identifies as Hispanic and enjoys reading, writing, cooking, and gardening.

FIGURE 6.18. Selfie by April McNary.

Can you share some examples of how you connect writers to opportunities and audiences beyond the classroom?

I tell the kids about [a novel writing challenge they can do in November]. The whole idea of writing a novel in a month seems overwhelming to them, but I say, "Look at what you were just able to accomplish in a few weeks." It's about being part of a bigger community of writers. The yearlong battle is getting kids to believe that they're readers and writers. "You really are. You're part of this world. And reading [and] writing is all communication. These are skills that you're going to need."

The school poetry contest happens every year in February. Kids are allowed to submit a couple of poems, and teachers vote on them. Then they go to the district level for another round of voting, and the district publishes the winning poems and has an award ceremony. I've attended that a couple of times for my kids. It's neat because kids who maybe don't do sports can find their way with writing, and they're like, "Oh, I can do this, and I like it." The kids like when you get them involved or make it something they could obtain. It's not on that bigger, national level. It's local.

I also share [outside] writing contest information and vet the contests as best I can. I tell students, "Look through this list. Some of them want a fee upfront. You may be competing with kids who are doing this on a regular basis, so you have to keep that in mind. Try to look for the free ones if you're just getting started. If you really want to take your writing to the next level, you need to polish it." I tell them they should pay attention to the dates because some have already passed, so maybe tuck those links away for next year.

My students have written pen-pal letters to students in third grade who were learning to write. I had a student who could decipher anything they had written. For us, it was a mentorship (a big brother, big sister type of) situation. My kids would write about what they were doing in school and ask the kids questions (e.g., What's your favorite color? What sport are you playing?). My friend said that when the kids got their letters, they would light up. When my sophomores received letters from the kids, they would melt. "They drew me a picture!" It was more the connection than anything else. They loved it. We protected the kids by not using full names or actual pictures of them.

They also wrote to college students. Both classes were reading *The Little Prince*. It was good for my students to have a view of the outside world and realize, "Oh, college kids are reading the same book that we're reading." It gave them confidence. They felt so cool being able to write to college students.

I have also used pen-pal letters here with a ninth-grade teacher. We made it anonymous and gave students numbers and colors. We paired them off, and they wrote five letters each. At the end, we had a breakfast in the library during Wednesday Learning Center [an optional time to be on campus when students can get extra help from teachers]. The library was packed with kids, and everybody brought food. All the administrators showed up. We had the students sign in and create name tags with their number, their color, and their real name. That way, they could go meet their pen pal. And it was the cutest experience. Some of them really bonded through their writing. There was one girl and boy who had been drawing pictures in their writing. The girl told me, "I didn't realize how much I needed this connection with somebody." It was interesting because they were all kids on the same campus. We're together. We should be building, communicating together, but we don't always do that authentically. And that's what we were attempting to do. The other teacher and I would meet at lunch, swap letters if we had them, and discuss the next prompt. We also wrote to each other. We learned a lot, even though we're already friends.

I invite my students and their parents to school for a Spoil Your Dinner family writing event. [There are snacks, so the event name is poking fun at the idea that attendees are going to spoil their dinner.] I did this for several years, and there was always a good turnout. I provided food, set up the tables in little pods with flowers, and gave them different prompts to get them writing or drawing. To watch kids working with their parents was very cool. At the end, they would write a letter to each other. One year I had a student, and I knew he was struggling. His mom had stage four cancer. She came to this event and said, "Thank you for giving me this opportunity." They wrote beautiful letters to each other. My mom would show up, you came, [our friend Tracey came], and my daughter. The kids are always worried about, "What if my parents don't speak English?"

I'm like, "Well, you get to translate when we're in there." And they're like, "What if my parents don't know how to write?" I say, "Then they can draw." I had a parent who was mapping out the neighborhood where she grew up. That was one of the activities we had done. And this daughter kind of looked over at her mom. "I didn't know my mom could draw!" She was drawing her home in Mexico and was teaching her daughter, "This is where I'm from. This is what it looked like." And it was really a cool kind of experience to watch.

I was participating in professional development workshops at the Phoenix Art Museum and decided to hold a Night at the Museum for my kids. Students could meet me there for free, and I took them to visit art pieces we had discussed in the workshops I attended. I would say, "Tell the story of that piece." They would all sit and write, and then we would talk about what we had written. The kids would come at it in different ways because they each bring their own life experience. I would give them a little bit of background on the piece, and they'd look closer.

I teach a unit on monsters, and the end product is to create a monster story (McNary, 2021). I tell the students, "I'm not the only one reading your monster story. Everybody will have access to your story. You are writing for a bigger audience than just me." They kind of panic at first and ask, "Wait. Who's going to have access?" I tell them, "Everybody in our class will be able to read your story with your names attached to it, and everybody's parents, including your own, will have access to your stories." Sometimes they also vote to give the faculty and staff access or to share the class anthology with other class periods. It's local, but for them, it's a big deal because a lot of them have never shared their writing beyond a teacher or a friend. The idea of having parents or other teachers reading their work is a little scary for them at first, but then their writing alters because they know that their name will be attached to it, and they want to be proud of what is shared with other people. I send out our class anthology when it's done. Teachers have commented, "Oh, so-and-so's story was great." I'm like, "Yeah, they're writers."

I remember when one of our students passed away. After the principal and social worker left my room, I looked at the kids and said, "What do we do?" And it was quiet for a long time. One of my girls raised her hand and said, "Can we write?" I said, "Yes. What do you want to write?" She said, "Can we write letters to his mom?" I said, "Absolutely." Somebody said, "Can we write about him and post it outside our classroom door?" We had a bulletin board outside my door. I turned on some music, put it on really low, and we just wrote. It took a kid to say it, but we write all the time to process. Why not write during this difficult situation? And the bulletin board outside did become like a makeshift memorial. You would see kids walk by and they would stop to read what people wrote. That was a very emotional, authentic situation where we were trying to process the death of the student.

We've also gone outside to write. At the end of the year, I take them around campus for a final writing tour of the school. I try to plant them in places where they have memories, like the football field. We go out to the bleachers. I give them prompts ahead of time. And then we move to different locations. I tell them, "Go look at Victor Viking [a statue of the school mascot]. You walk by him all the time. Do you ever look at him? What is he holding? What color are his eyes?" And then they sit at those tables and write about him. We go to the library where we can see "S Mountain" [there is an *S* painted on Sunnyslope Mountain in this neighborhood]. I ask, "What does it mean to be a Viking? Why are we here? What are we doing here? What legacy are we trying to leave for other people?" The last day of the school year, we read out loud something we wrote during the year. It could be what they wrote during that walking tour. It could be a goodbye letter. Everybody has to read something. We hear everybody's voice. Giving an actual final on final exam day seems terrible. We've spent so much time together, shared our writing, and done all this bonding, and we're going to spend the last day in complete silence? That seems wrong to me. So I started giving the final exam earlier so we can spend time together on the last day. I ask, "What else needs to be said that hasn't been said yet?" Some will say things to each other or to me. It's very sweet and good closure.

I want students to see that they can seek out opportunities for their writing (e.g., events, camps) if they really enjoy writing. Many of them say they don't think they are readers or writers in the beginning of the year, but then by the end they're like, "I can do this!" I'm like, "Yeah, you can!"

Why do you think it's important to connect students to writing and audiences beyond the classroom?
Why are we teaching them to read and write to begin with? Just to pass a test? I want it to be more real for them. You will eventually apply for something that you will need to write an essay for, or you're going to have to articulate why you're the best fit for a position. We need to connect students to writing and make it real for them. If all we're doing is giving them sentence starters or formulaic writing, it's not going to help them. It's important for us to bridge the academic side and show how they will be able to apply it later to benefit them.

When my dad passed away, I read part of what I had written for my dad's service to my students. And I said, "I didn't realize that I would be tapping into my own writing skills to process the death of my dad." In their personal lives when they're dealing with something difficult, writing can be an outlet. They write journals in my class every Friday, and they're learning they can express their emotions in a healthy way. I tell kids that when they're fighting with their parents, they should write them a letter. It's hard to argue with a letter because the person has to actually read it. And then maybe you can talk after they read what you had to say. You can get your feelings out without yelling. Giving students the space to write helps them. I model different ways they can use writing in life—not just in college, but when a parent passes away or you're going to have to say something in front of people.

What are the benefits of connecting students to writing opportunities and audiences beyond the classroom?
It helps their confidence. Connecting students to different opportunities makes them feel like, "I can do this! I can go for it, and if I get shot down, it's okay. I can bounce back from it. It's going to be okay."

Have you faced any challenges with this work?
It is a lot of work to match kids up for pen-pal letters, but I think some things warrant our time. We just have to figure out the balance. The kids keep their letters open. They have to be appropriate.

For the monster stories, I say, "Your parents are the boss, not me. When you go home, you need to run your story idea by your parents. And if there needs [to be] a content warning, you need to run that by your parents and explain why you wrote what you wrote." Some of them will continue to go that route, but others will change it completely because the parents will say, "Oh, you can't write about that." I tell students to remember that part of the audience for the monster story is their parents. The idea is, "Let's be respectful of your parents. We're not going to blindside them. Have the conversation." At the end, I say, "Here's what your kid did. Here's our anthology." They have a chance to be proud. You just have to figure out how to navigate things in a respectful way for everyone.

With the Spoil your Dinner event, it did cost money, and it took time setting everything up. However, I use Donors Choose. In the last few years, I've gotten smarter about trying to bulk up on materials [throughout the year].

How can teachers get started with this work?
Teachers need to talk to their kids. After a great writing assignment that kids feel proud of, start the conversation. They did a really nice job with this assignment. "What else could we do with the writing? Who needs to see our work? Where could we share it?" Kids are problem solvers. They may not realize it. Maybe we haven't been giving them the opportunity to realize it. They are already aware of different communities they could be part of. A student came to me and said, "My mom works for a nursing home and was wondering if your students would write to some of these people that don't have anybody to come visit during the holidays." I told the student, "Have your mom send me an email. We will definitely write to them."

What additional advice do you have for teachers?
Is the work really done once we slap a grade on it? I think that's detrimental to kids. They need to be proud of the work, and we need to see what else they can do with it, even if it's creating a portfolio digitally that is shareable for them later on. We have to ask, "Is the writing we are asking them to do going to benefit them later?" Yes, we have to follow standards. Yes, we have to do certain things, but could we also be writing pieces that students could use later for a resume or college admission essay or whatever they want to write for? I think we need to give students more opportunities to write. I would encourage teachers to think beyond what's expected and start creating assignments for the students more than for administrators and district officials.

Do you have any favorite resources on this topic?
I'm a big Kelly Gallagher and Peggy Kittle fan. I really love the idea of just sitting with the kids and writing. They do peer over your shoulder and want to see what you're doing. Teachers need to practice what they're teaching. We need to be willing to put ourselves out there. The National Writing Project changed my world. Also, National Endowment for the Humanities summer institutes have been important to me. We have to be willing to do professional development. Every year I've gone, I've met people I still talk to, and they become my resources. It's what other teachers are doing that has worked. We meet up again, and we write and talk together. I love the Penny Kittles, the Kelly Gallaghers of the world, but we are those people, too. We're just not published.

Do you have any cautions or warnings for teachers?
Do a bit of filtering to make sure you are passing along credible writing contests and other opportunities for kids (e.g., Scholastic, National Writing Project). That's safer than giving students random sites.

Do you have any words of encouragement for teachers as they embark on this work?
Teachers need to share their work, too. If the teacher is confident in their ability to share work, then they will pass on that attitude to their kids. "If I can do this, you can do this." Write with your kids and share your writing with others. Start local, like we're telling the kids. Then figure out how to branch out. Maybe reach

out to *English Journal*. Check the calls for manuscripts and see if you've done something that might fit that category. And if you get rejected, that's a lesson. Try again. Even with the poetry contest, I submitted my poetry just to see what would happen. [April placed first!] Teachers need to be willing to do the work they're asking of their students. If we're asking students to engage with writing beyond the classroom, teachers need to be willing to take that first step also. You are the leader. You do it first, see what happens, and open that door up for the kids.

Now You Try: Bringing Ideas to Life in the School Community

Classroom teachers can broker opportunities for writers in a variety of ways, and this work can begin on school campuses. In the following sections, I share tips for organizing writing celebrations, holding student film screenings, and filling the campus with words.

Writing Celebrations

One way teachers can bring writing to life on campus is to host a celebration of writing—perhaps a National Day on Writing event. According to the NCTE National Day on Writing website, October 20 is the day to "draw attention to the remarkable variety of writing" and to "transform the public's understanding of writing and the role it plays in society today" (see Figure 6.19).

FIGURE 6.19. Suggestions for hosting a National Day on Writing event.

Tips for Getting Started with a National Day on Writing Event

Toolkit: Go online to the NCTE website and download the National Day on Writing Toolkit (https://ncte.org/national-day-writing-toolkit/). It provides planning suggestions, a list of recommended activities, and printable tools.

Tables: At ASU, we have celebrated the National Day on Writing by having a table on campus that offers writing activities and games for students to play. What might this look like at your school? Could students be involved in planning and running different tables around campus at lunch?

Culminating Event: October 20 would be the perfect day to host an evening writing event. Perhaps students could participate in a special writing workshop with a local author or take part in an open mic event on campus.

Student Film Screenings

Holding a student film screening on campus is a fantastic way to communicate that multimodal composition matters at your school. These events give student filmmakers a larger audience than they would get in their English class (see Figure 6.20).

FIGURE 6.20. Suggestions for student film screenings.

Tips for Getting Started with Student Film Screenings

Teach the Elements of Film: Every aspect of a visual composition matters. Help students learn some basic film elements: shots (establishing, long, medium, close-up, extreme close-up), camera angles (bird's eye view, worm's eye view, Dutch angle), camera movement (pan, tilt, zoom), lighting, mise-en-scène, and editing (Golden, 2001). Access videos online that explain film elements with clips from popular movies; the Ultimate Guide series by StudioBinder is superb. Also, have students check out the Columbia Film Language Glossary (Trustees of Columbia University, 2015), which contains definitions along with stills and scenes from films.

Teach the Writing Process: Guide students through the work of brainstorming, composing, and editing their pieces. Prewriting should include scripts and storyboards.

Communicate the Film Screening Requirements: What are the minimum and maximum length requirements of the short films? What categories are being accepted? Do you need to articulate guidelines for acceptable content? When and where are entries to be submitted? How large can the student film crews be?

Decide on the Event Format: Will the screening event include an awards ceremony? If awards will be distributed, what will they recognize? Who will be on the awards committee?

Filling the Campus with Words

When you look around your school, do you see opportunities for students to fill the campus with their words? Goss (2019) has a great chapter on using the physical space of the school for "publishing." He tells the story of how he had students write SAT words on small bird-shaped pieces of paper to create a word wall, but these eventually covered the wall and then spilled out into the hallways, filling the campus with words. Later, he transformed this idea, having students write and post personal narratives on large cutouts in the shape of birds. Goss also writes about how his students selected one line or sentence each from Martin Luther King Jr.'s *Letter from Birmingham Jail* and put these on the risers of a stairway so students could see them as they went up the stairs. These examples are a wonderful reminder that there are physical areas of campus where we could post writing. If we think like a performance artist looking to get our work out to people who move through a space, where would we put it? Some ideas for filling the campus with words can be found in Figure 6.21. Teachers are advised to work with school administration when planning and implementing these sorts of projects.

FIGURE 6.21. Suggestions for filling the campus with words.

Tips for Getting Started with Filling the Campus with Words

Sidewalk Quotes: A temporary way to get words out into the world is to have students write them with sidewalk chalk. Perhaps students could share the best sentence from their piece.

Poetry in the Halls: Students could write short poems and post them in the halls of the school. This could involve using shapes, like Goss's (2019) birds. If plain paper is being used, how can it be enhanced with images or color to grab the attention of the people passing by?

Stories in 3D: After writing a short story, students could craft a figure or object that pertains to that narrative. They could then put that figure or object together with their story in a library display—or perhaps mix up the stories and figures/objects so that readers have to try to figure out what goes with what.

The Unique Opportunities Provided by Your Space: Take a close look at your campus. Where do you see unique opportunities to put student writing in front of a larger audience? I have seen poems posted as plaques along a river walkway, quotes on campus golf carts, and witty newsletters posted in bathrooms. Opportunities are all around us for students to go public with their work.

Final Thoughts

Some students already look beyond the classroom for writing opportunities. They may be part of a community of practice (Wenger, 2008) or an affinity space or group (Gee, 2004, 2018), such as a poetry club or an online fan fiction community. Some of our students are entering contests outside of school, sharing work through social media, or talking about their writing with friends. They may even participate in writing programs like YAS. Others may need assistance gaining access to such opportunities.

We know that students need to be able to "transfer their writing knowledge to new contexts, especially contexts beyond the classroom" (NCTE, 2022). Brokering writing opportunities for students is an important mentoring strategy because it puts students in touch with new purposes and audiences for writing. They may develop new friendships, gain skills, and learn practices that will enrich their lives. When teachers use this mentoring strategy, they support students in developing the motivation and confidence they need to come into their own as authors (or graphic novelists, filmmakers, songwriters . . .).

Six Strategies to Bring Out the Author in Every Student

This book considers how teachers can use six mentoring strategies to nurture the author (or graphic novelist, filmmaker, songwriter . . .) in every student. After all, our students have immense potential as creative thinkers, and they deserve to have access to authentic writing forms, opportunities, communities, and identities. This approach to teaching honors the unique resources that each student brings to the classroom, and it gives students space to make choices so they can grow into fulfilled individuals who can confidently communicate their ideas through a variety of modes and to a range of audiences. Mentors (more advanced practitioners) play an important role for students on this journey:

> We all encounter multiple roadblocks and constraints on the journey toward finding what we feel we were meant to do. Without a knowledgeable guide to aid us in identifying our passions, to encourage our interests, to smooth our paths, and to push us to make the most of our capacities, the journey is considerably harder. (Robinson, 2009, p. 184)

This book advocates for a shift in writing instruction, asking that teachers and scholars view education through a mentoring lens. Drawing on Young Authors' Studio data, research and theory including the NCTE *Position Statement on Writing Instruction in School* (2022), and the wisdom of secondary teachers, we have seen how teachers can mentor youth writers using six strategies (see Figure C.1).

FIGURE C.1. Six strategies to support student writers.

Six Strategies for Mentoring Youth Writers

1. Use a wide range of writing forms and modes with students.
2. Encourage student choice and decision-making.
3. Build a supportive writing community.
4. Honor student knowledge, experience, and interests.
5. Nurture students as writers.
6. Connect writers to opportunities beyond the classroom.

It goes without saying that mentors write alongside students, modeling writing as a practice and embracing vulnerability as they share their work. This dynamic of teacher and students writing together makes the classroom a more democratic, and less hierarchical, space (Kinloch, 2005; see Figure C.2).

FIGURE C.2. Writing together.

It is also worth pointing out that mentoring writers requires an asset-focused perspective. That is, we know that students *already* bring writing skills, valuable ideas and experiences, and unique interests and preferences to the classroom. Students may already see themselves as certain kinds of writers. Writing mentors notice where students are, support them, and guide them forward. They open doors to new adventures and possibilities.

This way of teaching can bring joy to students and teachers. In his book *Joy Write*, Ralph Fletcher (2017) suggests that writing workshops that invite choice, engagement, ownership, audience, invention, originality, and voice, as well as "fun, laughter, [and] a spirit of adventure" (p. 5), support students in their writing in school. Helping students develop a positive attitude toward writing can benefit them now and even into the future as they engage in writing in other contexts, whether they are writing in college, careers, or their personal lives. Confident writers are ready to communicate their ideas, tackle challenges, and advocate for themselves and others.

In this conclusion, I review the six strategies for mentoring youth writers, highlighting major themes and arguments and bringing in some additional comments from participants. Of particular interest, several comments by the youth writers echo ideas from NCTE's *Position Statement on Writing Instruction in School* (2022), reminding us that the suggestions for teachers outlined in this policy document are actually changes young people would like to see in schools as well.

Six Strategies for Mentoring Youth Writers

1. Use a Wide Range of Writing Forms and Modes with Students

As we saw in Chapter 1, exploring a wide range of writing forms and modes in the classroom helps students see that writing is varied, interesting, and meaningful. The writers in the YAS program enjoyed experimenting with different forms. One young writer reflected, "[I have learned] that there are many more forms of writing than I ever thought." The youth writers expressed disappointment with school-based writing that restricts them and limits their creativity. Instead, they recommended that schools include more creative writing, fiction, and varied forms (including screenwriting). They would like to write shorter pieces and not have so many essays assigned in school.

Some teachers already expose students to a variety of writing forms and modes. Recall that Carrie Deahl, the teacher I interviewed for Chapter 1, remarked, "I want to expose kids to as many types of writing as I can because the five-paragraph essay is so boring and outdated." This teacher has students compose novels, plays, graphic novels, poetry anthologies, and more. Carrie's approach to mentoring youth writers supports students in cultivating the habits of mind they will need for success in college and careers, habits such as curiosity, engagement, and flexibility (Council of Writing Program Administrators et al., 2011).

This first strategy for mentoring youth writers, using a wide range of writing forms and modes with students, is supported by the NCTE *Position Statement on Writing Instruction in School* (2022). This document advocates that a wider variety of forms, including visual and multimodal works, be used in writing instruction. Miranda, a mentor in the YAS program, found that teaching different writing forms and modes was not just beneficial for the youth writers. She wrote:

> These students [have] given me my imagination back. . . . [They] were making up stories about dogs who took over the world, secret agent robots, and even a musical! . . . They allowed us mentors to let loose for a second and rediscover our own creativity. For that, I can't be more thankful.

In other words, teachers benefit as well when many types of writing are explored in the classroom. Expanding our ideas about what counts as writing can result in a more interesting day, both for teachers and students. It also positions students well for a variety of careers that involve writing. Teachers, as you think about this first strategy, please consider the key questions in Figure C.3.

FIGURE C.3. Key questions for strategy #1.

Key Questions: Where are the opportunities in your curriculum to expand the writing forms and modes available to students? Do students have opportunities to experiment and play with writing in your classroom?

2. Encourage Student Choice and Decision-Making

In Chapter 2, we took a closer look at the second strategy for mentoring youth writers, encouraging student choice and decision-making in the writing classroom. We saw how in the YAS program, the physical space was configured in ways that facilitated conversation, which supported students as they engaged in complex decision-making about their writing. They could easily turn to a neighbor or mentor as they grappled with their pieces. In addition, students had a choice of short, high-interest writing activities they could participate in at the different breakout sessions. Having some choice in activities was exciting for these young writers. In a reflection, Emma commented, "A couple of the students even told me they were having trouble picking just two breakouts. . . . [T]hey want[ed] to go to all of them."

NCTE's *Position Statement on Writing Instruction in School* (2022) emphasizes that students need to be able to "make decisions about their own writing." Gallagher (2006) adds, "Choice fosters a feeling of ownership in the writer" (p. 91). Similarly, Scott Wade, the teacher I interviewed for Chapter 2, understands the importance of giving students some choice. He explained how secondary teachers could use choice boards to encourage students to make use of course content in personally meaningful ways. Recall that he stated, "I know that if students love [what they are doing], they will work harder. . . . And so you have that joy in the classroom because each person is doing things their own way."

When the youth writers in YAS thought about the ways they would like to see schools change, many of their responses dealt with choice (e.g., "Have free time to write anything." "I would like to change what we get to write or choose.") These students also admitted that they disliked having to write a minimum number of paragraphs or do timed writings in school.

When we give students the power to make choices, they will be more invested and engaged in course content. Making choices can also build their confidence, agency, and metacognitive skills, assets that will benefit these learners not just in school but also in their lives as adults. Teachers, as you think about this strategy for mentoring writers, please consider the key questions in Figure C.4.

FIGURE C.4. Key questions for strategy #2.

Key Questions: Which of your assignments could be adjusted to offer greater student choice? How could you organize the classroom space and lesson sequence to empower students as decision-makers?

3. Build a Supportive Writing Community

Chapter 3 explored the third strategy for mentoring youth writers, building a supportive writing community. Nari reflected, "It was so inspiring to see the young authors writing every Saturday and to also have the chance to write alongside them." The sense of wonder and awe she felt toward her fellow writers is the heart of building a community where the people in it feel respected and valued.

The teacher I interviewed for Chapter 3, Kimiko Warner-Turner, reminds teachers who are trying to build community in their classrooms, "You can do this while having fun." She recommends several theater books that have community-building activities but ultimately advises teachers to "let activities be led by the students [because] they have so many great ideas."

NCTE's *Position Statement on Writing Instruction in School* (2022) argues that students need to be able to write "within communities of other writers." In addition, community-of-practice theory (Wenger, 2008) helps explain why learning in these groups can be so valuable. Like other types of communities of practice, writing groups share practices and tools, allow for different kinds of participation, and provide access to experts. Members are able to consider different writing-related identities in these spaces, which can expand their ideas about who they are and who they could be.

In the YAS program, the youth writers were eager to return each week because the mentors helped create a positive atmosphere in which the students were seen, heard, and validated. These adolescents reflected at the end of the program: "I will miss coming here," and "Thank you for doing this class. I've enjoyed it." They appreciated learning to "collaborate with others on different ideas" and found that "sometimes as a writer, you have to exit your comfort zone." The YAS space was safe enough that these writers were willing to take risks and experiment with different kinds of writing. They also asked for help when they needed it. This community was made up of young people of different ages, interests, and backgrounds, but members were gathered together around a common practice (writing), and they supported each other in beautiful ways. Teachers, please consider the key questions in Figure C.5.

FIGURE C.5. Key questions for strategy #3.

Key Questions: How do you establish trust with students and validate them in your classroom? Do you group students in different configurations frequently to promote interaction?

4. Honor Student Knowledge, Experience, and Interests

In Chapter 4, we dove into the fourth strategy for mentoring youth writers, honoring student knowledge, experiences, and interests. An interview with Matt Hamilton highlighted how this teacher has invited students to tap into their knowledge and interests in the classroom as they compose works such as documentaries, plays, recipes, newspaper articles, websites, video games, board games, and more. Recall that Matt said, "Always have that teacher lens of 'How can this become a project?' I think it's really very cool that this author, artist, playwright, whatever, did this thing. I bet fifteen-year-olds could do it too." This teacher also pointed out, "We're building and iterating and creating ourselves, and teenagers are especially in that place."

FIGURE C.6. A YAS writer.

Again, the NCTE *Position Statement on Writing Instruction in School* (2022) urges teachers to support "diverse perspectives, voices, experiences, and linguistic practices in the classroom." In addition, Eisner (2002) recommends that teachers design learning activities to be enticing and meaningful to students. In the English classroom, this means assignments need to include opportunities for students to reflect on their own experiences and cultural knowledge, and students need to be able to make use of their languages. Furthermore, when students are able to explore their interests (comics, music, film, etc.) in classrooms, they are going to want to show up to learn. Students of all ages deserve to feel valued as the interesting, experienced, and knowledgeable people they are (see Figure C.6).

In the YAS program, students told us that they realized that "writing is meant to be fun and not boring" and "writing can be interesting." A student who had long wanted to learn how to write a screenplay was able to find support for that goal. When I asked these adolescents how they would like to see schools change, they recommended that teachers choose topics that are of interest to students. They also wished that schools would allow them some space to "work on any writing they wanted." Although Henry was brand new to teaching when he took part in the YAS internship, his perspective on teaching writing contains wisdom that even seasoned teachers can learn from. In a letter to future mentors, he wrote:

> Put the kids first. . . . Don't lose sight of what's really important. Pay attention to their wants and needs. Figure out what interests them about writing. If they want to share a novel with you that they wrote in their free time, by all means take the time to listen. By doing that, you show that you care, and you'll also encourage them to continue writing. Also, pay attention to the variety of skills and experiences [students bring to the classroom]. . . . Make sure that your curriculum has something for everybody. . . . Have fun with the curriculum. . . . The most fun that I had in [YAS] was preparing nerdy writing activities such as creating screenplays, graphic novels, and Dungeons & Dragons character sheets.

It is essential to honor students' interests, experiences, and knowledge in writing instruction. These assets, which include cultural and linguistic knowledge, are an important part of who our students are, and they are special resources that students should be encouraged to make use of in education. Attending to who students are and what they care about in their lives outside of school can support them in developing self-confidence and deepening their academic engagement, setting them up for success throughout their education and beyond. This approach makes learning more relevant, enjoyable, and exciting for students. In addition, it improves the lives of everyone in the writing community as we learn from one another. Teachers, please consider what this strategy could look like in your teaching (see Figure C.7).

FIGURE C.7. Key questions for strategy #4.

Key Questions: Where are the opportunities in the curriculum for students to draw on their interests, experiences, and knowledge (including cultural and linguistic knowledge)? Where are the opportunities for you to bring in these aspects of yourself as well?

5. Nurture Students as Writers

Chapter 5 looked at some ways teachers can nurture students as writers. This is the fifth strategy for mentoring youth writers. Readers were introduced to teacher Andrea Box, who uses feather circles and thank-you notes with writers in her classroom. This teacher emphasized the importance of writing alongside students and the need for teachers to take risks. Recall that she said, "In the end, you don't know how you will inspire a future author. It's an amazing process, and it's a privilege to be teaching kids how to write and how to find themselves as authors and writers and storytellers."

Emma from the YAS program emphasized how necessary it is to write with students. In her letter to future mentors, she wrote, "Whether you consider yourself a writer or not, you are a writer. . . . Writing with the students is one of the most important things you can do." In addition, she highlighted the need for teachers to really care about what they are teaching. She pointed out that the teacher's "excitement, or lack of, will rub off on [the students], and they will take on the attitude you have. Trust me, it's always better if you're excited. . . . You will . . . [help] these young people recognize their skill in writing and worth in life."

As we saw in this chapter, the NCTE *Position Statement on Writing Instruction in School* (2022) warns that a narrow curriculum and too much emphasis on standards and test preparation can harm students' attitudes toward writing. The document urges teachers not to lose sight of the writer. Related to this, Wenger (2008) recommends that schools give students opportunities to identify with different fields of study because identity and learning work together in powerful ways. Students benefit from reflecting on who they are as writers and imagining who they might become. In addition, taking students seriously as writers can help build their confidence, which is essential for those times when they will encounter new writing challenges down the road.

The YAS program honored writing identity. In this space, students were treated as real writers who had knowledge and skills that were worthy of respect. One student learned, "You don't have to be a certain age to write" and that "other children are writers." Another student concluded, "I am capable of writing anything." Interestingly, when we asked the youth writers how they would like to see schools change, two of them said, "More writing." Another recommended that students be able to write for at least two hours each day in school. When students enjoy the writing they are doing and are treated like real writers with important ideas to communicate, they want to write. Teachers, as you think about this fifth strategy for mentoring youth writers, please consider the key questions in Figure C.8.

FIGURE C.8. Key questions for strategy #5.

Key Questions: Do students have a chance to reflect on their writing histories, preferences, and attitudes? Is there space for working on out-of-school writing in the classroom?

6. Connect Writers to Opportunities beyond the Classroom

Chapter 6 explored the sixth and final strategy for mentoring youth writers, connecting writers to opportunities beyond the classroom. "Brokers are able to make new connections across communities of practice, enable coordination, and—if they are good brokers—open up new possibilities for meaning" (Wenger, 2008, p. 109). Teachers can broker new opportunities for students, putting them in touch with resources and audiences beyond their classroom, which can sustain these writers as they move into the world beyond high school. This work is in line with the NCTE *Position Statement on Writing Instruction in School*'s (2022) recommendations, including the need for students to be able to "transfer their writing knowledge to new contexts, especially contexts beyond the classroom."

The YAS study showed how mentors put students in touch with opportunities outside of the program space. They familiarized students with a national novel writing challenge and local writing groups and events. In addition, the mentors hosted a writing gallery and performance on campus to give students a chance to connect to larger audiences. Through these experiences, the youth writers learned that writing is "fun to share" and that performance, which may seem scary, can actually be rewarding. The program also made it easier for some students to share their writing. Emma reflected on the final performance:

> I was . . . pleasantly surprised to hear one parent say after the event that her son . . . wanted to participate in the program again next year! [The student] entered the program not interested in writing at all but told me he was not nervous about the performance when it came down to it. . . . To me, the whole program was about encouraging students who didn't like writing to learn to like it, and about encouraging those who already loved writing to continue doing so, and I think we succeeded in this.

These mentors helped students see themselves as writers, and they connected them to resources and opportunities that could nourish and sustain them.

In the teacher interview in this chapter, April McNary discussed some of the different ways she puts her students in touch with writing opportunities beyond the classroom. She connects students to new audiences through a class anthology and pen-pal letters. April has organized a Spoil Your Dinner family writing workshop and a Night at the Museum writing event, and she takes students around campus to reflect on their memories. She has demonstrated how students can use writing to process grief and honor loved ones. In addition, she connects these writers to contests and programs. Recall that in her interview, she said that this strategy helps students build their confidence. "Connecting students to different opportunities makes them feel like, 'I can do this! I can go for it, and if I get shot down, it's okay. I can bounce back from it. It's going to be okay.'" This mentoring strategy is all about immersing students in the wider world of writing so that students emerge as strong, confident writers with many options for using writing throughout their lives. The questions in Figure C.9 can help teachers consider how to implement this strategy.

FIGURE C.9. Key questions for strategy #6.

> **Key Questions:** How can you connect students to larger audiences on your school campus? What writing opportunities exist in your community?

An Invitation to Imagine and Inspire

As this book has shown, mentors are more experienced writers who guide students toward deeper participation in a practice. They help students become well versed in multiple forms, become more confident decision-makers, feel at ease among other writers, draw on their interests and experiences, cultivate writing identities, and connect to writing opportunities beyond the classroom. Along the way, mentors encourage, challenge, and inspire students.

Using a mentoring lens in education can help us see where we are going wrong. It can bring to light problems with outdated curricula, unfair distributions of power, poor allocations of resources and time, distance from content we teach, and more. It can expose problems with schooling that are sometimes taken for granted. At the same time, using a mentoring lens in education can illuminate the way forward. It can draw attention to the teacher as practitioner. It can prompt researchers to more closely examine the relationship between learning and identity, as well as the important role that mentors play in this work. In addition, concepts like agency and motivation can come into sharper focus through a mentoring lens.

In writing classrooms and community programs, a mentoring lens can help teachers and other leaders see where they could expand the forms of writing available, places where students could have more choice, ways to strengthen community, and so forth. You know the six strategies by now. You have the tools you need to mentor writers.

Now it is your turn to build the writing classroom of *your* dreams. Knowing everything that you know, what will that space look like? Who will you be there? What will be possible? How will you mentor writers?

Appendix A: Additional Information on the Program and the Study

This section of the book is for readers who are interested in additional information about the Young Authors' Studio program and the research study.

Young Authors' Studio

Program Origins

A few different ideas and programs helped shape the format of the Young Authors' Studio program. I first witnessed a program for youth run by university students who were earning course credit for their work when I was a doctoral student and my child participated in the Eleanor A. Robb Children's Art Workshop at Arizona State University (ASU). In that program, art education students were leading classes in pairs for kids in the community. The registration fee was nominal and covered the cost of the art supplies. At the time, I remarked to a colleague, whose child was also in the program, "Wow, how cool would it be to do this with *writing*?"

While I was reading for my literature review in the year before starting my dissertation research, I was deep in community-of-practice theory. Wenger's (2008) ideas about learning, participation, meaning, and identity really resonated with me. I wanted to do a study of a high school class with micro community-of-practice groups functioning inside of it, each focused on a different kind of writing (Williams, 2018). Students would first experiment with a wide range of writing forms and then gather around their favorite form. They would meet periodically in these groups to write, share mentor texts they had found, and support each other's writing. Although I changed course from that project, I held on to that vision. When I became a professor, I brought a version of that plan to life in the YAS program.

Superstition Review was another important influence on this program. A former colleague of mine at ASU founded this online literary journal. Each semester, she and her undergraduate students published one issue of the journal. They handled all aspects of running a publication (e.g., advertising, reviewing submissions, communicating with authors and artists, assembling issues, overseeing social media, etc.). The university students earned credit for their work through a two-course sequence, and they gained real-world experience through this innovative program. In fact, many of them leveraged that experience to get jobs in the publishing industry and other fields.

Finally, the National Writing Project (NWP) provided a valuable model for the work we did in YAS, especially in terms of the need for teachers to write alongside students. I participated in NWP summer institutes twice and was a guest lecturer for an NWP youth summer camp.

I started my job as a professor in August 2015, and in September 2016, I submitted my request to launch a new combined undergraduate-graduate internship course, ENG 484/584 Mentoring Youth Writers, for the following year. The title of this book comes from that internship course.

Different Iterations

The YAS program was offered in a face-to-face format twice (seven weeks on Saturday mornings in fall 2017; six weeks on Saturday afternoons in fall 2018). Then it was offered online twice. This is a strange coincidence, but the shift to online in spring 2020 had nothing to do with the COVID-19 pandemic; it was in response to a new "minors on campus" policy that prohibited students and employees from working with the same group of minors on campus for more than a stand-alone public event. That spring 2020 cohort of mentors built a website with writing activities, offered students writing feedback over email (to a parent's email account), and published an issue of an online journal for youth. In spring 2021, the program was online again, and we expanded it by adding four live writing workshops over Zoom; we also added writing activities to the website and published a second issue of the journal.

During the fifth iteration of the program, in spring 2023, an Arizona Humanities grant provided funding for two YA author events on Zoom (Garza, 2023; Leveen, 2023) and an in-person all-day event at ASU. Participants at the in-person event received a YA book, lunch, and writing supplies. Volunteer undergraduate and graduate students and professors served as writing mentors running the breakout sessions. They offered three rounds of twenty-five-minute breakout sessions, and their topics included animation short scripts, blackout poetry, songwriting, scar biographies, collage poetry, comic/manga character design, short story writing, and horror story competition. In the afternoon, a local teaching artist led a spoken word poetry workshop and open mic. I decided to bring the YAS program to a close after that series.

Challenges

I did not have a university mandate to start this writing program for youth, which was both a blessing and a curse. It was great because the mentors and I had freedom to design the program however we wanted. At the same time, it meant that I was really the only one pushing for the program. Building a new program and then sustaining it year after year was challenging. After five years of overseeing YAS on my own without allocated staff or resources, I dissolved the program. The behind-the-scenes work involved (recruiting ASU students and youth writers, meetings with lawyers, buying and organizing supplies, communicating with parents, etc.) was difficult to manage with my other commitments. It also became increasingly difficult to justify teaching a course with only five to seven university students in it. For those who are interested in starting a program like YAS, I recommend getting administrative buy-in, staff support, and funding prior to launching the program. Also, find a co-director right at the beginning of the process.

Study Design

The findings shared in this book come from a case study I did of the first year of the YAS program. Yin (2006) writes that case studies allow researchers to "examine, in-depth, a 'case' within its 'real-life' context" (p. 111). This type of research is appropriate for "descriptive or explanatory questions and . . . to produce a firsthand understanding of people and events" (p. 112). Using a case study approach allowed me to examine this program from multiple perspectives (mentors, students, my own) and through multiple data sources (creative writing, reflections, observations, planning/debrief sessions with mentors, surveys, course artifacts, etc.). The larger study looked at what went into building the program, as well as the experiences of the people in the space. This book shares findings that answer the research question, "How do mentors support youth writers in the YAS program?"

Site

The study took place on Arizona State University's Polytechnic campus in Mesa (see Figure A.1), where I work as an associate professor of English education. Founded in 1996, this campus was previously the site of Williams Air Force Base. These days there are many new buildings. Desert landscaping and wildlife, including roadrunners and javelina, can be found on this campus.

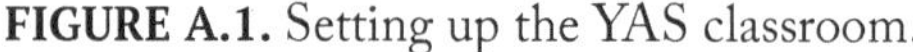

FIGURE A.1. Setting up the YAS classroom.

Figure A.2 shows the building where we held YAS. The two doors on the right lead to our main classroom (a double room). Occasionally we would offer noisier breakouts or quiet writing time in the classroom on the opposite side of the breezeway, just across from that main room. The large windows allowed us to see what was going on in each space, and I would move back and forth frequently between them when they were both in use (i.e., during the extended time to write stations and a couple of breakouts).

Participants

After the study received Institutional Review Board approval, mentors were recruited using IRB-approved consent forms. All five mentors in the internship joined the study. The youth participants were recruited during the YAS registration process using the IRB-approved child assent and parent consent forms. All eighteen youth who registered for the YAS program also joined the study. Data collection began after I had collected signed consent/assent forms from participants.

FIGURE A.2. External view of the building.

Data Sources

The study involved several data sources. Workshops and events were video-recorded and audio-recorded, and I wrote field notes while in the space. I routinely set up my Canon video recorder on a tripod at the back of the room, where its presence was obvious but not in participants' faces. After the study ended, I watched all of the videos and wrote video notes. Doing this after the program ended allowed me to revisit the earliest videos with knowledge of what would come later, which was useful for seeing patterns and trajectories.

I transcribed audio recordings myself using Express Scribe and a foot pedal. The recordings typically exceeded the lengths of our workshops and planning sessions because there were usually four small audio recorders going during breakout sessions, writing stations, and team time. These were placed on tables around the room. I did not record the writing gallery because it would have been impossible to separate out family members and friends from study participants. The lengths of the audio recordings were as follows:

Narratives Workshop	241 minutes
Poetry and Music Workshop	274 minutes
Art and Writing Workshop	325 minutes
Drama and Film Workshop	349 minutes
Genre Study Workshop	444 minutes
Revision and Rehearsal	243 minutes
Performance	52 minutes
Total:	1,928 minutes (32.13 hours)

During the mentor planning and debrief sessions, the mentors and I talked about things such as what they learned about the kids as writers, what went well in the workshop, what challenges they faced, and so forth. When someone talked about something they were struggling with, the other mentors were quick to ask clarifying questions and offer advice. Sometimes during these debriefs, I asked larger questions about the program, such as, "Are you seeing any benefits to mixing ages?" Sometimes I would ask questions about the youth writers in general, such as, "Are you seeing evidence that they are working their experiences and their cultures and languages into the writing they are doing here?" After reflecting on the day, we moved into planning for the next workshop, and mentors would continue to ask one another questions and offer advice. Audio-recording the mentor debrief and planning sessions was useful as it documented their celebrations, struggles, teamwork, and group problem-solving in action.

The mentors wrote twelve 300-word weekly reflections during the semester as part of their internship work (seven reflecting on the program and five reflecting on the planning sessions we held before the program started). They uploaded these reflections to Blackboard each week. Ultimately, there were fifty-seven completed mentor reflections at the end of the study that I collected. Mentors could write about whatever elements of the program they wanted to focus on, but later in the semester, I asked them to also address at least one of the following questions each week:

1. What experiences are you having in Young Authors' Studio?
2. What are you learning about youth, teaching, and building a writing program?
3. What experiences do the youth writers have in Young Authors' Studio?
4. What pieces do they create?
5. How do their texts draw on their experiences, cultures, and languages?
6. What significance does writing have in their lives?
7. Does this program change students' attitudes about writing or about themselves as writers?
8. What happens when writers of different ages come together in a writing program? What are the benefits? Challenges?

At the end of the internship, the mentors wrote a letter to me and a letter to future mentors (ten letters collected in total).

The youth writers completed an eighteen-item survey at the beginning and the end of the program. This survey contained thirteen statements to which participants could select "agree," "neutral," "or disagree"; one multiple-choice question about the amount of time they write each week; one question for which they could select and/or write in forms of writing they do outside of school; and three open-ended questions (about writing role models, writing they are proud of, and writing in school). Before I decided on this version of the survey, I asked my child, who was ten years old at the time, to take the survey and give me feedback on it. From that feedback, I realized having a traditional Likert scale with five options (from "strongly agree" to "strongly disagree") was too overwhelming for young people. Having three options (agree, neutral, disagree) worked better. That feedback also led me to reduce the number of questions and add options to the question about forms of writing done outside of school. All eighteen youth writers in the YAS program completed both the pre- and post-program surveys (see Chapter 5 for the survey).

Every week during the six weeks we were in our classroom for workshops, the youth writers filled out a short reflection (see Figure A.3). The top of this form asked background questions. Weeks one and six asked the identical question, "Who are you as a writer?," to ascertain if and/or how their attitudes changed during the program. Weeks two through five asked the youth writers a series of repeated questions. All eighteen youth participants completed the reflection; however, there were some blank weeks here and there due to some absences. I typed their reflection responses so these could be coded later.

FIGURE A.3. Weekly writing reflections.

Weekly Reflections

Writer's Name: ____________________

Age: ________ Grade: ________ Race/ethnicity: ____________________

Language(s) you can speak or read: ____________________

Hobbies and interests: ____________________

Reflection Workshop #1

Who are you as a writer?

____

____

____

____

____

Reflection Workshops #2–5 [section repeats; listed only one time here to save space]

What writing have you been working on today (or lately)?

____

What are you proud of in the piece?

____

List a writing goal you have.

____

Is there anything we can do to help you achieve that goal?

____

Reflection Workshop #6

What have you learned or realized in Young Authors' Studio?

____

____

____

____

____

Who are you as a writer?

____

____

____

____

____

I collected writing samples from the mentors and youth writers during workshops and events using photographs and audio recording. Performance comment cards were collected at the final event. For the program's social media posts, I took screenshots of pertinent material and cropped out or crossed out comments made by anyone outside of the study. Additional artifacts I collected for this study included writing workshop agendas, teaching materials mentors developed (e.g., PowerPoint slides), program fliers, any forms we created, and internship/course handouts I gave to the mentors. I collected digital or hard copies of items, depending on what was available.

Data Analysis

For the surveys, I typed participants' responses into pre- and post-sections of an Excel spreadsheet and then calculated totals and percentages for each response option using basic math (i.e., divide the number of people who answered that way by the total number of respondents for that question). Typically, there were eighteen responses total for each question (there were two blank responses across the surveys, which I noted). I designated the number of responses for each answer by putting that number in parentheses. This process resulted in the following chart (see Figure A.4). Please note: Not all rows total 100 percent as percentages have been rounded to the nearest tenth.

FIGURE A.4. Survey results (questions 1–14).

Question (n = 18)	Survey	Agree	Neutral	Disagree
1. I enjoy writing.	Pre-test	66.7% (12)	16.7% (3)	16.7% (3)
	Post-test	**83.3% (15)**	**16.7% (3)**	**0% (0)**
2. I have a hard time getting started with my writing.	Pre-test	22.2% (4)	55.6% (10)	22.2% (4)
	Post-test	**27.8% (5)**	**50% (9)**	**22.2% (4)**
3. I would like to publish or perform my writing.	Pre-test	55.6% (10)	16.7% (3)	27.8% (5)
	Post-test	**61.1% (11)**	**27.8% (5)**	**11.1% (2)**
4. I sometimes lose track of time when writing.	Pre-test	61.1% (11)	27.8% (5)	11.1% (2)
	Post-test	**66.7% (12)**	**27.8% (5)**	**5.6% (1)**
5. It is fun to share my writing with others.	Pre-test	27.8% (5)	38.9% (7)	33.3% (6)
	Post-test	**44.4% (8)**	**55.6% (10)**	**0% (0)**
6. I am sometimes scared to write.	Pre-test	5.6% (1)	33.3% (6)	61.1% (11)
	Post-test	**11.1% (2)**	**38.9% (7)**	**50% (9)**
7. Teachers seem to like the writing that I do.	Pre-test	66.7% (12)	16.7% (3)	16.7% (3)
	Post-test	**77.8% (14)**	**11.1% (2)**	**11.1% (2)**
8. I think of myself as a writer.	Pre-test	44.4% (8)	22.2% (4)	33.3% (6)
	Post-test	**55.6% (10)**	**44.4% (8)**	**0% (0)**
9. I would like to improve as a writer.	Pre-test	94.4% (17)	0% (0)	5.6% (1)
	Post-test	**94.4% (17)**	**5.6% (1)**	**0% (0)**
10. Writing is easy for me.	Pre-test	27.8% (5)	55.6% (10)	16.7% (3)
	Post-test	**55.6% (10)**	**44.4% (8)**	**0% (0)**
11. The writing we do at my school is fun.	Pre-test	33.3% (6)	38.9% (7)	27.8% (5)
	Post-test	**27.8% (5)**	**50% (9)**	**22.2% (4)**
12. I am really good at writing.	Pre-test	22.2% (4)	55.6% (10)	22.2% (4)
	Post-test	**38.9% (7)**	**50% (9)**	**11.1% (2)**
13. I hope to have a career that involves writing.	Pre-test (1 blank)	41.2% (7)	35.3% (6)	23.5% (4)
	Post-test	**38.9% (7)**	**38.9% (7)**	**22.2% (4)**

		2+ hours	1 hour	½ hour	0 hours
14. How much time do you spend writing your own pieces (not school assigned) each month?	Pre-test	33.3% (6)	27.8% (5)	16.7% (3)	22.2% (4)
	Post-test (1 blank)	**47.1% (8)**	**17.6% (3)**	**29.4% (5)**	**5.9% (1)**

Since questions 15–18 on the survey were more qualitative in nature, I uploaded those responses to NVivo, a data management program, to be coded with all of the other qualitative data from the case study.

I approached qualitative data analysis using grounded theory (Corbin & Strauss, 2008; Merriam, 2009). That is, I first read through materials and did open coding, which involves reducing chunks of content to the fewest words possible. Wherever possible, I used in vivo coding, which prioritizes using the language of participants when creating codes (Saldaña, 2009). Then I combined and collapsed the codes and matched these to the research questions they answered.

In answer to the research question "How do mentors support youth writers in the YAS program?", this study resulted in six key findings:

- Variation in activities (informs Chapter 1)
- Choice (informs Chapter 2)
- Community (informs Chapter 3)
- Funds of knowledge and student interests (informs Chapter 4)
- Supporting student writing attitudes and projects (informs Chapter 5)
- Brokering and performance (informs Chapter 6)

As demarcated in parentheses above, the theory of mentoring outlined in this book grew out of these six categories of study findings. The NCTE *Position Statement on Writing Instruction in School* (2022) helped me to articulate more clearly how these findings about mentoring are relevant to writing instruction in secondary schools.

The study findings I do not include in this book fall outside of the scope of mentoring youth writers. They deal with risk and reward in service learning and the program as a model for teacher education.

Appendix B: A Teacher Reflects on Authentic Writing

Authentic writing is a concept woven throughout this book. It appears in NCTE's *Position Statement on Writing Instruction in School* (2022), in the practices observed in the Young Authors' Studio program, and in the teacher interviews included in the previous chapters. In this final interview, a teacher who faces the constraints of a mandated curriculum reflects on the value of authentic writing.

Teacher Interview: Jennifer Ochoa on Authentic Writing

FIGURE B.1. Selfie by Jennifer Ochoa.

Jennifer Ochoa (see Figure B.1) has been teaching for thirty-three years and is currently an eighth-grade English teacher in New York City's Washington Heights. In addition, she teaches in the English education program at Lehman College, City University of New York, where she received an Adjunct of the Year award. Jennifer has served as the summer director for the New York City Writing Project. She is the author of the NCTE book *Already Readers and Writers: Honoring Students' Rights to Read and Write in the Middle Grade Classroom* (2020). She loves reading middle grade young adult literature.

Can you share some examples of how you engage students in authentic writing? At the beginning of the year, students are writing to know themselves and to tell other people who they are. Instead of just doing a memoir piece, they think, "Who am I as a reader? Who am I as a writer?" We also do a literary merit essay. The kids develop their criteria, and then we read all of these [published] short stories. They pick the one they think has the highest literary merit, and they write a letter to us arguing that we [should] keep it in the curriculum for next year's eighth graders. And we actually use those letters to develop the curriculum for the next year. We try to make spaces where students do school-like writing but for more authentic purposes.

One thing we did for many years was [performances fashioned after] TED Talks. There was this outside purpose and audience that wasn't just the teacher. The kids were so invested in revision that I didn't have to teach it at all. I didn't even have to mention that they needed to revise because the audience was so authentic and important to them. When the audience is personally high stakes, they care about the writing more. They want it to sound good when they say it out loud. And we talked about how when they write a text or a post, they do that same thing. They're very careful about what they say, read it, and might have someone else read it before they send it. Their TED talks are public performances. Parents come.

We do quick writes, too. Teenagers have a lot of big feelings. When they come together, their big feelings are magnified by ten million. They will get their notebook and write ten reasons why today was a bad day, and then ten reasons why today's a good day. We do a lot of social-emotional processing in their notebooks, so they have space to get that out. Then they can focus on whatever they need to focus on for school. It's hard to do your work when your brain is busy with something else. We also do a lot of opinion writing. All the time we talk about how people are more willing to listen to your opinion if you back it up with really solid evidence.

But I think for me it's about authentic *process*. When they go into other writing spaces with other teachers and tasks, they know, "This is how I do things when I write the best and when writing is important to me." We talk about at what point they want other people to read their drafts. And some people, their confidence might be greater or less depending on the audience. Sometimes they want people to read it every [time they write] two sentences and give them feedback, and sometimes they want to be finished with it. And so what kind of feedback helps them? No matter what the writing task is, they have a whole process in their brain. And it's good for them to know that because when they get into a class and somebody says, "You have to write an outline this way," if they know that's not how their brain starts thinking about a piece of writing, then they have a place to negotiate and start the conversation with their teacher: "This would work better for me."

Why do you think this kind of work is important?
My wife and I were in Florida for spring break. And when you're on vacation, you keep seeing the same families in the same places. So we kept going to the beach, and there was this family that was always at the beach and always kind of next to us. And one day I watched a boy spend probably an hour and a half at the very edge of the shore digging the deepest hole he could. And the entire point was, "How deep a hole can I dig in this space?" His family kept coming around and giving him pointers. And the sister wanted to help. He was like, "No, I'm doing this by myself." And the dad was a military dad, and he was standing in this military pose giving him pointers.

And I kept watching. I was just sitting there the whole time watching, and the kid would look up at his dad and listen. And then he'd just keep doing his own thing. And I mean, he was building up the walls. And then he would try and go a little closer to the water and then it would crash, and then he'd come back. I watched him engage in an activity that was of his own choosing and he was just trying it all out. There was no purpose other than he wanted to see if he could do this thing. And at a certain point, he just got up and walked away and went swimming. I'd been reading about Genius Hour, and I thought, "That's it right there."

It's not about authentic writing. It's about authentic thinking. Kids don't have the space in school to do the kind of trial-and-error thinking work that doesn't necessarily have a finished perfect purpose. It's the "trying it out." And that's what our society is missing. If we don't have people who can imagine a thing for themselves and try it out and not get frustrated, but keep going back and keep trying a little further this way and a little further this way. That's why play is so important. Who's going to invent new stuff? That's where that comes from. So I brought it back to my classroom and my grade team, and I was like, "We need to make this space for kids in school." So we would get done with a unit and we would do a thing called a *Make*. You could literally make anything you wanted that was somehow connected to this unit and represented your thinking around it. It didn't matter what it was, and you could do it by yourself or you could do it with other people.

And that space was the same space as the TED Talk space. It's the space where they have authentic composing experiences. They have the experience to build and try out and make a thing, whether it's a piece of writing, like a poem, whether it's making a whole book or a short story, whether it's making collages. And they were very invested in those projects. They were so excited to see what other people came up with. And sometimes the kid would be working on a thing for a whole week, and the thing that they imagined in their brain they couldn't make happen. They had to write about their process and how they came to the place where they didn't have anything and why. And they were never frustrated by that. They were just happy to talk about the process.

Sometimes they would make games. Sometimes they would make videos and skits. Sometimes they would write songs, sometimes they would write poetry. Sometimes they would write picturebooks. They would do pieces of art. They would make speeches. They would build weird, giant, incredible stuff. Some kids did the same thing every time; they liked to write poetry, so they always went to poetry, and some kids did a completely different thing every time.

What are the benefits of authentic writing?
It's one of the ways that human beings say to the world, "This is who I am, this is what I think, this is what I feel, and this is what I believe." And the more they get comfortable with themselves as a person who has a means of expression, the better they're going to be at that in the world.

Have you faced any challenges with this work?
In a space like New York City, the opportunities for authentic writing get narrower and narrower. This school year, our mayor has chosen four boxed curriculums. We're in the middle of the one that our superintendent picked. It's teaching students to write for a test. So lately the authentic purposes have been few. School accountability is so important right now across the country. You have to be proving that the time you're spending with kids is productive.

How can teachers get started with this work?
Think about what you do in your classroom and then think, "How is this similar to something that I do as a grown-up in the world, and how can I help kids move towards that?" So thinking about how they compose things, how they get started when they have to do a task, anything that they're writing for outside the classroom. What do they do when they want to change something? Do they try out a bunch of ideas, or do they think of one idea first and then try it out? Do they like things to be messy? Does it make them feel more anxious when something is messy? Everything won't feel like a struggle because they know themselves.

Do you have any additional advice for teachers?
It's okay if the idea doesn't sound perfect and you think to yourself, "I want kids to try this thing, but I don't really know what's going to happen when I try it. I don't know what it's going to look like. I don't have a good model. I don't have a rubric." You should just do that.

Do you have any favorite resources on authentic writing?
I love going back to Don Murray. I love Don Graves. I love—I just read the *Anti-Racist Writing Workshop*

(Chavez, 2021), which isn't really for teachers. It's about having a writing workshop in a community, but I loved how they were thinking about everyone as a real writer. My book is called *Already Readers and Writers* (Ochoa, 2020). I think that what happens when we get kids in our classroom is we think that we're the only people who have ever taught them, or who will ever teach them. And if they don't get it this year, everything's a disaster. But they already know how to read, and they already know how to write. They already have those experiences. And so [what we need is] to be thinking about them as people who are already writers and be drawing from those past experiences.

Do you have any cautions or warnings?
Yeah, people—especially [those who] are observers of your classroom. And I'm thinking of admin. Everyone thinks authentic writing comes to a point where there's something publishable, that's shiny, and there can be a party. And when the authentic writing is just practicing process or just trying stuff out, a lot of times administrators will come in and be like, "What are you doing?" And you'll get pushback. Tie it back, saying, "I'm helping them to learn how they're thinking."

And do you have any words of encouragement for teachers as they embark on this work?
Yeah, just keep trying and have fun. Do it with them. Be messy. Show them yourself. Bring your drafts, the really messy drafts.

Annotated Bibliography

The following resources are recommended for readers who seek additional information. These materials are grouped according to the chapter topics in this book.

Using a Wide Range of Writing Forms and Modes with Students (Chapter 1)

Serafini, Frank.
Reading the Visual: An Introduction to Teaching Multimodal Literacy
Teachers College Press, 2014

This book is essential reading for anyone interested in multimodal composition. The chapter "Elements of Art, Design, and Visual Composition" contains useful information on the ways particular art and design choices convey meaning to readers and viewers. These concepts are relevant to picturebooks, comics, graphic novels, manga, animation, and more.

Trustees of Columbia University.
The Columbia Film Language Glossary
https://filmglossary.ccnmtl.columbia.edu

This comprehensive online glossary of film terminology includes definitions with excerpts from films. It is a wonderful resource to help students learn about film concepts before composing short films of their own.

Encouraging Student Choice and Decision-Making (Chapter 2)

AVID.
Empower Students through Creativity and Choice
AVID Open Access, 2025. https://avidopenaccess.org/resource/empower-students-through-creativity-and-choice/

This AVID resource contains the handy chart "A Teacher's Guide to Student Voice and Choice" to assist teachers in thinking through the points at which they could allow for more student choice, whether it be in the project's audience, message, format, materials, logistics, timeline, assessment, etc.

Dobbs, Meredith.
"15 Ways to Integrate Student Choice into the Secondary ELA Classroom."
Bespoke ELA, 2018. www.bespokeclassroom.com/blog/2018/5/17/15-ways-to-integrate-student-choice-into-the-secondary-ela-classroom

This blog post by teacher Meredith Dobbs offers many suggestions to help teachers integrate more choice into their classes. She recommends providing choice in essay topics and using genius hours and passion projects, "I wonder" statements, choice boards, and more.

Building a Supportive Writing Community (Chapter 3)

Muhammad, Gholdy.
"We Must Create an Environment Where Writing Incites Knowledge and Joy"
Education Week, 2022. https://www.edweek.org/teaching-learning/opinion-how-to-build-a-culturally-responsive-community-of-writers/2022/11

Gholdy Muhammad shares her thoughts on ways teachers can foster culturally responsive spaces, including by focusing on identity, skills, intellect, criticality, and joy. She writes, "We must create an environment where writing incites knowledge and joy—not just an assignment"; in addition, "we must connect writing to a participation of celebration and transformation."

Zemelman, Steven, & Harvey Daniels.
A Community of Writers: Teaching Writing in the Junior and Senior High School
Heinemann, 1988

This book discusses how to create a community of writers in the classroom. It includes sections on classroom climate, how to plan for a writing-focused course, what to do starting in week one, writing workshops and journals, how to design activities and assignments, and tips for publishing and evaluating student work.

Honoring Student Knowledge, Experience, and Interests (Chapter 4)

Christensen, Linda, & Dyan Watson, editors.
Rhythm and Resistance: Teaching Poetry for Social Justice
Rethinking Schools, 2015

The poetry forms discussed in this book honor students' experiences and cultures. There are examples of the "I am from . . ." poem, the metaphor poem, the "What if?" poem, and more.

Nelson, G. Lynn.
Writing and Being: Embracing Your Life through Creative Journaling
Inner Ocean Publishing, 2004

G. Lynn Nelson provides teachers with a wide array of writing prompts they can use with students. Maps and memories, autobiographical poems, scar stories, heart stories, memories that sustain us, mythography, and many other activities are included in this practical guide to creative writing.

Nurturing Students as Writers (Chapter 5)

Ivanič, Roz.
Writing and Identity: The Discoursal Construction of Identity in Academic Writing
John Benjamins, 1998

This book is recommended for scholars who are interested in learning more about the complex relationship between writing and identity. Roz Ivanič distinguishes between four aspects of writing identity: the autobiographical self, discoursal self, self as author, and possibilities for self-hood.

Kittle, Penny.
Write beside Them: Risk, Voice, and Clarity in High School Writing
Heinemann, 2008

Penny Kittle offers instructional strategies that nurture students as writers. See her explanations of the writer's notebook, quick writes, the writers workshop, and portfolios.

Connecting Writers to Opportunities beyond the Classroom (Chapter 6)

Reyes, Gerald T.
"Finding the Poetic High: Building a Spoken Word Poetry Community and Culture of Creative, Caring, and Critical Intellectuals"
Multicultural Education, vol. 14, no. 2 (2006), pp. 10–15

This article does a wonderful job of explaining how to create an authentic space for young people to perform their pieces.

Wenger, Etienne.
Communities of Practice: Learning, Meaning, and Identity
Cambridge University Press, 2008

This groundbreaking work describes useful concepts such as brokering and trajectories, and it explains how learning and identity work together. In magnificent detail, it outlines the features of a community of practice. Readers who make it to the end will be rewarded with a chapter on education that is everything. If *Mentoring Youth Writers* motivates you to pick up just one other book, I hope it will be this one.

References

Alim, H. S., & Paris, D. (2017). What is culturally sustaining pedagogy and why does it matter? In D. Paris and H. S. Alim (Eds.), *Culturally sustaining pedagogies: Teaching and learning for justice in a changing world* (pp. 1–21). Teachers College Press.

Anyon, J. (1980). Social class and the hidden curriculum of work. *Journal of Education, 162*(1), 67–92.

Atwell, N. (1998). *In the middle: New understandings about writing, reading, and learning* (2nd ed.). Heinemann.

Bacalja, A. (2020). Digital writing in the new literacies age: Insights from an online writing community. *Literacy Learning, 28(*2), 33–43.

Baker-Bell, A. (2020). *Linguistic justice: Black language, literacy, identity, and pedagogy.* Routledge and NCTE.

Bakhtin, M. M. (1986). *Speech genres and other late essays* (V. W. McGee, Trans.; C. Emerson & M. Holquist, Eds). University of Texas Press.

Barry, L. (2020). *Making comics.* Drawn & Quarterly.

BBC Ideas. (2018). *Lotte Reiniger: The animation genius you've probably never heard of* [Video]. YouTube. BBC Ideas. Retrieved April 18, 2025, from https://www.youtube.com/watch?v=3Gm9kZLP0uE

Beach, R., with Caraballo, L. (2022). *Drawing on students' worlds in the ELA classroom: Toward critical engagement and deep learning*. Routledge.

Behizadeh, N. (2014). Adolescent perspectives on authentic writing instruction. *Journal of Language and Literacy Education, 10*(1), 27–44.

Beucher, B., & Seglem, R. (2019). Black male students negotiate ways of knowing themselves during digital storytelling. *LEARNing Landscapes, 12*(1), 47–62.

Blasingame, J., & Bushman, J. H. (2005). *Teaching writing in middle and secondary schools.* Pearson/Merrill/Prentice Hall.

Boal, A. (2021). *Games for actors and non-actors* (A. Jackson, Trans.; 3rd ed.). Routledge.

Bonnet, T. (2017, October 4). Filmmaking can help develop young people's creativity and improve their soft skills. *TES Magazine.* Retrieved from https://www.tes.com

Boscolo, P., & Gelati, C. (2007). Best practices in promoting motivation for writing. In S. Graham, C. A. MacArthur, & J. Fitzgerald (Eds.), *Best practices in writing instruction* (pp. 202–221). Guilford Press.

Brosgol, V. (2011). *Anya's ghost.* First Second.

Brunetti, I. (2011). *Cartooning: Philosophy and practice.* Yale University Press.

Bunting, J. (n.d.). *Once upon a time: Pixar prompt.* The Write Practice. Retrieved April 18, 2025, from https://thewritepractice.com/once-upon-a-time-pixar-prompt/

Burn, A. (2016). Making machinima: Animation, games, and multimodal participation in the media arts. *Learning, Media and Technology, 41*(2), 310–329.

Bush, J., & Zuidema, L. A. (2011). Professional writing in the English classroom: Beyond language—the grammar of document design. *English Journal, 100*(4), 86–89.

Chavez, F. R. (2021). *The anti-racist writing workshop: How to decolonize the creative classroom.* Haymarket Books.

Christensen, L. (2000). *Reading, writing, and rising up: Teaching about social justice and the power of the written word.* Rethinking Schools.

Clark, J. (2016, May 27). *Bakunawa: The moon eating dragon of Philippine mythology.* The Aswang Project. Retrieved April 18, 2025, from https://www.aswangproject.com/bakunawa/

Common Core State Standards Initiative. (2010). *Common Core State Standards for English Language Arts.* Retrieved April 18, 2025, from https://corestandards.org/

Coppola, S. (2017). *Renew! Become a better—and more authentic—writing teacher.* Stenhouse Publishers.

Coppola, S. (2019). *Writing, redefined: Broadening our ideas of what it means to compose.* Stenhouse Publishers.

Corbin, J., & Strauss, A. (2008). *Basics of qualitative research: Techniques and procedures for developing grounded theory* (3rd ed.). SAGE.

Council of Writing Program Administrators, National

Council of Teachers of English, and National Writing Project. (2011). *Framework for success in postsecondary writing*. Retrieved April 18, 2025, from https://wpacouncil.org/aws/CWPA/asset_manager/get_file/350201?ver=7548

Cremin, T. (2006). Creativity, uncertainty and discomfort: Teachers as writers, *Cambridge Journal of Education, 36*(3), 415–433.

Csikszentmihalyi, M. (1990). *Flow: The psychology of optimal experience.* HarperPerennial.

Daly, J. A., & Miller, M. D. (1975). The empirical development of an instrument to measure writing apprehension. *Research in the Teaching of English, 9*(3), 242–249.

Darrington, B., & Dousay, T. (2014). Using multimodal writing to motivate struggling students to write. *TechTrends: Linking Research and Practice to Improve Learning, 59*(6), 29–34.

Deahl, C. (2020). Bracing for NaNoWriMo. *English Journal, 110*(1), 109–110.

Dean, D. (2017). *Strategic writing: The writing process and beyond in the secondary English classroom* (2nd ed.). National Council of Teachers of English.

Eisner, E. W. (2002). *The arts and the creation of mind.* Yale University Press.

Elbow, P. (1998). *Writing without teachers* (2nd ed.). Oxford University Press.

Evans, R. A., Goering, C. Z., & French, S. D. (2021). Soundtracks, songwriting, and soundscapes: Producing the podcast of our lives. *English Journal, 110*(4), 69–76.

Felten, P. (2008). Visual literacy. *Change: The Magazine of Higher Learning, 40*(6), 60–64.

Fisher D., Frey, N., & Almarode, J. (2020). *Student learning communities: A springboard for academic and social-emotional development*. Association for Supervision and Curriculum Development.

Fisher, M. T. (2007). *Writing in rhythm: Spoken word poetry in urban classrooms.* Teachers College Press.

Fleischer, C., & Andrew-Vaughan, S. (2009). *Writing outside your comfort zone: Helping students navigate unfamiliar genres.* Heinemann.

Fletcher, R. (1993). *What a writer needs.* Heinemann.

Fletcher, R. (2017). *Joy write: Cultivating high-impact, low-stakes writing.* Heinemann.

Freedom Writers, with Gruwell, E. (2009). *The Freedom Writers diary: How a teacher and 150 teens used writing to change themselves and the world around them* (10th Anniv. ed.). Broadway Books.

Gallagher, K. (2006). *Teaching adolescent writers.* Stenhouse Publishers.

Gallagher, K. (2011). *Write like this: Teaching real-world writing through modeling and mentor texts.* Stenhouse Publishers.

Gallagher, K., & Kittle, P. (2018). *180 days: Two teachers and the quest to engage and empower adolescents.* Heinemann.

Gardner, P. (2014). Becoming a teacher of writing: Primary student teachers reviewing their relationship with writing. *English in Education, 48*(2), 128–148.

Garza, X. (2011). *Maximilian and the mystery of the guardian angel.* Cinco Puntos Press.

Garza, X. (2023, February 4). *Visual storytelling* [Video]. YouTube. Retrieved April 18, 2025, from https://www.youtube.com/watch?v=CNcSsDAa61Y

Gee, J. P. (2004). *Situated language and learning: A critique of traditional schooling.* Routledge.

Gee, J. P. (2018). Affinity spaces: How young people live and learn online and out of school. *Phi Delta Kappan, 99*(6), 8–13.

George, D. (2002). From analysis to design: Visual communication in the teaching of writing. *College Composition and Communication, 54*(1), 11–39.

Golden, J. (2001). *Reading in the dark: Using film as a tool in the English classroom.* National Council of Teachers of English.

Gorman, A. (2021, January 20). *The hill we climb* [Video]. YouTube. Retrieved April 18, 2025, from https://www.youtube.com/watch?v=LZ055ilIiN4

Goss, S. (2019). Putting the public in publication: Guerilla art in ELA classrooms. In K. J. Macro & M. Zoss (Eds.), *A symphony of possibilities: A handbook for arts integration in secondary English language arts* (pp. 157–175). National Council of Teachers of English.

Graves, D. H. (1994). *A fresh look at writing.* Heinemann.

Gutiérrez, K. D. (2011). Developing a sociocritical literacy in the third space. *Reading Research Quarterly, 43*(2), 148–164.

Haddix, M. M. (2018). What's radical about youth writing? Seeing and honoring youth writers and their literacies. *Voices from the Middle, 25*(3), 8–12.

He, A. E. (2009). Bridging the gap between teacher educator and teacher in a community of practice: A case of brokering. *System, 37*(1), 153–163.

Heath, S. B. (1983). *Ways with words: Language, life, and work in communities and classrooms.* Cambridge University Press.

Hill, M. L. (2009). *Beats, rhymes, and classroom life: Hip-hop pedagogy and the politics of identity.* Teachers College Press.

Hughes-Roberts, T., Brown, D., Boulton, H., Burton, A., Shopland, N., & Martinovs, D. (2020). Examining the potential impact of digital game making in curricula based teaching: Initial observations. *Computers & Education, 158*, 1–15.

Hull, G., & Schultz, K. (2001). Literacy and learning out of school: A review of theory and research. *Review of Educational Research, 71*(4), 575–611.

Ivanič, R. (1998). *Writing and identity: The discoursal construction of identity in academic writing.* John Benjamins.

Iyengar, S. S., & Lepper, M. R. (2000). When choice is demotivating: Can one desire too much of a good thing? *Journal of Personality and Social Psychology, 79*(6), 995–1006.

Jocson, K. M. (2008). *Youth poets: Empowering literacies in and out of schools.* Peter Lang.

Kagan, S., & Kagan, M. (2009). *Kagan cooperative learning.* Kagan Publishing.

Kahn, P., Robinson, C., & Levin, A. M. (2022). Three lives revolutionized through spoken word poetry. *English Journal, 111*(3), 101–103.

Kinloch, V. F. (2005). Poetry, literacy, and creativity: Fostering effective learning strategies in an urban classroom. *English Education, 37*(2), 96–114.

Kittle, P. (2008). *Write beside them: Risk, voice, and clarity in high school writing.* Heinemann.

Kovacs, M. (2017). *What makes a poem . . . a poem?* [Video]. TED Ed/YouTube. Retrieved April 18, 2025, from https://www.youtube.com/watch?v=JwhouCNq-Fc

Lave, J., & Wenger, E. (1991). *Situated learning: Legitimate peripheral participation.* Cambridge University Press.

Leveen, T. (2013). *Sick.* Abrams.

Leveen, T. (2023, February 11). *Novel writing.* YouTube. Retrieved April 18, 2025, from https://www.youtube.com/watch?v=ot0Cw9EhyIE

Lukpat, A. (2022, February 1). *An 8-year-old wrote a book and hid it on a library shelf. It's a hit.* New York Times. Retrieved April 18, 2025, from https://www.nytimes.com/2022/02/01/books/crismis-book-school-library.html

Lyiscott, J., Mirra, N., & Garcia, A. (2021, April). *Critical media literacy and popular culture in ELA classrooms.* National Council of Teachers of English. Retrieved April 18, 2025, from https://ncte.org/critical-media-literacy/

Macro, K. J., & Zoss, M. (Eds.). (2019). *A symphony of possibilities: A handbook for arts integration in secondary English language arts.* National Council of Teachers of English.

Maldonado, R., & DeHart, J. D. (2021). Creating graphic novels to inspire the superhero within. *English Journal, 111*(2), 96–98.

McCloud, S. (2006). *Making comics: Storytelling secrets of comics, manga, and graphic novels.* William Morrow.

McMahon, K. (2018). *The elements of art . . . defined!* YouTube. Retrieved April 18, 2025, from https://www.youtube.com/watch?v=iSbm21bhXVk

McNary, A. Z. (2021). Writing a monster's story. *English Journal, 111*(1), 85–88.

Merriam, S. B. (2009). *Qualitative research: A guide to design and implementation.* Jossey-Bass.

Metzger, K., Box, A., & Blasingame, J. (2013). Embracing intercultural diversification: Teaching young adult literature with Native American themes. *English Journal, 102*(5), 57–62.

Moll, L. C., Amanti, C., Neff, D., & Gonzalez, N. (1992). Funds of knowledge for teaching: Using a qualitative approach to connect homes and classrooms. *Theory into Practice, 31*(2), 132–141.

Morales, A., & Hanson, W. (2005). Language brokering: An integrative review of the literature. *Hispanic Journal of Behavioral Sciences, 27*(4), 471–503.

Morrell, E., & Duncan-Andrade, J. M. R. (2002). Promoting academic literacy with urban youth through engaging hip-hop culture. *English Journal, 91*(6), 88–92.

Muhammad, G. (2023). *Unearthing joy: A guide to culturally and historically responsive teaching and learning.* Scholastic.

National Council of Teachers of English. (2022).

Position statement on writing instruction in school. Retrieved April 18, 2025, from https://ncte.org

Nelson, G. L. (2004). *Writing and being: Embracing your life through creative journaling.* Inner Ocean Publishing.

New London Group. (1996). A pedagogy of multiliteracies: Designing social futures. *Harvard Educational Review, 66*(1), 60–92.

Ng, S. H., He, A., Loong, C. (2004). Trigenerational family conversations: Communication accommodation and brokering. *British Journal of Social Psychology, 43*(3), 449–464.

Ochoa, J. (Ed.) (2020). *Already readers and writers: Honoring students' rights to read and write in the middle grade classroom.* National Council of Teachers of English.

Osorio, J. (2009, May 12). *Kumulipo* [Video]. YouTube. Retrieved April 18, 2025, from https://www.youtube.com/watch?v=kc176yYdcxY

Paris, D. (2012). Culturally sustaining pedagogy: A needed change in stance, terminology, and practice. *Educational Researcher, 41*(3), 93–97.

Patall, E. A., Cooper, H., & Robinson, J. C. (2008). The effects of choice on intrinsic motivation and related outcomes: A meta-analysis of research findings. *Psychological Bulletin, 134*(2), 270–300.

Patall, E. A., Cooper, H., & Wynn, S. R. (2010). The effectiveness and relative importance of choice in the classroom. *Journal of Educational Psychology, 102*(4), 896–915.

Pérez, C. C. (2018). *The first rule of punk.* Puffin Books.

Pilkey, D. (1993). *Dogzilla.* Clarion Books.

Pilkey, D. (2003). *Kat Kong.* Clarion Books.

Prior, P. (2006). A sociocultural theory of writing. In C. A. MacArthur, S. Graham, and J. Fitzgerald (Eds.), *Handbook of writing research* (pp. 54–66). Guilford Press.

Pytash, K. E., Testa, E., Geise, K., and Kovalchick, C. (2017). Guide on the side: Collaboratively writing and revising with students. *Voices from the Middle, 25*(2), 24–27.

Reyes, G. T. (2006). Finding the poetic high: Building a spoken word poetry community and culture of creative, caring, and critical intellectuals. *Multicultural Education 14*(2), 10–15.

Rhodes, J. P. (2012). *Ninth ward.* Little, Brown Books for Young Readers.

Robb, L. (2010). *Teaching middle school writers: What every English teacher needs to know.* Heinemann.

Robinson, C. (n.d.). *Does offering students a choice in assignments lead to greater engagement?* Digital Promise. Retrieved April 18, 2025, from https://researchmap.digitalpromise.org

Robinson, K. (2011). *Out of our minds: Learning to be creative.* Capstone.

Robinson, K., with Aronica, L. (2009). *The element: How finding your passion changes everything.* Penguin Books.

Rohd, M. (1998). *Theatre for community, conflict, and dialogue: The hope is vital training manual.* Heinemann.

Romano, T. (1987). *Clearing the way: Working with teenage writers.* Heinemann.

Roode, D. M. (2020). *38 questions to prompt food memories.* Modern Heirloom Books. Retrieved April 18, 2025, from https://www.modernheirloombooks.com/new-blog/2020/9/3/38-questions-to-prompt-food-memories

Ryder, D. (2020, August 18). *Creating comics in the classroom.* Edutopia. Retrieved April 18, 2025, from https://www.edutopia.org/article/creating-comics-classroom/

Saldaña, J. (2009). *The coding manual for qualitative researchers.* SAGE.

Sanchez, N., Corbin, M., & Norka, A. (2019). Use of "comment bubbles" in a writing-intensive, social and economic justice course. *Advances in Social Work, 19*(2), 463–477.

Sandven, M. L., Goering, C. Z., & Montgomery, A. (2023). Choice, agency, engagement: Choosing intellect through a menu approach. *Voices from the Middle, 30*(3), 50–53.

Selznick, B. (2007). *The invention of Hugo Cabret.* Scholastic Press.

Serafini, F. (2014). *Reading the visual: An introduction to teaching multimodal literacy.* Teachers College Press.

Skerrett, A., & Bomer, R. (2013). Recruiting languages and lifeworlds for border-crossing compositions. *Research in the Teaching of English, 47*(3), 313–337.

Smitherman, G. (1977). *Talkin and testifyin: The language of Black America.* Wayne State University Press.

Spolin, V. (1986). *Theater games for the classroom: A*

teacher's handbook. Northwestern University Press.
Stockman, A. (2022). *The writing workshop teacher's guide to multimodal composition (6–12)*. Routledge.
Street, C., and Stang, K. K. (2009). In what ways do teacher education courses change teachers' self confidence as writers? *Teacher Education Quarterly, 36*(3), 75–94.
Suh, E. K., Hoffman, L., Wade, S., & Maher, S. C. (2022). Offering emergent multilingual students the freedom to choose. *English Journal, 111*(5), 90–92.
Tan, S. (2007). *The arrival*. Arthur A. Levine Books.
Trustees of Columbia University. (2015). *The Columbia film language glossary*. Retrieved April 18, 2025, from https://filmglossary.ccnmtl.columbia.edu/
UNC Writing Center. (2023). *Writing as decision-making*. Retrieved April 18, 2025, from https://writingcenter.unc.edu/tips-and-tools/writing-as-decision-making/
Vetter, A., Lambert, C., Lejeune, M., Consalvo, A., David, A., & McDaniel, D. (2022). Asking teens about their writing lives: The writing identity work of youth. *Literacy Research and Instruction, 61*(4), 315–338.
Vološinov, V. N. (1973). *Marxism and the philosophy of language* (L. Matejka & I. R. Titunik, Trans). Harvard University Press.
Vygotsky, L. S. (1978). *Mind in society: The development of higher psychological processes*. Harvard University Press.
Wahleithner, J. M. (2018). Five portraits of teachers' experiences teaching writing: Negotiating knowledge, student need, and policy. *Teachers College Record, 120*(1), 1–60.
Weinstein, S. (2006). A love for the thing: The pleasures of rap as a literate practice. *Journal of Adolescent & Adult Literacy, 50*(4), 270–281.
Weinstein, S. (2009). *Feel these words: Writing in the lives of urban youth*. SUNY Press.
Weiss, J., & Herndon, S. (2001). *Brave new voices: The Youth Speaks guide to teaching spoken word poetry*. Heinemann.
Wenger, E. (2008). *Communities of practice: Learning, meaning, and identity*. Cambridge University Press.
Williams, W. R. (2013). "Untold stories to tell": Making space for the voices of youth songwriters. *Journal of Adolescent & Adult Literacy, 56*(5), 369–379.
Williams, W. R. (2015). Every voice matters: Spoken word poetry in and outside of school. *English Journal, 104*(4), 79–84.
Williams, W. R. (2018). *Listen to the poet: Writing, performance, and community in youth spoken word poetry*. University of Massachusetts Press.
Williams, W. R. (2019). Attending to the *visual* aspects of visual storytelling: Using art and design concepts to interpret and compose narratives with images. *Journal of Visual Literacy, 38*(1–2), 66–82.
Williams, W. R. (2020). Examining Studio Ghibli's animated films: A study of students' viewing paths and creative projects. *Journal of Adolescent & Adult Literacy, 63*(6), 639–650.
Williams, W. R., & Reid, S. F. (2019). Young Authors' Studio: Writing and learning together in Arizona. *Literacy Today (Jan./Feb.)*, 44–45.
Woodson, J. (2016). *Brown girl dreaming*. Nancy Paulsen Books.
Wortham, S. (2006). *Learning identity: The joint emergence of social identification and academic learning*. Cambridge University Press.
Wright, K. L., Hodges, T. S., & McTigue, E. M. (2019). A validation program for the Self-Beliefs, Writing-Beliefs, and Attitude Survey: A measure of adolescents' motivation toward writing. *Assessing Writing, 39*, 64–78.
Yang, G. L. (2021). *American born Chinese*. First Second.
Yeh, H. C., Chang, W. Y., Chen, H. Y., & Heng, L. (2021). Effects of podcast-making on college students' English speaking skills in higher education. *Educational Technology Research and Development, 69*(5), 2845–2867.
Yin, R. K. (2006). Case study methods. In J. L. Green, G. Camilli, & P. B. Elmore (Eds.), *Handbook of complementary methods in education research* (pp. 111–122). Lawrence Erlbaum.
Zdanowicz, C. (2022, February 7). *An 8-year-old boy snuck a book he wrote onto a library shelf. More than 100 people are waiting to check it out*. CNN. Retrieved April 18, 2025, from https://www.cnn.com/2022/02/07/us/boy-writes-book-library-trnd/index.html

Index

Note: An *f* following a page number indicates a figure.

Author

Wendy R. Williams is an associate professor of English education at Arizona State University. This is her second book. She is also the author of *Listen to the Poet: Writing, Performance, and Community in Youth Spoken Word Poetry* (2018) and numerous articles and chapters. Her current projects address visual and multimodal storytelling and food studies in English language arts. Williams is co-chair of the ELATE Commission on Arts and Literacies and past editor of *English Journal*'s Teaching Creative Writing column. At her university, she has organized community writing events, designed new academic programs, and developed and taught courses on narrative research, visual narratives, Studio Ghibli films, children's literature, and food writing. Before becoming a professor, she taught high school and middle school English for nine years. She is a cellist, certified Maricopa County Master Gardener, and classically trained chef.

This book was typeset in Adobe Caslon Pro and PT Serif by Barbara Frazier.

Typefaces used on the cover include
Chronicle Display Semibold and Avenir Next Medium.